fine Cooking Cookies

fine Cooking
Cookies

200 favorite recipes
for cookies, brownies, bars & more

Editors and Contributors of *Fine Cooking*

The Taunton Press
Inspiration for hands-on living®

The Taunton Press
Inspiration for hands-on living®

The Taunton Press, Inc.
63 South Main Street
PO Box 5506, Newtown, CT 06470-5506
e-mail: tp@taunton.com

Copy editor: Li Agen
Indexer: Heidi Blough
Cover design: Alison Wilkes
Cover food stylist: Allison Ehri Kreitler
Cover photographer: Scott Phillips, © The Taunton Press, Inc.
Interior design: Kimberly Adis
Layout: Sandra Mahlstedt

Fine Cooking® is a trademark of The Taunton Press, Inc., registered in the U.S. Patent and Trademark Office.

The following names/manufacturers appearing in *Fine Cooking Cookies* are trademarks: Bailey's®, Coco Lopez®, Doughmakers®, Frangelico®, Godiva®, Grand Marnier®, Guittard®, Heath Bar®, Jif®, Kahlúa®, Kraft®, Lindt®, Maker's Mark®, Nestlé®, Parrish®, Philadelphia®, Quaker®, King Arthur Flour®, Silpat®, Sugar in the Raw®

Library of Congress Cataloging-in-Publication Data

Fine cooking cookies : 200 favorite recipes for cookies, brownies, bars & more / editors and contributors of Fine cooking.
       p. cm.
   Includes index.
   ISBN 978-1-60085-369-2
   1. Cookies. 2. Cookbooks. I. Fine cooking.
   TX772.F56 2011
   641.8'654--dc23
                          2011021258

Printed in the United States of America
10 9 8 7 6 5 4 3 2 1

contents

classic cookies & confections

dark chocolate crackles

YIELDS ABOUT 5 DOZEN COOKIES

11¼ oz. (2½ cups) unbleached all-purpose flour

1 tsp. baking soda

¼ tsp. table salt

½ lb. (1 cup) unsalted butter, softened at room temperature

2 cups firmly packed light brown sugar

2 oz. (⅔ cup) natural, unsweetened cocoa powder, sifted if lumpy

2 tsp. finely grated orange zest

1 tsp. pure vanilla extract

3 large eggs

8 oz. bittersweet chocolate, melted and cooled until barely warm

6 oz. white, bittersweet, or semisweet chocolate, chopped

⅓ cup granulated sugar; more as needed

A tiny hint of orange zest makes these cookies a knockout. They're fragile when hot, so be sure to let them cool on the cookie sheet for 5 minutes before moving them.

1. Position a rack in the center of the oven and heat the oven to 350°F. Line three large cookie sheets with parchment or nonstick baking liners.

2. In a medium bowl, whisk together the flour, baking soda, and salt. In the bowl of a stand mixer fitted with the paddle attachment (or in a large bowl with a hand mixer), beat the butter, brown sugar, cocoa, orange zest, and vanilla on medium speed until well combined, about 4 minutes. Add the eggs one at a time, beating briefly between additions. Add the melted chocolate and mix until blended, about 1 minute. Add the flour mixture and mix on low speed until almost completely blended, about 1 minute. Add the chopped chocolate and mix until blended, about 15 seconds.

3. Shape the dough into 1¼-inch balls with a small ice cream scoop or two tablespoons.

4. Pour the granulated sugar into a shallow dish. Dip the top of each ball in the sugar and set the balls, sugar side up, about 1½ inches apart on the prepared cookie sheets. Bake one sheet at a time until the cookies are puffed and cracked on top, 11 to 12 minutes. Let the cookies cool on the sheet for 5 minutes before transferring them to a rack to cool completely.
—*Abigail Johnson Dodge*

PER COOKIE: 110 CALORIES | 2g PROTEIN | 16g CARB | 5g TOTAL FAT | 3g SAT FAT | 1.5g MONO FAT | 0g POLY FAT | 20mg CHOL | 45mg SODIUM | 1g FIBER

Make Ahead

The balls of dough may be frozen for 1 month. Thaw them overnight in the refrigerator before proceeding with the recipe.

classic cut–out cookies

YIELDS ABOUT 3½ DOZEN
2-INCH COOKIES

- **9** oz. (2 cups) unbleached all-purpose flour; more for rolling
- **1½** tsp. baking powder
- **½** tsp. kosher salt
- **6** oz. (¾ cup) unsalted butter, softened at room temperature
- **¾** cup granulated sugar
- **1** large egg
- **1** tsp. pure vanilla extract
- **2** Tbs. heavy cream
- **½** tsp. finely grated lemon zest
- Sanding sugars or other decorations (optional)

Make Ahead

If you wrap small batches of these cookies in plastic and put them in a larger plastic container, you can freeze them for several weeks. They thaw in minutes.

To decorate these simple Christmas cookies, dip the tops in a confectioners'-sugar glaze and sprinkle with colored sanding sugars.

1. In a small bowl, whisk the flour, baking powder, and salt to blend. Using a stand mixer fitted with the paddle attachment (or in a large bowl with a hand mixer), beat the butter and sugar on medium-high speed until well creamed. Add the egg and beat until the mixture is light and fluffy. Add the vanilla, cream, and lemon zest and mix just until well combined. Reduce the speed to medium low and gradually add the flour mixture. Mix just until well combined. Portion the dough into thirds, shape each third into a disk, and wrap with plastic. Chill in the refrigerator until firm enough to roll out (or chill overnight).

2. When ready to bake, line several baking sheets with parchment and heat the oven to 350°F. Flour a work surface. Working with one dough disk at a time, roll the dough to ³⁄₁₆ to ¼ inch thick, lightly flouring the rolling pin, the dough, and the work surface as needed to prevent sticking. Using a variety of cookie cutters, cut out shapes as close together as possible. Combine and reroll scraps as necessary. Using a thin metal spatula, transfer the cut–outs to the baking sheet and decorate with sanding sugars or other decorations. Bake one sheet at a time until the edges of the cookies are just beginning to turn golden, 9 to 10 minutes. Watch carefully—the cookies should remain pale except for the golden edges. Let cool completely on racks. Store the cookies, well wrapped in airtight containers, for up to a few days. —*Susie Middleton*

vanilla slice and bake cookies

15	oz. (3⅓ cups) unbleached all-purpose flour
¾	tsp. baking powder
½	tsp. table salt
9	oz. (1 cup plus 2 Tbs.) unsalted butter, softened at room temperature
1½	cups granulated sugar
1	large egg
1	large egg yolk
1½	tsp. pure vanilla extract

flavor variation: ginger-spiced

Adding crystallized ginger to this recipe may cause the dough to crumble as you slice the cookies; if that happens, just press them back together.

Add to the flour mixture:

¾	cup finely chopped crystallized ginger
2	tsp. ground ginger
1	tsp. ground cinnamon
	Pinch of ground black pepper

Break out your favorite cookie cutters or keep it simple and make rounds. These cookies stack and wrap beautifully.

1. In a medium bowl, whisk the flour, baking powder, and salt until well blended.

2. Using a stand mixer fitted with the paddle attachment (or in a large bowl with a hand mixer), beat the butter and sugar on medium speed until fluffy and well blended, about 3 minutes. Scrape the bowl and the beater. Add the egg, egg yolk, and vanilla. Continue mixing on medium until well blended, about 1 minute. Add the flour mixture and mix on low speed until the dough is well blended and forms moist clumps, about 1 minute.

3. Gently knead the dough by hand in the bowl until smooth. Shape it into 2 square or round logs, each about 10 inches long, and wrap in plastic. Refrigerate until chilled and very firm, about 4 hours.

4. Position a rack in the center of the oven and heat the oven to 350°F. Line two or three cookie sheets with parchment or nonstick baking liners. Using a thin-bladed, sharp knife and a ruler, mark off ³⁄₁₆-inch-wide slices on the top of the log. Using the same knife, cut straight down to form cookies. Arrange the cookies about 1 inch apart on the lined cookie sheets.

5. Bake the cookies one sheet at a time until the edges are golden brown, 11 to 13 minutes (for even browning, rotate the sheet after about 5 minutes). Let the cookies cool on the sheet for about 10 minutes and then transfer them to a rack to cool completely. —*Abigail Johnson Dodge*

PER COOKIE: 50 CALORIES | 1g PROTEIN | 6g CARB | 2.5g TOTAL FAT | 1.5g SAT FAT | 0.5g MONO FAT | 0g POLY FAT | 10mg CHOL | 15mg SODIUM | 0g FIBER

Make Ahead

The dough logs may be refrigerated for up to 3 days or frozen for 1 month. Thaw overnight in the refrigerator before proceeding with the recipe.

Tricks and Tips for Shaping "Logs" of Dough

Once your dough is mixed, make sure it's not too soft to shape. Stash it in the refrigerator for 20 to 30 minutes or until it's firm enough to handle. If it becomes too firm, just let it stand at room temperature until it's malleable.

• When shaping dough into cylinders, sprinkling a thin dusting of flour (no more than a teaspoon) on the rolling surface can help make the logs easier to handle.

• Moistening your hands ever so slightly can make shaping easier.

• Put the cylinders of dough on plastic wrap at least 6 inches longer than the length of the log.

• Take care not to roll the logs any longer than 10 inches; dough that you'll roll in nuts or other coatings will lengthen when coated, so start them off slightly shorter.

• As you wrap the log in plastic, roll tightly and tug on the ends to tighten the plastic and to smooth any creases.

• To secure the plastic, twist the ends well; then roll the dough back and forth to eliminate any air pockets.

• To compact the log, push the ends of the cylinder firmly toward the center.

ginger-spiced slice and bake cookies

vanilla slice and bake cookies

soft and chewy vanilla cookies

YIELDS ABOUT 2½ DOZEN COOKIES

- 6¾ oz. (1½ cups) unbleached all-purpose flour
- ½ tsp. table salt
- ¼ tsp. baking powder
- 6 oz. (¾ cup) unsalted butter, softened at room temperature
- 1¼ cups granulated sugar
- Seeds scraped from 1 vanilla bean, or 1½ tsp. pure vanilla extract
- 2 large eggs

Make Ahead

Store cookies in an airtight container at room temperature for up to 3 days or freeze for up to a month.

These thin, delicate rounds have a heady vanilla perfume. They can be eaten on their own or sandwiched with a touch of your favorite fruit preserves.

1. Position racks in the upper and lower thirds of the oven and heat the oven to 375°F. Line two cookie sheets with parchment.

2. In a medium bowl, whisk the flour, salt, and baking powder until well blended. In another medium bowl, using a stand mixer fitted with the paddle attachment (or in a large bowl with a hand mixer), beat the butter on medium-high speed until smooth. Add the sugar and vanilla bean seeds or extract and continue beating until well combined, about 2 minutes. Add the eggs and beat until well blended, about 1 minute longer. Add the flour mixture and mix on low speed until just blended, about 30 seconds.

3. Using a 1-tablespoon cookie scoop or 2 tablespoons, arrange heaping tablespoonfuls of the dough in mounds about 3 inches apart on the prepared cookie sheets. Bake two sheets at a time, swapping the sheets' positions halfway through baking, until the edges are golden brown, 10 to 14 minutes.

4. Set the sheets on racks and let cool for 5 minutes before transferring the cookies to the racks to cool completely. Using cooled cookie sheets, bake the remaining cookie dough. *—Abigail Johnson Dodge*

PER COOKIE: 100 CALORIES | 1G PROTEIN | 13G CARB | 5G TOTAL FAT | 3G SAT FAT | 1G MONO FAT | 0G POLY FAT | 25MG CHOL | 50MG SODIUM | 0G FIBER

Buying and Storing Vanilla Extract and Beans

EXTRACT

Buying: Always buy pure vanilla extract, never imitation, which can have an off-putting chemical flavor.

Storing: Sealed and stored in a cool, dark spot, vanilla extract will last almost forever—the flavor may even improve with age. That's good news if you like to buy in large quantities. Many good brands are available in larger volumes at discounted rates.

BEANS

Buying: Selecting vanilla beans is much like choosing fruit—look for size, shape, feel, and smell. The perfect bean is 5 to 7 inches long, plump, and has very dark brown skin; it should feel moist and supple (not dry and brittle) when rolled between your fingers. And be sure it passes the sniff test: Even through heavy plastic, the aroma should be close to intoxicating.

Storing: Store vanilla beans in a sealed container in a cool, dark place. They should stay moist for up to six months. If they begin to dry out, add them to your vanilla extract or a jar of vodka. And don't discard the used beans: The seeded pods still have tons of flavor. Add them to your sugar container, coffee beans, or favorite liqueur.

Vanilla Varieties

Just like wine or olive oil, the flavor of vanilla beans varies depending on where they're grown, so it's likely that in your supermarket you'll see vanilla beans and extract labeled Madagascar, Tahitian, or Mexican. If you're confused about which type to buy, consider their flavor profiles. Tahitian vanilla is known for its fragrant floral aroma, Mexican vanilla is nutty, and Madagascar vanilla is typically sweet and buttery. Choose one to suit your taste.

checkerboard cookies

YIELDS ABOUT 18 DOZEN COOKIES

FOR THE VANILLA DOUGH

- **6 oz. (¾ cup) unsalted butter, softened at room temperature**
- **½ tsp. table salt**
- **3½ oz. (1 cup) confectioners' sugar**
- **1½ oz. (⅓ cup plus 1 Tbs.) finely ground almonds**
- **1 large egg yolk, at room temperature**
- **1 tsp. pure vanilla extract**
- **9 oz. (2 cups) unbleached all-purpose flour**

FOR THE CHOCOLATE DOUGH

- **6 oz. (¾ cup) unsalted butter, softened at room temperature**
- **½ tsp. table salt**
- **3½ oz. (1 cup) confectioners' sugar**
- **1 oz. (¼ cup) finely ground almonds**
- **1 oz. (¼ cup) natural cocoa powder**
- **1 large egg yolk, at room temperature**
- **9 oz. (2 cups) unbleached all-purpose flour**

FOR THE EGG WASH

- **1 large egg, whisked well**

You'll end up with a little chocolate dough left over. The yield is big for this recipe, but the dough keeps for months in the freezer as long as you wrap it well.

MIX THE VANILLA DOUGH

1. With an electric mixer fitted with the paddle attachment, cream the butter on medium speed until soft and creamy but not melted. Add the salt and confectioners' sugar; mix on medium-low speed until thoroughly combined, about 5 minutes, scraping the bowl as needed. Reduce the speed to low and add the ground almonds, egg yolk, and vanilla extract; mix until blended. Add the flour; as soon as the dough comes together, stop the mixer.

2. Roll the dough between two sheets of parchment or waxed paper into an 8½ x 11-inch rectangle that's ⅓ inch thick; try to get the thickness very even. Transfer the dough to a baking sheet; refrigerate for several hours until hardened.

MIX THE CHOCOLATE DOUGH

Follow the instructions for the vanilla dough, adding the cocoa along with the ground almonds. Roll and chill as for the vanilla dough.

ASSEMBLE THE COOKIES

1. Remove the dough from the refrigerator, peel off the paper from both sides, and set the dough onto a fresh sheet of parchment. Using a sharp, thin knife, slice both doughs lengthwise into square strips about ⅓ inch thick. If the dough starts to soften, freeze it briefly to firm it up.

2. Set up your workspace so that you have a baking sheet to work on in front of you, both doughs to one side, and the egg wash with a pastry brush to the other side. Lay a strip of vanilla dough lengthwise on the baking sheet; then lay a strip of chocolate dough next to the vanilla; finally lay another strip of vanilla next to the chocolate. Press the three strips gently together so that they stick to one another. Brush the tops with the egg wash.

3. Lay a strip of chocolate directly on top of the first strip of vanilla, lay a strip of vanilla next to that, and a strip of chocolate next to that. Again, gently but firmly press together and down to ensure that all the strips are stuck to one another. Brush this layer with more egg wash. Finish with another layer of vanilla-chocolate-vanilla. Gently press the log together on all sides. Make more logs with the remaining strips. Chill the logs for at least an hour.

BAKE THE COOKIES

Position a rack in the center of the oven and heat the oven to 375°F. Line cookie sheets with parchment. When the logs are hard enough to slice, remove them from the refrigerator. Slice into cookies about ¼ inch thick. Set the squares ½ inch apart on the cookie sheets. Bake one sheet at a time until the vanilla parts are lightly browned, about 8 minutes, rotating the sheet halfway through. Let cool on the cookie sheet until cool enough to handle (about 10 minutes) and then transfer the cookies to a rack. —*Joanne Chang*

PER COOKIE: 25 CALORIES | 0g PROTEIN | 3g CARB | 1.5g TOTAL FAT | 1g SAT FAT | 0.5g MONO FAT | 0g POLY FAT | 5mg CHOL | 10mg SODIUM | 0g FIBER

how to shape and slice checkerboard cookies

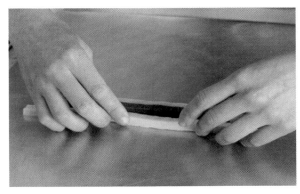

To build the first layer, sandwich one strip of chocolate between two vanilla strips. Press the strips together.

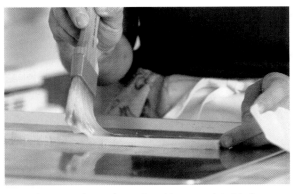

Brush the pressed-together strips with egg wash to bind them and the next layer. Brush each succeeding layer with more egg wash.

Don't worry if the strips break; gently press the pieces together as you build a 3x3 checkerboard.

Press the log firmly together on all sides to join the strips and square it up.

With a sharp knife, cut the chilled log into ¼-inch-thick slices and space them ½ inch apart on the parchment-lined sheet.

pinwheel cookies

YIELDS ABOUT 10 DOZEN
2-INCH COOKIES

- 13½ oz. (3 cups) unbleached all-purpose flour
- ½ tsp. table salt
- ¼ tsp. baking soda
- 10 oz. (1¼ cups) unsalted butter, slightly softened
- 1¼ cups granulated sugar
- 1 large egg
- 1½ tsp. pure vanilla extract
- 1 tsp. instant espresso powder
- 2 Tbs. boiling water
- 3 Tbs. unsweetened Dutch-processed cocoa powder
- 3 oz. bittersweet chocolate, melted and still warm (see p. 23 for tips on how to melt chocolate)

Store cooled cookies between sheets of waxed paper in an airtight container for up to 2 weeks, or freeze for up to 3 months.

MIX THE DOUGH

1. Sift together the flour, salt, and baking soda. Using a stand mixer fitted with the paddle attachment (or in a large bowl using a hand mixer), beat the butter on medium-low speed until smooth, about 2 minutes. Add the sugar in a steady stream and mix for another 2 minutes. Add the egg and vanilla and mix until well combined, scraping the bowl as needed. Reduce the speed to low and add the dry ingredients in two additions, mixing just until combined. Remove 2 cups less 2 Tbs. of the dough and set aside.

2. Dissolve the espresso powder in the boiling water and set aside briefly to cool. Then mix the espresso and cocoa powder into the remaining dough in the bowl. Reduce the mixer speed to low, add the melted chocolate, and mix just until thoroughly combined. To portion and shape the dough and roll it into pinwheel logs, see the instructions on the facing page.

BAKE THE COOKIES

Position racks in the upper and lower thirds of the oven and heat the oven to 350°F. Line two rimmed baking sheets with parchment. Working with one log at a time, use a sharp, thin-bladed knife to slice the dough into ³⁄₁₆-inch rounds. Set the rounds about 1 inch apart on the prepared sheets and bake until the tops of the cookies feel set, 12 to 14 minutes (don't let the edges become too brown). To ensure even browning, rotate the sheets as needed during baking. Let the baked cookies stand for 1 minute on the sheet. While they're still warm, use a thin metal spatula to transfer them to racks. —*Carole Walter*

how to layer and roll a pretty pinwheel cookie

Portion each flavor of dough into three equal pieces. (For accuracy, use a scale.) Shape each piece into a 5x5-inch square on a piece of plastic wrap and wrap well. The chocolate will be thicker than the vanilla. Refrigerate the dough for 30 minutes. (If the dough becomes too hard, let it stand at room temperature for a few minutes before rolling.)

While the dough is chilling, tear off twelve 12-inch squares of waxed paper. Roll each piece of dough into a 7x7-inch square between two sheets of the waxed paper. Without removing the waxed paper, layer the squares of dough on a baking sheet and refrigerate for 10 to 15 minutes. Have ready three 15-inch sheets of plastic wrap.

To shape the cookies, remove one square of the vanilla dough and one square of the chocolate dough from the refrigerator and peel off the top sheet of waxed paper from each. Invert the chocolate over the vanilla (or vice versa), aligning the two layers evenly. Gently roll over the dough to seal the layers together. Peel off the top layer of waxed paper.

Starting with the edge of the dough closest to you, carefully curl the edge of the dough up and over with your fingertips, so no space is visible in the center of the pinwheel.

Using the waxed paper as an aid, continue rolling the dough into a tight cylinder. After the cylinder is formed, roll it back and forth on the counter to slightly elongate it and compact it. Transfer the log to the plastic wrap. Roll tightly, twisting the ends of the plastic firmly to seal. With your hands on either end of the log, push firmly toward the center to compact the dough. It should be about 9 inches long and 1½ inches thick. Repeat with remaining dough. Refrigerate the logs until firm enough to slice, about 3 hours, or freeze for up to 3 months.

chocolate-chunk cookies

YIELDS ABOUT 40 COOKIES

- 9½ oz. (2 cups plus 2 Tbs.) unbleached all-purpose flour
- 1 tsp. baking soda
- ½ tsp. table salt
- ½ lb. (1 cup) unsalted butter, softened at room temperature
- ¾ cup granulated sugar
- ¾ cup plus 2 Tbs. very firmly packed light brown sugar
- 2 large eggs
- ½ tsp. pure vanilla extract
- 9 oz. bittersweet chocolate, coarsely chopped
- 2½ oz. milk chocolate, coarsely chopped

A mix of milk and dark chocolate chunks makes for a doubly tasty version of chocolate-chip cookies. Chopping your own chocolate into chunks gives the pieces a welcome lack of uniformity: Some bites yield especially big "chips."

1. Position a rack in the center of the oven and heat the oven to 350°F. In a medium bowl, whisk the flour, baking soda, and salt to blend. Using a stand mixer fitted with the paddle attachment (or in a large bowl with a hand mixer), beat the butter and both sugars on medium speed until light and fluffy, 4 to 5 minutes. Scrape the bowl with a rubber spatula. Beat in the eggs and vanilla until thoroughly combined, about 2 minutes. Scrape the bowl again. With the mixer on low speed, slowly blend in the flour mixture until incorporated, about 30 seconds. Fold in the chopped chocolate mixture with the spatula, making sure all the flour and butter are thoroughly combined.

2. Drop the dough by rounded tablespoonfuls about 3 inches apart on ungreased cookie sheets. Bake until the cookies are golden brown on the edges and slightly soft in the center, about 15 minutes. Let the cookies cool on the sheet for 1 minute before transferring them to a rack to cool.
—*Joanne Chang*

tips for evenly baked cookies

- Be sure that unbaked cookies are all about the same size or rolled to an even thickness; that way, they'll all finish baking around the same time.

- Use cookie sheets, not rimmed baking pans. Unrimmed sheets allow better air circulation around the cookies while they're in the oven.

- Be sure to use heavy-duty cookie sheets that won't warp. If the sheets warp, your cookies will slide around and bake unevenly.

- Bake cookies one sheet at a time, unless you're using a convection oven. If the dough doesn't fit onto one cookie sheet, drop the remaining batter onto a second sheet and bake it after the first batch comes out of the oven. If you're reusing cookie sheets, be sure to let them cool down before putting more dough on them.

chewy chocolate-chip cookies

**YIELDS ABOUT 9 DOZEN
2½-INCH COOKIES**

10¾ oz. (1⅓ cups) cold unsalted
butter

1½ cups packed light brown
sugar

1 cup granulated sugar

2 large cold eggs

1 Tbs. pure vanilla extract

17 oz. (3¾ cups) unbleached
all-purpose flour

1¼ tsp. table salt

1 tsp. baking soda

12 oz. semisweet chocolate
chips

*Use butter and eggs right out
of the refrigerator so the dough
stays cool and the cookies maintain their thickness during baking.*

1. Position racks in the upper and
center portions of the oven and
heat the oven to 375°F.

2. Using a stand mixer fitted with
the paddle attachment (or in a
large bowl with a hand mixer),
beat the butter and both sugars,
starting on low speed and gradu-
ally working your way up to high speed until the mixture is light and fluffy,
about 3 minutes once you reach high speed. Scrape the bowl and beater. Add
the eggs and vanilla and beat on low until blended. Beat on high until light and
fluffy, about 1 minute. Scrape the bowl and beater.

3. In a medium bowl, whisk the flour, salt, and baking soda. Add this to the
butter mixture and stir with a wooden spoon until just blended; the dough will
be stiff. Stir in the chocolate chips.

4. Drop rounded measuring teaspoons of dough about 2 inches apart onto
two ungreased cookie sheets. Refrigerate any unused dough.

5. Bake until the bottoms of the cookies are golden brown, 8 to 10 minutes,
rotating the sheets halfway through for even baking. Remove the sheets from
the oven, let sit for 3 to 5 minutes, and then transfer the cookies with a spatula
to a rack to cool completely. Let the cookie sheets cool completely before
baking the remaining dough. *—Bonnie Gorder-Hinchey*

PER COOKIE: 70 CALORIES | 1g PROTEIN | 10g CARB | 3.5g TOTAL FAT | 2g SAT FAT
| 1g MONO FAT | 0g POLY FAT | 10mg CHOL | 40mg SODIUM | 0g FIBER

**Your kitchen's temperature will affect the temperature of the
dough, as will dropping cookies onto still-hot cookie sheets: For
chewy cookies, be sure to bake them on cool sheets or else the heat
from the pan will spread them thin and they'll turn out crispy. To
keep the cookies soft after baking, store them in an airtight container along with a slice of bread.**

crisp chocolate-chip cookies

YIELDS ABOUT 6 DOZEN 3-INCH COOKIES

- **12 oz. (1½ cups) unsalted butter, softened at room temperature; more for the cookie sheets**
- **1 cup granulated sugar**
- **¾ cup packed light brown sugar**
- **2 large eggs, at room temperature**
- **2 tsp. pure vanilla extract**
- **13½ oz. (3 cups) unbleached all-purpose flour**
- **1 tsp. table salt**
- **1 tsp. baking soda**
- **12 oz. semisweet chocolate chips**

Humid weather will soften even the crispiest cookies in as little as a day, so store them well wrapped.

Using more white sugar than brown sugar increases the crispiness of these wafer-thin cookies. Be sure the butter and eggs are at room temperature before mixing to help the cookies spread thinner as they bake. Greased baking sheets encourage the cookies to spread even more.

1. Position racks in the upper and center portions of the oven and heat the oven to 375°F. Butter two cookie sheets.

2. Using a stand mixer fitted with the paddle attachment (or in a large bowl with a hand mixer), beat the butter and both sugars on high speed until light and fluffy, about 1 minute. Scrape the bowl and beater. Add the eggs and vanilla and beat on low until blended. Beat on high until light and fluffy, about 1 minute. Scrape the bowl and beater.

3. In a medium bowl, whisk together the flour, salt, and baking soda. Add this to the butter mixture and beat on medium low until just blended. Stir in the chocolate chips with a wooden spoon. Drop rounded measuring teaspoonfuls of dough 2 inches apart onto the prepared cookie sheets.

4. Bake until deep golden brown around the edges and golden in the center, 8 to 10 minutes, rotating the cookie sheets halfway through for even baking. Remove the sheets from the oven, let sit for 3 to 5 minutes, and then transfer the cookies with a spatula to a rack to cool completely. Repeat until all the dough is baked. *—Bonnie Gorder-Hinchey*

PER COOKIE: 100 CALORIES | 1g PROTEIN | 12g CARB | 5g TOTAL FAT | 3.5g SAT FAT | 1.5g MONO FAT | 0g POLY FAT | 15mg CHOL | 55mg SODIUM | 0g FIBER

chocolate-chip tips

Chocolate chips are specially formulated morsels that retain their shape and creamy texture without burning, making them ideal mix-ins for cookies. Here is some useful information about these marvelous morsels:

- Though most chips are semisweet or bittersweet, there are also milk chocolate morsels, as well as miniature and oversize ones and chocolate "chunks."

- Don't have chips on hand? You can usually substitute coarsely chopped semi- or bittersweet chocolate with decent results.

- Avoid substituting chocolate chips when the recipe calls for bitter- or semisweet chocolate; since chocolate chips contain significantly less cocoa butter than bar chocolate, they behave differently when melted.

- Store chocolate chips as you would all chocolate, well sealed in a cool place away from light and heat and strong-flavored foods.

Control the Amount and Temperature of Key Ingredients to Get the Cookie You Like

Sugar The moisture in sugar affects chewiness: The relative amount of white vs. brown sugar you use has a great effect on texture because each type has a different moisture content (brown sugar is much wetter than white). Using more brown sugar will produce a softer, chewier cookie, while using more white sugar will turn out cookies that are sandier in texture and crisper overall.

Flour Keep in mind that the way you measure flour makes a big difference. Too much flour will make the cookie firm, dry, and tough, while too little flour will cause the cookie to spread too much and lose structure. Always use a scale to measure flour so your results are as consistent as possible. If you do use a measuring cup, here's how to do it: First, always use a true dry measure—not a Pyrex® cup. Fluff the flour with a fork to avoid densely packed flour. Then, spoon the flour from the bag into the measuring cup and level it with a knife—never scoop right from the bag, which would compact too much flour into the cup. And be careful not to shake or tap the cup as you add the flour, as this would pack down the flour as well.

Butter and Eggs Baking recipes usually specify the temperature for butter and eggs, but does it really matter? Absolutely. The temperature of these ingredients helps control how much the dough spreads. Cool ingredients will keep your dough cooler, which means it will spread more slowly in the oven, letting the oven's heat "set" the cookie while it's still thick, and producing a denser, chewier cookie. Warm dough spreads more quickly in the oven, which makes the cookies thinner and crisper. A high proportion of butter to flour in the dough will also allow it to spread quickly.

Warming eggs quickly is as easy as dunking them in warm water for a minute or two. Butter presents a bigger problem. Some people warm butter in the microwave, but just a few seconds too long and it's melted. It's best just to plan ahead.

gingerbread cookies

YIELDS THIRTY 4-INCH COOKIES
OR FORTY 3-INCH COOKIES

- 10½ oz. (2⅓ cups) unbleached all-purpose flour; more for rolling
- 1 tsp. baking soda
- ½ tsp. table salt
- 2 tsp. ground ginger
- 1 tsp. ground cinnamon
- ½ tsp. ground cloves
- 4 oz. (½ cup) unsalted butter, softened at room temperature
- ½ cup packed dark brown sugar
- ½ cup molasses
- 1 Tbs. grated or finely minced fresh ginger
- 1 large egg

Because they're rolled so thin, these gingerbread cookies feel more sophisticated than most, even when shaped like little people. Lightly flour the sharp edge of your cookie cutters to keep the dough from sticking.

1. In a medium bowl, combine the flour, baking soda, salt, ground ginger, cinnamon, and cloves. Using a stand mixer fitted with the paddle attachment, beat the butter and brown sugar until light and fluffy, scraping the bowl from time to time with a rubber spatula. Beat in the molasses, fresh ginger, and egg, again scraping down the sides of the bowl to blend the mixture. Beat in the flour mixture just until combined. Remove the dough from the bowl (it will be somewhat sticky), divide it in half, wrap each half in plastic, and chill until firm, at least 3 hours.

2. Position a rack in the center of the oven and heat the oven to 325°F. Line two or three cookie sheets with parchment. Generously flour a work surface. Remove the dough from the refrigerator. It may be stiff and hard to roll at first; let it sit for a few minutes. Roll the dough ³⁄₁₆ inch thick. Cut out the shapes with cookie cutters and arrange them on the cookie sheets about 1 inch apart. Reroll the scraps to make more cookies. Bake until the undersides are browned, 12 to 14 minutes. Let cool on the sheets before transferring or decorating. *—Joanne Chang*

PER COOKIE: 100 CALORIES | 1g PROTEIN | 15g CARB | 3.5g TOTAL FAT | 2g SAT FAT | 1g MONO FAT | 0g POLY FAT | 15mg CHOL | 85mg SODIUM | 0g FIBER

Make Ahead

These cookies can be stored in an airtight container for 3 to 4 days.

black and white crescents

YIELDS ABOUT FORTY-TWO
3-INCH COOKIES

- 6 ¾ oz. (1½ cups) unbleached all-purpose flour
- ¼ tsp. table salt
- ⅓ cup unsweetened cocoa powder
- ½ tsp. baking soda
- 4 oz. (½ cup) unsalted butter, softened at room temperature
- ½ cup plus 2 Tbs. granulated sugar
- 1 large egg
- 1 tsp. pure vanilla extract
- 2 oz. white chocolate

cookie shaping tips

- Chill the dough until firm before shaping.
- Work with half the dough at a time, keeping the rest chilled.
- If the dough sticks to your hands, try wetting your hands lightly with cold water.
- Shape the cookies identically so that they bake for the same amount of time.

For the best flavor, use good-quality white chocolate for the drizzle decoration.

SEVERAL HOURS BEFORE BAKING

1. In a medium bowl, combine the flour and salt. Sift in the cocoa and baking soda; stir well to mix.

2. Using a stand mixer fitted with the paddle attachment (or in a large bowl with a hand mixer), beat the butter and sugar on medium speed until light and fluffy. Beat in the egg and vanilla, scraping the bowl, until smooth and blended. Add the flour mixture and beat on low until well combined. Wrap the dough in plastic and chill for at least 2 hours.

BAKE THE COOKIES

1. Heat the oven to 350°F. Line two cookie sheets with parchment. Scoop the dough into pieces about the size of a heaping teaspoon. Roll each piece between your palms to form balls. Roll each ball into a 3-inch-long cylinder, tapering the ends slightly. Put the cylinders about ¾ inch apart on a cookie sheet and curve the ends to make crescent shapes. When one sheet is filled, bake for 8 minutes while filling the other sheet. Bake the second batch for 8 minutes. (They'll be puffed, covered with tiny cracks, and dry on top.) Let cool on the sheets.

2. When the cookies are completely cooled, melt the white chocolate in the microwave or in the top of a double boiler over barely simmering water. Put the melted chocolate into a small zip-top plastic bag. Snip a tiny hole in one bottom corner of the bag. Pipe the chocolate across the cookies to make thin zigzag stripes. Let the stripes harden at room temperature or in the refrigerator before serving or storing the cookies. *—Elaine Khosrova*

peanut butter cookies

YIELDS 4½ DOZEN COOKIES

- **13 oz. (2¾ cups plus 1 Tbs.) unbleached all-purpose flour**
- **1 tsp. baking soda**
- **½ lb. (1 cup) unsalted butter, softened at room temperature**
- **1 cup granulated sugar**
- **1 cup very firmly packed light brown sugar**
- **2 large eggs**
- **1 lb. (1¾ cups) smooth peanut butter (such as Skippy® or Jif®)**
- **¼ tsp. pure vanilla extract**
- **½ cup salted peanuts, chopped**

To make it easier to measure the peanut butter, lightly coat your measuring cup with oil or cooking spray and the peanut butter will slide out smoothly.

1. Position a rack in the center of the oven and heat the oven to 350°F. Sift together the flour and baking soda. Using a stand mixer fitted with the paddle attachment (or in a large bowl with a hand mixer), beat the butter and both sugars on medium speed until light and fluffy, 4 to 5 minutes. Scrape the bowl with a rubber spatula. Beat in the eggs until thoroughly combined, 1 to 2 minutes. Scrape the bowl again. Beat in the peanut butter and vanilla until blended, about 1 minute. Scrape the bowl again. With the mixer on low speed, slowly add the flour until incorporated, about 30 seconds. Mix in the peanuts.

2. Drop the dough by rounded tablespoonfuls about 3 inches apart on ungreased cookie sheets and flatten each cookie slightly with the palm of your hand. Using the tines of a fork, make a crisscross pattern on top of each cookie. Bake until the cookies are golden brown on the edges and slightly soft in the center, 15 to 18 minutes. Let the cookies cool on the sheet for 1 minute before transferring them to a rack to cool. —*Joanne Chang*

Make Ahead

These cookies can be stored in an airtight container for up to 3 days.

Natural vs. Emulsified Peanut Butter

At its most basic, peanut butter is simply ground peanuts and salt, which is all you'll find in many natural peanut butters. Super-smooth emulsified peanut butters contain sweeteners, oils, and ingredients that keep the peanut oil and nut mass from separating. The two kinds differ enormously in texture and flavor, with the natural peanut butters having a more coarse texture.

vanilla sugar cookies

YIELDS ABOUT 2 DOZEN
COOKIES

- 8½ oz. (1¾ cups) unbleached all-purpose flour
- ½ tsp. baking powder
- ½ tsp. table salt
- ½ lb. (1 cup) unsalted butter, softened at room temperature
- 1 cup granulated sugar; more for coating
- 1 large egg
- ½ tsp. pure vanilla extract

Be sure to bake these cookies on a cookie sheet, not a rimmed baking sheet; otherwise, the dough will spread too much, and the cookies won't retain a nice, round shape.

1. Position a rack in the center of the oven and heat the oven to 350°F. In a medium bowl, whisk the flour, baking powder, and salt to blend. Using a stand mixer fitted with the paddle attachment (or in a large bowl with a hand mixer), beat the butter and sugar on medium speed until light and fluffy, about 3 minutes. Scrape the bowl with a rubber spatula. Beat in the egg and vanilla until thoroughly combined, about 2 minutes. Scrape the bowl again. With the mixer on low speed, slowly blend in the flour mixture until incorporated, about 30 seconds.

2. Drop the dough by rounded tablespoonfuls into a bowl of granulated sugar and roll to coat; then set the coated balls about 3 inches apart on ungreased cookie sheets.

3. Bake one sheet at a time until the cookies are golden brown on the edges and slightly soft in the center, 15 to 18 minutes. Let the cookies cool on the sheet for 1 minute before transferring them to a rack to cool completely.
—Joanne Chang

Make Ahead

These cookies can be stored in an airtight container for up to 3 days.

double chocolate cookies

- **5** oz. unsweetened chocolate, chopped
- **½** lb. bittersweet or semisweet chocolate, coarsely chopped
- **¼** lb. (½ cup) unsalted butter, cut into four pieces
- **4** large eggs
- **1½** cups granulated sugar
- **¼** tsp. pure vanilla extract
- **2½** oz. (½ cup plus 2 Tbs.) unbleached all-purpose flour
- **½** tsp. baking powder
- **¼** tsp. table salt
- **3** oz. (¾ cup) walnuts, toasted and chopped

These cookies can be stored in an airtight container for up to 3 days or frozen for about a month.

1. Melt the unsweetened chocolate, 4 oz. of the bittersweet or semisweet chocolate, and the butter in a small saucepan over low heat (or in a bowl in the microwave) and set aside to cool slightly.

2. Using a stand mixer fitted with the whisk attachment (or in a large bowl with a hand mixer), whip the eggs and sugar on medium-high speed until thick and light, about 10 minutes. With the mixer on low speed, add the melted chocolate mixture and the vanilla and mix until blended.

3. With a rubber spatula, fold in the flour, baking powder, and salt and scrape the bowl. Fold in the remaining chopped chocolate and the walnuts. Refrigerate the dough until it's firm enough to scoop, about 1½ hours.

4. Position a rack in the center of the oven and heat the oven to 350°F. Drop the chilled dough by rounded tablespoonfuls about 3 inches apart on ungreased cookie sheets. Bake one sheet at a time until the cookies are cracked on top and feel dry on the surface but still soft inside, about 15 minutes. Let the cookies cool on the sheet for 1 minute before transferring them to a rack to cool completely. —*Joanne Chang*

Tips for Melting Chocolate

Chop white and milk chocolate finely. White and milk chocolates are delicate; if they get too hot they can get gritty or scorch. Chopping them finely and stirring frequently helps melt them quickly and evenly with minimal heat.

Chop dark chocolate coarsely. It's more forgiving than white or milk chocolate, so chop it into coarse pieces. It will take a little longer to melt than if it were finely chopped, but it means less knife work up front, and less frequent stirring.

Watch out for water. Unless you're melting chocolate along with a significant amount of water or another ingredient like butter or cream, just a few drops of water (like what might be in a wet bowl) can make the chocolate seize into an unworkable mass. Be sure that all the tools that come in contact with the chocolate are bone-dry before you start, and to avoid condensation, don't cover melting chocolate.

snickerdoodles

YIELDS ABOUT 3 DOZEN COOKIES

- ½ lb. (1 cup) unsalted butter, softened at room temperature; more for the cookie sheets
- 12 oz. (2⅔ cups) unbleached all-purpose flour
- 2 tsp. cream of tartar
- 1 tsp. baking soda
- ¼ tsp. table salt
- 1¾ cups granulated sugar
- 2 large eggs
- 2 Tbs. ground cinnamon

Make Ahead

These cookies can be stored in an airtight container for up to 3 days.

Buttery, soft, and cinnamon scented, these are great cookies to give as a gift. Present a few in a pretty teacup (or coffee mug) with a ribbon tied around it.

1. Position a rack in the center of the oven and heat the oven to 350°F. Grease a cookie sheet with butter.

2. In a medium bowl, whisk the flour, cream of tartar, baking soda, and salt to blend. Using a stand mixer fitted with the paddle attachment (or in a large bowl with a hand mixer), beat the butter and 1½ cups of the sugar on medium speed until light and fluffy, about 3 minutes. Scrape the bowl with a rubber spatula. Beat in the eggs until thoroughly combined, about 2 minutes. Scrape the bowl again. With the mixer on low speed, slowly blend in the flour mixture until incorporated, about 30 seconds.

3. In a small bowl, mix the cinnamon and remaining ¼ cup sugar. Drop the dough by rounded tablespoonfuls into the cinnamon sugar and roll around to coat. Set the coated balls of dough about 3 inches apart on the prepared cookie sheet. Bake until golden brown on the edges and slightly soft in the center, 15 to 18 minutes. Let the cookies cool on the sheet for 1 minute before transferring them to a rack to cool completely. Repeat with the remaining dough. —*Joanne Chang*

Ingredient Profile: Cinnamon

Made from rolled, pressed, and dried tree bark, both cinnamon and its more common relative cassia have a pleasing, woody fragrance and sweet flavor in both stick and ground form. The widely available brands tend to be made from cassia (*Cinnamomum cassia*). For cassia, look for names such as Korintje (from Indonesia) or Saigon cinnamon (from Vietnam), varieties that tend to possess the fullest and finest flavor. The best true cinnamon (*Cinnamomum zelanicum*) comes from Ceylon and India.

Whole cinnamon sticks work well for infusing subtle flavor into custard sauce, hot cider, and poaching syrups, but ground cinnamon is what you want for cookies.

classic lace cookies

YIELDS ABOUT 3 DOZEN 3-INCH COOKIES

2 oz. blanched almonds (to yield ½ cup ground almonds)

2½ oz. (5 Tbs.) unsalted butter

⅓ cup granulated sugar

2 Tbs. light corn syrup

1½ oz. (⅓ cup) unbleached all-purpose flour

   Pinch of table salt

1 tsp. pure vanilla extract

flavor variations

• Add ½ tsp. almond extract for more almond flavor.

• Add 1 tsp. grated lemon zest or orange zest.

• Replace the ground almonds with ground hazelnuts.

• Dissolve 1 tsp. instant coffee with the sugar.

• Mix in 3 Tbs. very finely diced crystallized ginger.

For a slightly thicker cookie that's easier to handle, melt four tablespoons of butter rather than five, which makes a thicker batter but still gives you lacy results.

1. Position racks in the center and upper third of the oven and heat the oven to 350°F. Line two baking sheets with nonstick liners, or with parchment. Line a wire rack with paper towels.

2. In a food processor, grind the almonds finely and measure out ½ cup. In a medium saucepan, heat the butter, sugar, and corn syrup over low heat, stirring often, until the butter melts and the sugar dissolves. Increase the heat to medium high and, stirring constantly, bring the mixture just to a boil. Remove the pot from the heat and stir in the flour and salt until incorporated. Stir in the ground almonds and vanilla.

3. Drop the batter by the teaspoon 3 inches apart on the baking sheets, about ½ dozen cookies per baking sheet. Bake the cookies until evenly light brown, about 10 minutes total. About 6 minutes into baking, switch the sheets from top to bottom and back to front to promote even baking.

4. Remove the cookies from the oven and let them cool on the baking sheets for a few minutes, until firm. Then use a wide spatula to transfer them to the paper-towel-lined rack to cool completely. Bake off the remaining cookies; the batter will have firmed up a bit, but that's fine. —*Elinor Klivans*

PER COOKIE: 40 CALORIES | 0g PROTEIN | 4g CARB | 2.5g TOTAL FAT | 1g SAT FAT | 1g MONO FAT | 0.5g POLY FAT | 5mg CHOL | 10mg SODIUM | 0g FIBER

cream cheese spritz cookies

YIELDS ABOUT 100 COOKIES, DEPENDING ON SIZE AND STYLE

- ½ lb. (1 cup) unsalted butter, softened at room temperature
- 3 oz. cream cheese (preferably Philadelphia® brand), softened at room temperature
- 1 cup granulated sugar
- 1 large egg yolk
- 1 tsp. pure vanilla extract
- 11¼ oz. (2½ cups) unbleached all-purpose flour, sifted
- 1 egg white, lightly beaten

  Colored sugars or other decorations for sprinkling (optional)

The original recipe for these sweet and slightly tangy cookies dates back to the 1960s. Luckily, today's cookie presses are much easier to use than the old hand-crank variety, so baking dozens of pretty little cookies is a snap.

1. Position a rack in the center of the oven and heat the oven to 375°F. Using a stand mixer fitted with the paddle attachment (or in a large bowl using a hand mixer), beat the butter, cream cheese, and sugar on medium speed until light and fluffy, about 4 minutes. Add the egg yolk and vanilla and beat again until blended. Add the flour and mix on low speed until blended.

2. Fit a cookie press with a die plate. Scoop up about a quarter of the dough and, using a small amount of flour if needed, shape the dough into a log just narrower than the barrel of the cookie press. Slide the log into the cookie press and spritz the cookies directly onto ungreased baking sheets about 1 inch apart. Brush the tops with the beaten egg white and sprinkle with colored sugar or other decorations, if using. Repeat with the remaining dough.

3. Bake one sheet at a time until the cookies are just golden around the edges, 10 to 12 minutes. Let the cookies cool on the baking sheet on a rack for 5 minutes before transferring them to a rack to cool completely. Be sure the baking sheet is cool before spritzing more cookies. Store at room temperature or freeze in an airtight container, separating the cookie layers with waxed paper. *—Jennifer Weglowski*

potato-chip cookies

- ½ lb. (1 cup) unsalted butter, softened at room temperature; more for shaping
- ½ cup granulated sugar; more for shaping
- 1 tsp. pure vanilla extract
- ½ lb. (scant 2 cups) unbleached all-purpose flour
- 2 oz. (½ cup) finely chopped pecans
- ½ cup finely crushed potato chips

Don't refrigerate or freeze the unbaked dough, as the potato chips will become soggy.

Potato chips in a cookie? You bet. This recipe adds a new and delicious crunch to the traditional pecan sandie, resulting in a buttery cookie with a light and flaky texture that's destined to be a staple on your cookie tray.

1. Position racks in the center and upper third of the oven and heat the oven to 350°F. Line two large baking sheets with parchment.

2. Using a stand mixer fitted with the paddle attachment (or in a large bowl with a hand mixer), beat the butter and sugar on medium speed until creamy and well blended, about 4 minutes, scraping the bowl as needed. Add the vanilla and beat again until blended. Add the flour, pecans, and potato chips and mix on low speed until just blended.

3. Shape heaping teaspoons of dough into 1-inch balls. Arrange the balls about 2 inches apart on the prepared baking sheets. Put some sugar in a shallow bowl. Lightly grease the bottom of a glass or measuring cup with soft butter. Dip the glass into the sugar and press the glass down on a dough ball until it's about ¼ inch thick. Repeat dipping and pressing with the remaining balls.

4. Bake until the cookies look dry on top and the edges are light golden, 10 to 12 minutes, rotating and swapping the positions of the sheets for even baking. Let the cookies cool on the sheets on racks for 5 minutes before transferring them to racks to cool completely. Store at room temperature or freeze in an airtight container, separating the cookie layers with waxed paper.
—Candice Clauss

marbled chocolate-vanilla cookies

YIELDS ABOUT THIRTY-SIX
2½-INCH COOKIES

- 6¾ oz. (1½ cups) unbleached all-purpose flour
- ½ tsp. baking powder
- ¼ tsp. table salt
- ¼ lb. (½ cup) unsalted butter, softened
- ¾ cup granulated sugar
- 1 large egg
- 1 tsp. pure vanilla extract
- 2 Tbs. unsweetened cocoa powder
- 2 oz. semisweet chocolate (preferably high quality), melted and cooled slightly

For tips and tricks on how to shape logs of dough, see p. 6.

For a very distinct marbled pattern, handle this dough as little as possible.

SEVERAL HOURS OR THE DAY BEFORE BAKING

1. In a medium bowl, sift together the flour, baking powder, and salt. Using a stand mixer fitted with the paddle attachment (or in a large bowl with a hand mixer), beat the butter and sugar until light and fluffy. Beat in the egg and vanilla, scrape the bowl, and beat again until blended. Lower the speed and add the flour mixture, beating just until combined. Remove half the dough (about 9 oz.); and set it aside. Whisk the cocoa into the melted chocolate; add to the dough remaining in the mixing bowl and beat briefly to blend.

2. Portion the chocolate and vanilla doughs into eight pieces each, more or less the same size. Recombine the pieces, alternately pressing the chocolate and vanilla pieces together, to create a marbled ball. On a lightly floured surface, roll and shape the ball into a 9-inch-long log. Wrap in plastic and chill until very firm, 2 to 3 hours.

BAKE THE COOKIES

Heat the oven to 350°F. Line baking sheets with parchment. Unwrap the firm dough and roll the log briefly on the counter to make it more evenly round. Cut it crosswise into ¼-inch-thick slices; arrange the slices 1½ inches apart on the sheets. Bake until the edges are lightly browned, 9 to 11 minutes, rotating the sheets from the top to bottom racks after 5 minutes for even baking. Let cool on the baking sheets for 5 minutes and then transfer the cookies to a rack to cool completely. *—Elaine Khosrova*

chocolate fudge cookies

**YIELDS ABOUT 3 DOZEN
2¾-INCH COOKIES**

- **8½ oz. (1¾ cups) unbleached
  all-purpose flour**

- **⅓ cup unsweetened cocoa
  powder**

- **½ tsp. baking soda**

- **½ tsp. table salt**

- **6 oz. (¾ cup) unsalted butter,
  slightly softened**

- **1 cup packed dark brown sugar**

- **½ cup granulated sugar**

- **2 large eggs**

- **1 tsp. pure vanilla extract**

- **9 oz. (1½ cups) semisweet
  chocolate chunks**

- **3½ oz. (about ¾ cup) coarsely
  chopped pecans**

*These cookies are especially good and chewy if underbaked using the short
time indicated in the baking instructions below; otherwise the cookies will be
overly crisp and hard when cooled.*

1. Heat the oven to 350°F. Line cookie sheets with parchment. In a
medium bowl, mix the flour, cocoa powder, baking soda, and salt. Using a
stand mixer fitted with the paddle attachment (or in a large bowl with a hand
mixer), beat the butter and both sugars on medium-high speed until light and
fluffy, scraping the bowl as needed. Beat in the eggs, one at a time, and then
the vanilla, scraping the bowl. Add the flour mixture and mix on medium-low,
just until combined. Scrape down the bowl and stir in the chocolate
and pecans.

2. Drop the dough by the heaping tablespoonful about 2 inches apart onto
the cookie sheets. Bake until they're still very soft but no longer look wet,
about 8 minutes. Let cool on the cookies sheets for 5 minutes and then
transfer the cookies to a rack to cool completely. *—Elaine Khosrova*

technique tips for drop cookies

- Before mixing, your butter should be malleable but not very
  soft. If it's too soft, it will spread too much during baking, and the
  cookies may become too thin and delicate to handle. Generally,
  30 to 60 minutes at room temperature is enough time to slightly
  soften the butter.

- To make chewy drop cookies, underbake them slightly so that
  they're still quite soft and not yet browned, but no longer look
  wet in the center. For crisper cookies, bake them longer, letting
  the cookies become lightly browned all over.

- Use a spring-loaded 1¼-inch ice-cream scoop for ease and
  consistency when dropping dough onto the baking sheets.

chocolate cut-outs

YIELDS ABOUT 4 DOZEN
2½-INCH COOKIES

10 oz. (2¼ cups) unbleached all-purpose flour; more for rolling

1½ oz. (½ cup) natural unsweetened cocoa

Pinch of table salt

½ lb. (1 cup) unsalted butter, softened at room temperature

¾ cup granulated sugar

1½ tsp. pure vanilla extract

These cookies are a perfect "canvas" for decorating. Pipe on Royal Icing (see below), or even use edible gold leaf, applied with a small paintbrush.

1. In a medium bowl, combine the flour, cocoa, and salt. Using a stand mixer fitted with the paddle attachment (or in a large bowl with a hand mixer), beat the butter, sugar, and vanilla on medium speed until well blended. Add the flour mixture; beat until well blended. Halve the dough and shape it into two flat disks; wrap one in plastic while you work with the other.

2. Position a rack in the center of the oven and heat the oven to 350°F. On a lightly floured surface, roll one disk ⅜ inch thick. Cut out shapes and set them 1 inch apart on parchment-lined baking sheets. Repeat with the other disk. Combine the scraps, chill them if they feel warm, and re-roll. Bake the cookies one sheet at a time until the tops look dry and you see flaky layers when you break a cookie in half. Transfer to a rack to cool completely. Decorate the cooled cookies. —*Abigail Johnson Dodge*

PER COOKIE: 70 CALORIES | 1g PROTEIN | 8g CARB | 4g TOTAL FAT | 2.5g SAT FAT | 1g MONO FAT | 0g POLY FAT | 10mg CHOL | 5mg SODIUM | 0g FIBER

royal icing

YIELDS ABOUT 3 CUPS

3 large egg whites (or 2 Tbs. powdered egg whites or meringue powder plus 6 Tbs. warm water)

1 lb. (4 cups) confectioners' sugar

Food coloring (optional)

1. If using the powdered egg whites or meringue powder and warm water, combine them in the bowl of a stand mixer or in a large bowl. Let stand, whisking frequently, until the powder is dissolved, about 5 minutes. If using fresh egg whites, just put them in the bowl.

2. Using a stand mixer fitted with the whisk attachment (or in a large bowl with a hand mixer), begin mixing on medium speed until frothy. Add the confectioners' sugar and continue beating until blended. Increase the speed to high and beat until the mixture is thick and shiny, about 3 minutes for fresh eggs and 5 minutes for powdered. Stir in food coloring (if using). Put a damp paper towel directly on the icing to keep a skin from forming. If not using within 2 hours, cover the bowl with plastic and refrigerate. —*Abigail Johnson Dodge*

Risk-free Royal Icing

Royal icing carries a very slight risk of salmonella infection from the raw egg whites used to make it. If you want to eliminate that risk completely, use pasteurized whites, which are available either dried or fresh. Look for dried egg white powder or meringue powder (dried egg white powder plus sugar and stabilizers) in the baking section of the market. You'll need to reconstitute the powder before making the icing, as described in the recipe on the facing page.

Fresh pasteurized egg whites are kept in the dairy case near the other eggs and egg products. Depending on your store, you may find cartons of whole in-shell pasteurized eggs (look closely at all the cartons because they're packaged just like regular eggs and are sometimes hard to notice), or you may find containers of liquid egg whites. Use fresh pasteurized egg whites just as you would use regular egg whites.

cream cheese swirls

YIELDS ABOUT 4 DOZEN COOKIES

½ lb. (1 cup) unsalted butter, softened at room temperature

8 oz. cream cheese, softened at room temperature

1 cup granulated sugar

1 tsp. pure vanilla extract

10 oz. (2¼ cups) unbleached all-purpose flour

Apricot or raspberry preserves

Piping is easier if the butter and cream cheese are at room temperature and if you work with small amounts of dough in the piping bag. For these cookies to look and taste their best, dab on the preserves right before serving or giving.

Position a rack in the center of the oven and heat the oven to 350°F. Using a stand mixer fitted with the paddle attachment (or in a large bowl with a hand mixer), beat the butter, cream cheese, and sugar on medium speed until very smooth, scraping the bowl often. Stir in the vanilla. Add the flour; mix until just combined. Fit a pastry bag with a wide star tip and fill the bag with the dough. On parchment-lined cookie sheets, pipe the dough in 1½-inch "S" shapes about 1½ inches apart. Press your thumb into each end of the "S," leaving a small indentation. Bake one sheet at a time until the cookies turn light brown around the edges, 17 to 19 minutes. Transfer the cookies to a rack to cool completely. Fill each indentation with about ⅛ tsp. of preserves.
—*Abigail Johnson Dodge*

PER COOKIE: 90 CALORIES | 1g PROTEIN | 9g CARB | 6g TOTAL FAT | 3g SAT FAT | 2g MONO FAT | 0g POLY FAT | 15mg CHOL | 15mg SODIUM | 0g FIBER

how to fill a pastry bag

If you've never done it before, the idea of working with a pastry bag might seem a little daunting. But it's actually quite fun, especially once you get the hang of loading the filling into the bag. Here's how to make this potentially messy step neat and easy.

Attach the piping tip, using a plastic coupler if need be (consult the instructions that came with your tips). Fold the top of the bag into a wide cuff, and hold the bag under this cuff.

Using a long spatula, transfer the filling into the bag. With the hand holding the bag, pinch the spatula as you pull it out of the bag to slide the filling off the spatula. Once the bag is half full—don't fill it more than halfway or it will be hard to pipe—unfold the cuff, lay the bag on the counter, and use a bench knife or the side of your hand to force the filling into the tip of the bag.

Twist the bag closed and, before you begin piping, squeeze a little of the filling into a small bowl to force out any air trapped near the tip.

classic butter cookies

YIELDS ABOUT 6 DOZEN
2-INCH COOKIES

½ lb. (1 cup) unsalted butter, softened

4½ oz. (1 cup) confectioners' sugar, sifted after measuring

1 tsp. vanilla extract

¼ tsp. almond extract

10½ oz. (2⅓ cups) unbleached all-purpose flour

½ tsp. table salt

This dough works great for a marathon cookie-baking session because it allows for variations of shape and flavor (see variations below). If you're mailing the cookies as a gift, keep the shapes simple.

1. Cream the butter and sugar together with a mixer or a wooden spoon until well blended. Add the vanilla and almond extracts. Sift the flour with the salt; gradually add the flour to the butter mixture until you have a firm but silky dough that does not stick to your hands. If necessary, add more flour a little at a time until you've reached the right consistency. Chill the dough for at least an hour before rolling and shaping.

2. Position racks in the upper and lower thirds of the oven and heat the oven to 350°F. Divide the dough and roll each half between sheets of waxed paper to about ¼ inch thick. Lightly dust the dough with flour. If the dough becomes sticky, chill it for about 10 minutes. Press the dough with cookie cutters and arrange them 2 inches apart on parchment-lined cookie sheets. Reroll the scraps and cut more shapes. Repeat the process with the second half of the dough.

3. Bake the cookies until they turn light brown, 10 to 12 minutes. Remove from the cookie sheet immediately and cool on a wire rack. When completely cooled, decorate with Royal Icing (see p. 30) or other decorations, if desired.
—*Margery K. Friedman*

PER COOKIE: 45 CALORIES | 0g PROTEIN | 5g CARB | 2.5g TOTAL FAT | 1.5g SAT FAT | 1g MONO FAT | 0g POLY FAT | 5mg CHOL | 15mg SODIUM | 0g FIBER

Mix and Match Your Batch

Instead of baking the basic, shaped butter cookies, try these style and flavor variations.

Sandwich cookies Make the dough as directed but roll it to about ⅛ inch thick. Press cookies with a 2-inch circular cutter. Using a smaller cookie cutter of the same or a different shape, cut holes in half of the 2-inch circles. (Use scraps from the holes to make a few more cookies.) Bake as directed above. When the cookies are cool, spread about 1 tsp. ganache (recipe on facing page) or fruit preserves on one side of a whole cookie. Press on a cookie with a cut-out center. Repeat with the rest of the cookies. Yields about 30 sandwich cookies.

Bar cookies Shape the dough into a brick about 3 inches wide, 9½ inches long, and 1¼ inches thick. Chill for at least an hour. Cut the brick into ¼-inch slices. Bake in a 350°F oven until golden brown, about 12 to 15 minutes. Yields about 40 cookies.

Nutty flavor Omit the almond extract and add 1 cup toasted chopped hazelnuts to the dough.

Cardamom flavor Omit the almond extract and add ½ tsp. ground cardamom to the dough. This tastes great paired with orange marmalade in a cookie sandwich (as described above).

homemade graham crackers

YIELDS FORTY-FIVE
2X2-INCH-SQUARE CRACKERS

- 5 oz. (1 cup) whole-wheat graham flour
- 5 oz. (1 cup plus 2 Tbs.) unbleached all-purpose flour
- ⅓ cup packed light brown sugar
- ¾ tsp. baking powder
- ½ tsp. baking soda
- ½ tsp. kosher salt
- ⅛ tsp. ground cinnamon
- 3 oz. (6 Tbs.) cold unsalted butter, cut into small pieces
- 3 Tbs. buttermilk
- 3 Tbs. honey
- 1½ Tbs. molasses
- ½ tsp. pure vanilla extract

You can bake half a batch of dough and save the rest for later use. Divide the dough in two before rolling it, wrap one-half well, and refrigerate for up to 3 days or freeze for up to 1 week. Remove the dough at least a couple of hours before you plan to bake so it will soften slightly.

1. Position a rack in the center of the oven and heat the oven to 350°F.

2. Put both flours, the sugar, baking powder, baking soda, salt, and cinnamon in a food processor and pulse until combined. Add the butter and pulse until the mixture resembles coarse meal. In a small bowl, whisk the buttermilk, honey, molasses, and vanilla. Add the wet ingredients to the dry and pulse until a dough begins to form.

3. Remove the dough from the food processor and transfer to a large piece of parchment. Lay another piece of parchment over it. Roll the dough into a ⅛-inch-thick, 16x13-inch rectangle. Remove the top sheet of paper, trim the rough edges, and transfer the dough along with the bottom layer of parchment to a baking sheet.

4. With a pizza cutter, cut the dough into 2-inch squares (press just hard enough to cut the dough and not the paper). With a fork, prick each square 3 or 4 times. Bake until golden brown, 15 to 20 minutes. Let cool on the sheet.
—*Yasmin Lozada-Hissom*

PER CRACKER: 50 CALORIES | 1g PROTEIN | 8g CARB | 1.5g TOTAL FAT | 1g SAT FAT | 0g MONO FAT | 0g POLY FAT | 5mg CHOL | 35mg SODIUM | 0g FIBER

What Is Whole Wheat Flour?

Whole wheat flour is flour that still contains the wheat germ and bran (as opposed to white flour, which is ground from only the wheat's starchy endosperm). As a result, whole-wheat flour has more fiber and nutrients than all-purpose white flour, and whole-wheat baked goods have a more interesting flavor and chewier texture.

truffles

YIELDS ABOUT 45 TRUFFLES

FOR THE GANACHE

- 12 oz. semisweet chocolate (55% to 60% cacao), coarsely chopped or broken into pieces
- 1 cup heavy cream
- 2 Tbs. unsalted butter, softened at room temperature

FOR THE COATING

- 1 cup cocoa powder (preferably Dutch-processed); more as needed
- 8 oz. semisweet chocolate, chopped (about 1½ cups)

If you're not using the ganache right away, transfer it to a bowl, cover, and refrigerate. To reheat, warm it gently in a double boiler or in the microwave.

Making truffles is not as difficult as you might think, and this recipe has a shortcut to make it even easier. While pastry chefs temper the chocolate they use to coat truffles so that they look smooth and shiny, skip the tricky tempering and roll the truffles in cocoa powder or ground nuts right after coating them with melted chocolate. The truffles look great and any imperfections in the chocolate coating are hidden.

MAKE THE GANACHE

1. Grind the chocolate in a food processor until it reaches the consistency of coarse meal, about 30 seconds.

2. Bring the cream to a boil in a small saucepan over medium heat. Add the cream to the food processor and process until smooth, about 10 seconds.

3. Add the butter to the warm ganache still in the food processor. Process until smooth, about 10 seconds. Transfer to a medium bowl, cover tightly with plastic wrap, and refrigerate until firm, at least 2 hours or overnight.

MAKE THE TRUFFLES

Follow the steps on the facing page. After truffles are made, let them sit at room temperature for at least 15 minutes before serving. If not serving right away, store them in an airtight container in the refrigerator, where they will keep for up to 5 days. Bring them to room temperature before serving.
—*Greg Case & Keri Fisher*

PER TRUFFLE, BASED ON 45 SERVINGS: 90 CALORIES | 1g PROTEIN | 9g CARB | 7g TOTAL FAT | 4g SAT FAT | 2g MONO FAT | 0.2g POLY FAT | 10mg CHOL | 4mg SODIUM | 1g FIBER

Truffle Variations

Liqueur filling Add 3 Tbs. of a flavored liqueur to the ganache before refrigerating. Try Frangelico®, Bailey's®, Godiva®, Kahlúa®, or amaretto.

Nut coating After coating the truffles with melted chocolate, coat them with 1 cup (6 oz.) of your choice of finely chopped toasted nuts instead of cocoa powder. Try almonds, hazelnuts, walnuts, pecans, peanuts, or pistachios. When you use nuts for the coating, you will still need cocoa to shape the truffles.

Mexican Chocolate Add 2 Tbs. Kahlúa liqueur, 2 tsp. instant espresso, and ½ tsp. ground cinnamon to the ganache. Coat the truffles with 1 cup (6 oz.) ground toasted almonds.

Toffee & Fleur de Sel Add ½ cup ground toffee bits (or six 1.4-oz. Heath® Bars ground coarsely in a food processor) and ¼ tsp. fleur de sel to the ganache. Use 1¼ cups finely ground toffee bits mixed with 1 tsp. fleur de sel for the coating.

Peanut Butter and Jelly Add ⅔ cup strawberry jam to the ganache and process until smooth. Coat the truffles with 2 cups (10 oz.) ground salted peanuts. (Yields about 54 truffles because of the added jam.)

Mint Add ½ tsp. pure peppermint extract to the ganache.

Coating Truffles

When coating the truffles, it's important to work quickly and in batches so the coating doesn't harden before you roll them in the cocoa powder. Any leftover cocoa powder can be sifted and saved. Dutch-processed cocoa powder is the best choice to coat the truffles with because it's brighter in color and less acidic than natural cocoa powder. But if you can find only natural cocoa, you can use it instead.

how to make truffles

Put the cocoa powder in a large bowl. Using two teaspoons, drop rounded, heaping teaspoonfuls of truffle mixture onto a large, parchment-lined baking sheet.

When all of the truffles are scooped, dip them in the cocoa and use your palms to roll the truffles into smooth 1-inch balls (don't worry about making them perfect; slightly irregular truffles have an appealing homemade appearance). Transfer the truffles to the refrigerator.

Melt the chocolate in a medium heatproof bowl set in a small skillet of barely simmering water, stirring occasionally until smooth. Transfer the bowl to a work surface. Working in batches, use your fingers or a couple of forks to coat the truffles with the melted chocolate.

Coat the truffles again with cocoa or nuts, (see the sidebar on the facing page for variations) and return them to the baking sheet. If using your hands, you'll have to stop and wash off the chocolate in between batches.

toffee-chocolate candy

YIELDS ABOUT THIRTY-FIVE 2-INCH PIECES

- 6 oz. semisweet chocolate, chopped
- 6 oz. bittersweet chocolate, chopped
- ½ lb. (1 cup) unsalted butter
- 1 cup granulated sugar
- 1 tsp. light corn syrup
- ½ tsp. kosher salt
- 1 tsp. pure vanilla extract
- ½ cup finely chopped toasted pecans

For a variation, use 12 oz. semisweet or even milk chocolate instead of 6 oz. each of semisweet and bittersweet chocolate. For easier cleanup when chopping chocolate, line a rimmed baking sheet with parchment and put your cutting board on top of it. Use the paper to gather the shards.

1. Combine the chocolates and set aside. Set a small bowl of water and a pastry brush next to the stove. In a heavy saucepan fitted with a candy thermometer, cook the butter, sugar, ¼ cup water, corn syrup, and salt over medium heat. Stir frequently with a wooden spoon until the butter melts and the sugar dissolves; then stir gently and only occasionally as the mixture approaches 300°F and begins to darken. Brush the sides of the pan down with a little water every once in a while to keep the sugar from crystallizing. When the mixture reaches 300°F (this will take about 18 to 20 minutes), remove the pan from the heat, carefully add the vanilla, and stir it in. With a heatproof rubber spatula, scrape the mixture into a metal 9x11-inch baking pan set on a rack. Tilt the pan until the toffee covers the bottom of the pan evenly. Let cool for 2 minutes.

2. Sprinkle with the chopped chocolate and let it melt for a few minutes (cover with another baking pan to help it melt). Smooth the chocolate with a spatula (use a narrow offset spatula if you have one) and sprinkle on the pecans. Let cool completely (3 to 4 hours) and then break or chop into pieces; use a metal spatula or a blunt knife to pry the toffee out of the pan. To help the chocolate set faster on a warm day, refrigerate the candy. —*Susie Middleton*

Choosing Chocolate for Baking

Semisweet & Bittersweet Chocolate Traditionally, these can be used interchangeably, with semisweet giving a slightly sweeter result. Bittersweet generally contains less sugar than semisweet, but the distinction between the two types becomes hazy between brands.

Milk Chocolate Although popular to eat out of hand, milk chocolate is used less widely in baking than semi- or bittersweet chocolate. In the U.S., milk chocolate must contain a minimum of 10% chocolate liquor and 12% milk solids.

traditional peanut brittle

Unflavored vegetable oil, for greasing the slab

¾ tsp. baking soda

½ tsp. table salt

1 tsp. pure vanilla extract

¾ cup light corn syrup

2 cups granulated sugar

1½ cups raw peanuts (Spanish or blanched)

2 Tbs. unsalted butter, softened

The relatively large proportion of corn syrup in this recipe prevents the sugar syrup from crystallizing. There's no need to wash down the sides of the pan.

1. Generously oil an 18x18-inch marble slab (or an inverted baking sheet) and a thin metal spatula. Sift the baking soda and salt onto a small sheet of waxed paper. Measure the vanilla extract into a small container. Set all of these near your work area, along with a pair of rubber gloves. In a heavy, deep, 4-quart saucepan, combine ½ cup water with the corn syrup and sugar. Stir over medium-low heat until the sugar dissolves, 10 to 12 minutes. When the solution is clear and begins to boil, increase the heat to high and stop stirring. Put a candy thermometer in the solution, holding it with a mitt to protect your hand. When the mixture registers 265°F on the thermometer, (8 to 10 minutes later), add the nuts and stir gently to disperse them through the mixture.

2. Continue cooking, stirring occasionally, until the mixture reaches the hard-crack stage, 305°F to 310°F, about another 5 minutes. Remove the pan from the heat. Stir in the softened butter, the vanilla extract, and then the baking soda and salt. The mixture will begin to foam. Stir just until the mixture foams evenly, and without delay pour it onto the oiled marble slab. The mixture should spread to about 14 inches in diameter. Slip the oiled spatula under the hot candy to loosen the edges and bottom.

3. Put on the gloves and as soon as the candy is firm enough on the bottom to be picked up (the top won't be hard yet), lift the edges and turn the entire piece of brittle over. With gloved hands, stretch the brittle to extend it so it's as thin as you can get it, about 17 inches in diameter. Let the candy cool undisturbed for at least 1 hour and then break it into small pieces. Store the brittle in airtight containers for up to 10 days. —*Flo Braker*

PER 1-OZ PIECE: 120 CALORIES | 2g PROTEIN | 20g CARB | 4g TOTAL FAT | 1g SAT FAT | 2g MONO FAT | 1g POLY FAT | 5mg CHOL | 75mg SODIUM | 1g FIBER

bars, brownies & bites

creamy chocolate fudge

YIELDS TWENTY-FIVE 1½-INCH PIECES

- **3** Tbs. cold unsalted butter; more at room temperature for buttering the thermometer and pan
- **3¾** cups granulated sugar
- **1½** cups heavy cream
- **4** oz. unsweetened chocolate, coarsely chopped
- **3** Tbs. light corn syrup
- **1** tsp. table salt

This melt-in-your-mouth chocolate fudge is simple to make and keeps for up to 10 days in an airtight container, making it perfect for gift-giving.

1. Lightly butter the face of a candy thermometer and set aside.

2. Put the sugar, cream, chocolate, corn syrup, and salt in a large (4-quart) heavy-duty saucepan and stir with a spoon or heatproof spatula until the ingredients are moistened and combined. Stirring gently and constantly, bring the mixture to a boil over medium heat, 7 to 12 minutes. Cover the saucepan and let the steam clean the sides of the pan for 2 minutes.

3. Clip the candy thermometer to the pot, being careful not to let the tip of the thermometer touch the bottom of the pot, or you might get a false reading. Let the mixture boil without stirring until it reaches 236°F to 238°F, 2 to 5 minutes. Take the pan off the heat and add the butter, but do not stir it into the mixture. Set the pan on a rack in a cool part of the kitchen. Don't disturb the pan in any way until the mixture has cooled to 110°F, 1 to 1½ hours.

4. Meanwhile, line the bottom and sides of an 8x8-inch baking pan with foil, leaving a 2-inch overhang on two opposite sides of the pan. Butter the foil. Set the pan aside.

5. Remove the thermometer from the fudge mixture. Using a hand mixer, beat the mixture on high speed until it is a few shades lighter in color and thickens enough that the beaters form trails that briefly expose the bottom of the pan as they pass through, 10 to 20 minutes. Pour the thickened fudge into the prepared pan, using a rubber spatula to help nudge it out of the pot. You can scrape the bottom of the pot but not the sides; any crystals that stick to the pot stay in the pot. Smooth the top of the fudge with the spatula. Set the pan on a rack and let the fudge cool completely, about 2 hours. The fudge will be slightly soft the day it's made but will firm up overnight.

6. Turn the fudge out onto a clean cutting board and peel off the foil. Turn the slab of fudge right side up and cut it into 25 equal pieces.
—*Bonnie Gorder-Hinchley*

PER SERVING: 190 CALORIES | 1g PROTEIN | 30g CARB | 9g TOTAL FAT | 6g SAT FAT | 2.5g MONO FAT | 0g POLY FAT | 25mg CHOL | 100mg SODIUM | 1g FIBER

Give Your Homemade Fudge a Flavor Twist

Peppermint-Chocolate Fudge After beating the fudge, stir in ½ cup crushed peppermint candy. Sprinkle an additional ¼ cup crushed candy over the fudge after smoothing the top.

Chocolate-Coconut Fudge After beating the fudge, stir in 2¼ cups toasted sweetened coconut flakes. Sprinkle an additional ¼ cup of the coconut over the fudge after smoothing the top.

Rocky Road Fudge After beating the fudge, stir in 2 cups mini marshmallows and 1⅓ cups toasted slivered almonds.

Mocha-Chocolate Fudge Add 2 Tbs. instant espresso or coffee to the chocolate-cream mixture and cook as directed in the recipe. After beating the fudge, stir in ½ cup cocoa nibs. After smoothing the top and scoring the pieces, place a coffee bean in the center of each piece.

how to make smooth fudge

Making melt-in-your-mouth chocolate fudge is simple: You boil sugar, heavy cream, and chocolate, let the mixture cool, and then beat it to the right consistency. As the mixture boils, the sugar crystals dissolve, and the sugar concentration gradually increases. Then, once beating starts, the sugar begins to recrystallize. If the crystals stay small, the result is a smooth fudge. But if larger crystals form, the fudge will be grainy. Because large crystals can form at any time during fudge making, you need to be vigilant. Here's what to do every step of the way for perfect results.

Both corn syrup and butter interfere with sugar crystallization, so adding them to the fudge prevents the crystals from growing too large. Butter should be added only after the boiling is done. If added before boiling, it coats the crystals and keeps them from dissolving, resulting in grainy fudge.

It's important to keep the boiling mixture from coming in contact with sugar crystals on the sides of the pan; otherwise, the sugar will start to recrystallize too soon, causing large crystals to form. To prevent this, cover the pot with a lid for two minutes after it starts boiling—the steam will wash the crystals down the sides.

Boiling the mixture to 236°F to 238°F (known as the soft-ball stage) results in the correct concentration of sugar, so the fudge sets up to the proper firmness after beating. Fudge boiled below this temperature is too soft to hold its shape, and fudge boiled above this point becomes too firm.

Don't stir the fudge; shaking or stirring the fudge mixture while it's boiling or cooling causes premature crystal growth. If the crystals form too early, they continue to grow and become too large.

Start beating the fudge only when it has cooled down to 110°F. It will be glossy and dark brown. If it's hotter, the crystals will form too fast and the fudge will be grainy. If the fudge is too cool, it will set up and be difficult to beat.

Beat the fudge vigorously to form many small crystals and create a smooth texture; stop beating when it turns a lighter brown and becomes more opaque, and when the ripples made by the beaters hold their shape long enough to briefly expose the bottom of the pan.

chocolate brigadeiros

YIELDS ABOUT 3 DOZEN BRIGADEIROS

- **1 14-oz. can sweetened condensed milk**
- **2 Tbs. unsalted butter**
- **2 Tbs. heavy cream**
- **1 tsp. light corn syrup**
- **1½ oz. semisweet or bittersweet chocolate (preferably 60% to 62% cacao), chopped**
- **1 tsp. Dutch-processed cocoa powder**
- **1 cup chocolate sprinkles (preferably Guittard®)**

Brigadeiros, a popular Brazilian treat, may look like truffles, but they're more like little fudge balls made with sweetened condensed milk and covered with sprinkles instead of cocoa powder.

1. Put the condensed milk, butter, cream, and corn syrup in a 3-quart heavy-duty saucepan and bring to a boil over medium heat, whisking constantly. Add the chocolate and cocoa powder and continue to whisk, making sure there are no pockets of cocoa powder. As soon as the mixture comes back to a boil, turn the heat to medium low and cook, whisking constantly, until the mixture thickens and pulls together into a dense, fudgy batter, about 8 minutes. When the mixture is ready, the whisk will leave trails in the batter, allowing you to briefly see the pan bottom, and when you tilt the pan, the mixture should slide to the side in a blob, leaving a thick residue on the bottom of the pan.

2. Slide the mixture into a bowl. (Don't scrape the pan—you don't want to use any of the batter stuck to the bottom.) Let the mixture cool to room temperature and then refrigerate uncovered until very firm, 3 to 4 hours.

3. Put the sprinkles in a bowl. Using a teaspoon or a melon baller, scoop the mixture by the teaspoonful, and with your hands, roll each into a ball about 1 inch in diameter. Place each ball into the bowl with the sprinkles as you finish rolling it. When you've placed 4 to 6 brigadeiros in the bowl, toss them around in the sprinkles to coat. You may need to exert a little pressure to ensure that the sprinkles stick. *—Leticia Moreinos*

PER PIECE: 50 CALORIES I 1g PROTEIN I 8g CARB I 2.5g TOTAL FAT I 1.5g SAT FAT I 0.5g MONO FAT I 0g POLY FAT I 5mg CHOL I 15mg SODIUM I 0g FIBER

Make Ahead

Store brigadeiros in a tightly covered container at room temperature for up to 2 days or in the refrigerator for up to 2 weeks. If refrigerating, bring to room temperature before serving for the best flavor and texture.

pistachio brigadeiros

YIELDS ABOUT 3 DOZEN BRIGADEIROS

- **1 14-oz. can sweetened condensed milk**
- **⅔ cup heavy cream**
- **½ cup plus 2 Tbs. finely ground pistachios**
- **2 tsp. light corn syrup**
- **1 tsp. unsalted butter**

If the pistachios don't stick to the outside of the balls the first time, roll the balls briefly between your hands to rewarm them and then reroll in the nuts to coat.

1. Put the condensed milk, cream, 6 Tbs. ground pistachios, corn syrup, and butter in a 3-quart heavy-duty saucepan and bring to a boil over medium heat. Turn the heat to medium low, and cook, whisking constantly, until the mixture thickens and pulls together into a dense batter, about 12 minutes. When the mixture is ready, the whisk will leave trails in the batter, allowing you to briefly see the pan bottom, and when you tilt the pan, the mixture should slide to the side in a blob, leaving a thick residue on the bottom of the pan.

2. Slide the mixture into a bowl. (Don't scrape the pan—you don't want to use any of the batter stuck to the bottom.) Let the mixture cool to room temperature and then refrigerate until very firm, 3 to 4 hours.

3. Put the remaining ¼ cup ground pistachios in a bowl. Using a teaspoon or a melon baller, scoop the mixture by the teaspoonful, and with your hands, roll each into a ball about 1 inch in diameter. Place each ball into the bowl with the pistachios as you finish rolling it. When you've placed 4 to 6 brigadeiros in the bowl, roll them in the pistachios and lift them out with your fingers semi-open, carefully shaking off the excess. *—Leticia Moreinos*

PER PIECE: 70 CALORIES | 1g PROTEIN | 7g CARB | 3.5g TOTAL FAT | 2g SAT FAT | 1.5g MONO FAT | 0g POLY FAT | 10mg CHOL | 15mg SODIUM | 0g FIBER

coconut brigadeiros

YIELDS ABOUT 3 DOZEN BRIGADEIROS

- **1 cup sweetened condensed milk**
- **½ cup coconut milk**
- **2 Tbs. unsalted butter**
- **2 tsp. light corn syrup**
- **1 cup finely shredded, unsweetened coconut (toasted, if desired)**

If you can't find finely shredded unsweetened coconut, you can buy coconut chips or flaked coconut and run it through a food processor until it looks like it was grated on the smallest holes of a box grater. Be sure it's unsweetened, or the brigadeiros will be much too sweet.

1. Put the condensed milk, coconut milk, butter, corn syrup, and ½ cup of the coconut in a 3-quart heavy-duty saucepan and bring to a boil over medium heat. Turn the heat to medium low and cook, whisking constantly, until the mixture thickens and pulls together into a dense batter, about 8 minutes. When the mixture is ready, the whisk will leave trails in the batter, allowing you to briefly see the pan bottom, and when you tilt the pan, the mixture should slide to the side in a blob, leaving a thick residue on the bottom of the pan. (It's OK if the residue is slightly brown.)

2. Slide the mixture into a bowl. (Don't scrape the pan—you don't want to use any of the batter stuck to the bottom.) Let the mixture cool to room temperature and then refrigerate until very firm, 3 to 4 hours.

3. Put the remaining ½ cup coconut in a bowl. Using a teaspoon or a melon baller, scoop the mixture by the teaspoonful, and with your hands, roll each into a ball about 1 inch in diameter. Place each ball into the bowl with the coconut as you finish rolling it. When you've placed 4 to 6 brigadeiros in the bowl, roll them in the coconut and lift them out with your fingers semi-open, carefully shaking off the excess. —*Leticia Moreinos*

PER PIECE: 50 CALORIES | 1g PROTEIN | 6g CARB | 3.5g TOTAL FAT | 2.5g SAT FAT | 0g MONO FAT | 0g POLY FAT | 5mg CHOL | 10mg SODIUM | 0g FIBER

how to make brigadeiros

Bring condensed milk, butter, cream, and corn syrup to a boil over medium heat, whisking constantly. Then add the chocolate and cocoa powder and continue to whisk until boiling.

Reduce the heat to medium low and keep whisking the mixture until it begins to thicken and starts to feel like fudge. The batter is almost ready when the whisk leaves trails in it.

Pour the mixture into a bowl. Use only the portion of the batter that slides out easily; do not scrape the pan.

Scoop up the batter using a small ice-cream scoop, a melon baller, or a teaspoon.

Roll the scooped-up batter between the palms of your hands until you get a smooth, even ball.

Cover the ball with sprinkles (or another garnish of your choice) and then roll it gently in your hands, exerting slight pressure, to make sure the topping adheres well and evenly.

ultimate fudgy brownies

YIELDS 2 DOZEN

- **12 oz. (1½ cups) unsalted butter, cut into 9 pieces; more softened for the pan**
- **3¾ oz. (1¼ cups) natural unsweetened cocoa powder, sifted if lumpy**
- **2¾ cups granulated sugar**
- **½ tsp. table salt**
- **5 large eggs**
- **2 tsp. pure vanilla extract**
- **7½ oz. (1⅔ cups) unbleached all-purpose flour**

You won't find the secret to rich, fudgy chocolate brownies in a box: Make them from scratch for the best flavor and texture. This one-pot batter comes together in minutes and there's a good chance you already have all the ingredients on hand.

1. Position a rack in the center of the oven and heat the oven to 325°F. Line the bottom and sides of a 9x13-inch straight-sided metal baking pan with heavy-duty aluminum foil, leaving about a 2-inch overhang on the short sides. Lightly butter the foil.

2. Put the butter in a large (4-quart) saucepan over medium-low heat and stir occasionally until melted, about 2 minutes. Off the heat, whisk in the cocoa powder until smooth, 1 minute. Add the sugar and salt, and whisk until well blended. Use your fingertip to check the temperature of the batter—it should be warm, not hot. If it's hot, set the pan aside for a minute or two before continuing.

3. Whisk in the eggs, two and then three at a time, until just blended. Whisk in the vanilla until the batter is well blended. Sprinkle the flour over the batter and stir with a rubber spatula until just blended.

4. Scrape the batter into the prepared pan and spread evenly. Bake until a toothpick inserted in the center comes out with small bits of brownie sticking to it, 35 to 45 minutes. For fudgy brownies, do not overbake. Cool the brownies completely in the pan on a rack, about 3 hours.

5. When the brownies are cool, use the foil overhang to lift them from the pan. Invert onto a cutting board and carefully peel away the foil. Flip again and cut into 24 squares. Serve immediately or wrap in plastic and store at room temperature for up to 3 days. They can also be frozen in an airtight container or freezer bag for up to 1 month. —*Abigail Johnson Dodge*

PER BROWNIE: 250 CALORIES | 3g PROTEIN | 32g CARB | 14g TOTAL FAT | 8g SAT FAT | 3.5g MONO FAT | 0.5g POLY FAT | 75mg CHOL | 65mg SODIUM | 2g FIBER

This recipe calls for natural unsweetened cocoa powder, which has a much stronger chocolate flavor than melted bittersweet chocolate. (Cocoa powder is chocolate with most of its cocoa butter pressed out, hence its big chocolate punch.) Don't substitute Dutch-processed cocoa; it has a milder flavor and so will your brownies.

Tips for Better Brownies

• For brownies with sharp, clean edges, use a straight-sided rectangular metal baking pan and line it with aluminum foil for easy brownie removal. The foil also helps with cleanup.

• Whisking cocoa powder into melted butter—instead of stirring it in—helps break up any lumps for a smooth brownie batter.

• Once you've combined the hot melted butter with the cocoa, sugar, and salt, check the batter with your fingertip before adding the eggs. It should be warm—not hot—or your eggs will cook and curdle. Set it aside to cool for a few minutes if necessary.

• The key to brownies with a moist, fudgy interior is to bake them just until a toothpick inserted in the center comes out with small bits of brownie attached. Baking any longer will result in dry, overbaked brownies.

banana split brownies

FOR THE BROWNIES

½ lb. (1 cup) unsalted butter; more for the pan

3 oz. (⅔ cup) unbleached all-purpose flour; more for the pan

1¾ cups granulated sugar

½ tsp. table salt

3 large eggs

½ cup coarsely mashed overripe banana (about 1 medium)

½ tsp. pure vanilla extract

2¼ oz. (¾ cup) natural unsweetened cocoa powder

FOR THE TOPPING

¾ cup plus 2 Tbs. heavy cream

½ cup coarsely chopped ripe banana (about 1 medium)

7 oz. semisweet or mildly bittersweet chocolate (55% to 62% cacao), finely chopped

2 cups mini marshmallows

¼ cup sliced almonds

With a topping of marshmallows, crunchy almonds, and banana-infused ganache, these brownies are like a classic banana split, minus the ice cream. Adding an overripe banana to the batter keeps the brownies moist for up to 5 days.

MAKE THE BROWNIES

1. Position a rack in the center of the oven and heat the oven to 350°F. Line a 9x9-inch metal baking pan with foil, leaving an overhang on two sides for easy removal of the brownies. Butter and flour the bottom and sides of the foil, tapping out the excess flour.

2. Melt the butter in a 3-quart saucepan over medium heat until it smells nutty and turns golden, 4 to 5 minutes. Remove the pan from the heat and let cool for 5 minutes. Whisk in the sugar and salt, followed by the eggs, banana, and vanilla. Whisk in the cocoa powder and flour, mixing slowly at first and then more vigorously until the batter is combined.

3. Spread the batter in the prepared baking pan, smoothing it so it fills the pan evenly. Bake until a toothpick or a skewer inserted in the center of the pan comes out with just a few moist clumps clinging to it, 40 to 45 minutes. Let the brownies cool in the pan before topping.

MAKE THE TOPPING

1. While the brownies cool, bring the cream to a boil in a small saucepan over medium-high heat. Remove from the heat. Stir the chopped banana into the cream; let the mixture steep for 1 hour.

2. Put the chopped chocolate in a medium heatproof bowl. Bring the cream to a boil over medium-high heat, stirring occasionally. Pour the cream mixture through a strainer held directly over the bowl of chopped chocolate. Discard the banana. Let the chocolate mixture stand for 1 minute; then stir until smooth. Pour the ganache evenly over the cooled brownies.

3. Position a rack 6 inches from the broiler and heat the broiler on high. Cover the ganache with the marshmallows and almonds. Broil, rotating the pan every 20 seconds or so to keep the marshmallows from burning, until browned. Using a knife, free the marshmallow topping from the sides of the pan. Let the brownies cool in the pan until the ganache is set, at least 1½ hours. Using the foil overhang, remove the brownies from the pan and cut into 16 squares (use a wet knife to keep the marshmallows from sticking). —*Nicole Rees*

PER BROWNIE: 370 CALORIES | 4g PROTEIN | 44g CARB | 23g TOTAL FAT | 14g SAT FAT | 7g MONO FAT | 1g POLY FAT | 90mg CHOL | 100mg SODIUM | 3g FIBER

chocolate brownie cookies

YIELDS ABOUT 4½ DOZEN COOKIES

- 2 oz. (¼ cup) unsalted butter; more for the pan
- 12 oz. bittersweet chocolate, chopped
- 3 large eggs, at room temperature
- ¾ cup granulated sugar
- 2 tsp. pure vanilla extract
- 1½ oz. (⅓ cup) unbleached all-purpose flour
- ¼ tsp. baking powder
- ¼ tsp. table salt
- 4 oz. (1 cup) chopped toasted pecans

These cookies are crackly outside, gooey inside. Each one is a bite's worth of brownie, in cookie form. A pastry bag is faster than a spoon for piping the cookie batter; use a #4 tip. It's fine to pipe the cookies close together; they won't spread much during baking.

1. Position a rack in the center of the oven and heat the oven to 350°F. Line two baking sheets with parchment (or grease and flour the pan). In a double boiler over simmering water, melt the butter and chocolate. Stir to combine; let cool. Using a stand mixer with the whisk attachment (or in a large bowl with a hand mixer), beat the eggs and sugar on medium high to a ribbon consistency, 3 to 4 minutes. Take the bowl off the mixer. Add the cooled chocolate mixture and the vanilla; stir to combine.

2. Sift the flour, baking powder, and salt together. Stir the flour mixture and the nuts into the batter; let the batter rest for 5 minutes. Spoon the batter into a pastry bag fitted with a #4 tip (or into a heavy-duty zip-top bag; with one bottom corner snipped to create a ⅔-inch-diagonal opening). For each cookie, pipe 1 Tbs. batter onto the lined baking sheet. While you pipe the second tray, bake the first until the cookies are puffed and cracked and the tops barely spring back when pressed, 8 to 10 minutes. The cracks should be moist but not wet. Cool the cookies on a wire rack. —*Cindy Mitchell*

PER COOKIE: 70 CALORIES | 1g PROTEIN | 7g CARB | 5g TOTAL FAT | 2g SAT FAT | 1g MONO FAT | 1g POLY FAT | 15mg CHOL | 15mg SODIUM | 0g FIBER

For a minty variation, substitute 1½ tsp. mint extract for the vanilla and the nuts.

caramel-pecan brownies

YIELDS 36 BROWNIES

FOR THE BROWNIES

- 6 oz. (¾ cup) unsalted butter, cut into ½-inch pieces; more softened for the pan
- 4 oz. unsweetened chocolate, coarsely chopped
- 4 large eggs
- 1¾ cups granulated sugar
- 1½ tsp. pure vanilla extract
- ¼ tsp. table salt
- 3½ oz. (¾ cup) unbleached all-purpose flour
- ¾ oz. (¼ cup) natural unsweetened cocoa powder
- 1½ cups pecans, coarsely chopped

FOR THE TOPPING

- 1 recipe Basic Caramel (recipe on the facing page)
- ½ cup heavy cream
- 3 Tbs. unsalted butter, cut into 3 pieces
- 1 tsp. pure vanilla extract
- ¼ tsp. table salt

FOR THE GARNISH

- 2 oz. bittersweet chocolate, coarsely chopped
- 1 Tbs. heavy cream
- ½ cup pecans, toasted and chopped

Serve these brownies chilled or at room temperature. Well-covered brownies will keep at room temperature for up to 2 days and in the refrigerator for up to 5 days.

MAKE THE BROWNIES

1. Position a rack in the center of the oven and heat the oven to 350°F. Butter the bottom and sides of a 9x13-inch baking pan.

2. Put the butter and chocolate in a medium heavy-duty saucepan over low heat and stir constantly until melted and smooth. Remove from the heat and set aside.

3. In a medium bowl, whisk the eggs until well blended. Gradually whisk in the sugar and then whisk vigorously until well blended. Whisk in the melted chocolate mixture, vanilla, and salt. Whisk in the flour and cocoa powder until blended. Stir in the pecans and then scrape the batter into the prepared pan, smoothing it into an even layer with a spatula.

4. Bake until a toothpick inserted in the center of the brownies comes out with a few moist crumbs clinging to it, 20 to 22 minutes. Transfer the pan to a wire rack and, if necessary, gently press down any puffed areas with a spatula to make the top level. Let cool for about 5 minutes.

MAKE THE TOPPING

While the brownies are baking, make the Basic Caramel (recipe on the facing page). Remove the pan from the heat and carefully add the cream—the mixture will bubble up furiously. Once the bubbling has subsided, add the butter and gently whisk until completely melted. Whisk in the vanilla and salt. Pour the caramel topping over the brownies, using a spatula to spread it evenly over the entire top. Let the brownies cool on the rack for 45 minutes and then refrigerate until the caramel topping is set, at least 1 hour.

GARNISH THE BROWNIES

Combine the chocolate and heavy cream in a small saucepan over low heat and stir constantly until melted and smooth. Pour the chocolate into a small piping bag fitted with a ⅛-inch plain tip. (Or put it in a small zip-top bag and seal the bag. Using scissors, snip off a corner of the bag to make a small hole.) Drizzle the chocolate over the brownies in a zigzag pattern. Sprinkle the chopped pecans over the top. Refrigerate until the chocolate is set, about 30 minutes. Cut the brownies into 36 rectangles. —*Tish Boyle*

PER BROWNIE: 210 CALORIES | 2g PROTEIN | 21g CARB | 14g TOTAL FAT | 6g SAT FAT | 5g MONO FAT | 2g POLY FAT | 40mg CHOL | 45mg SODIUM | 2g FIBER

basic caramel

YIELDS ⅔ CUP

1   cup granulated sugar

¼   tsp. fresh lemon juice

The longer you cook caramel, the darker it gets. For the Caramel-Pecan Brownies, cook it to medium amber. The caramel will harden quickly upon cooling.

1. Fill a cup measure halfway with water and put a pastry brush in it; this will be used for washing down the sides of the pan to prevent crystallization.

2. In a heavy-duty 2-quart saucepan, stir the sugar, lemon juice, and ¼ cup cold water. Brush down the sides of the pan with water to wash away any sugar crystals. Bring to a boil over medium-high heat and cook, occasionally brushing down the sides of the pan, until the mixture starts to color around the edges, 5 to 8 minutes. Gently swirl the pan once to even out the color and prevent the sugar from burning in isolated spots. Continue to cook until the sugar turns medium amber, about 30 seconds more. (Once the mixture begins to color, it will darken very quickly, so keep an eye on it.)

quick caramel cleanup

After you make the Basic Caramel, you'll have a very sticky pan to clean. The easiest way to clean a caramel-coated pan is to boil water in it until the sugar has completely dissolved. Then just pour out the water, let the pan cool, and wash with soap and water.

For ramekins or other vessels that can't go directly on the stovetop, pour boiling water into them, let soak until cool, and repeat as necessary until all the caramel is gone.

5 Tips for Perfect Caramel

One of two things can go wrong when making caramel: The caramel burns, or sugar crystals form, so the caramel goes from liquid and smooth to crystallized and solid. Here are a few pointers for making a perfectly smooth caramel every time:

Watch bubbling caramel like a hawk. Caramel cooks quickly and will turn from golden amber to a smoking mahogany in seconds. Burnt caramel has an unpleasantly bitter taste.

Use clean utensils. Sugar crystals tend to form around impurities and foreign particles.

Acid helps. Adding lemon juice to the sugar and water helps break down the sucrose molecules and prevents sugar crystals from forming.

Swirl, don't stir. Stirring tends to splash syrup onto the sides of the pan, where sugar crystals can form. So once the sugar is completely dissolved in water, just gently swirl the pan to caramelize the sugar evenly.

A pastry brush is your friend. Keep a pastry brush and some water next to the stove; you'll need it to wash off any crystals that might form on the sides of the pan.

port ganache–glazed brownies with dried cherries

YIELDS SIXTEEN 2¼-INCH SQUARE BROWNIES

FOR THE PORT-SOAKED DRIED CHERRIES

½   cup dried cherries, very coarsely chopped (or whole dried cranberries)

⅓   cup tawny port

FOR THE BROWNIES

½   lb. (1 cup) unsalted butter; more softened butter for the pan

3   oz. (⅔ cup) unbleached all-purpose flour; more for the pan

2   cups granulated sugar

4   large eggs, at room temperature

½   tsp. pure vanilla extract

2¼   oz. (¾ cup) natural unsweetened cocoa powder

½   tsp. baking powder

½   tsp. table salt

FOR THE PORT-GANACHE TOPPING

½   cup tawny port

½   cup heavy cream

6   oz. semisweet chocolate, finely chopped

A port-ganache topping and port-soaked dried cherries transform the classic fudgy brownie into an elegant, grown-up dessert, but you can also omit them for an indulgent afternoon snack.

SOAK THE CHERRIES

In a small saucepan, bring the cherries and port to a boil over medium heat. Reduce the heat to low and cook for 2 minutes. Take the pan off the heat and let cool to room temperature.

MAKE THE BROWNIES

1. Position a rack in the center of the oven and heat the oven to 350°F. Butter and flour a 9x9-inch metal baking pan, tapping out the excess flour.

2. Melt the butter in a medium saucepan over medium heat. Remove the pan from the heat. Whisk or stir in the sugar, followed by all four of the eggs and the vanilla. Stir in the flour, cocoa, baking powder, and salt, starting slowly to keep the ingredients from flying out of the pan and stirring more vigorously as you go. Stir until the batter is smooth and uniform, about 1 minute. Stir in the port-soaked cherries, along with any remaining liquid from the saucepan.

3. Spread the batter into the prepared baking pan, smoothing it so it fills the pan evenly. Bake until a toothpick or a skewer inserted ¾ inch into the center of the brownies comes out with just a few moist clumps clinging to it, about 40 minutes. Let the brownies cool completely in the pan on a rack.

MAKE THE TOPPING

1. In a small saucepan over medium heat, bring the port to a boil. Boil until the port is reduced to 2 Tbs., 3 to 6 minutes. Pour it into a small cup or bowl. Thoroughly rinse the pan. Bring the heavy cream to a boil in the pan over medium-high heat, stirring occasionally. Take the pan off the heat. Stir in the chopped chocolate and reduced port until the mixture is smooth and the chocolate is melted.

2. Pour the ganache into a bowl and cover the surface with plastic wrap to prevent a skin from forming. Put the bowl in a cool part of the kitchen and let the ganache cool to room temperature, stirring occasionally. When it's cool, spread it evenly over the cooled brownies and give the ganache about an hour to set (it will still be quite soft and gooey). Cut into 16 squares. Keep the brownies at room temperature, well wrapped. You can freeze them, too.
—*Nicole Rees*

PER BROWNIE: 360 CALORIES | 4g PROTEIN | 44g CARB | 19g TOTAL FAT | 11.5g SAT FAT | 8g MONO FAT | 2.5g POLY FAT | 95mg CHOL | 110mg SODIUM | 2g FIBER

double chocolate chunk fudge brownies

YIELDS 12 BROWNIES

- 6 oz. (¾ cup) unsalted butter, cut into six pieces; more for the pan
- 2 oz. (⅔ cup) unsweetened cocoa powder (natural or Dutch-processed)
- 1⅔ cups granulated sugar
- ¼ tsp. table salt
- 2 large eggs
- 1 tsp. pure vanilla extract
- 4½ oz. (1 cup) unbleached all-purpose flour
- 4 oz. very coarsely chopped semisweet or bittersweet chocolate
- 2 oz. (½ cup) coarsely chopped walnuts or pecans (optional)

The cooler the brownie is, the cleaner the cutting will be, but these fudgy brownies will always leave some sticky crumbs on the knife.

If you use a metal pan, the edges of these brownies will be flat and the texture will be even. If you use a Pyrex baking pan, your brownies will have puffier, drier edges, but it will be easier to get the brownies out of the pan.

1. Position a rack in the center of the oven and heat the oven to 350°F. Generously butter the bottom and sides of an 8x8-inch Pyrex or metal baking pan.

2. Melt the butter in a medium saucepan over medium heat, stirring occasionally. Turn off the heat and add the cocoa. Whisk until smooth. Add the sugar and salt and whisk until blended. Add one egg and whisk until just blended. Whisk in the vanilla and the second egg until just blended. Sprinkle the flour over the mixture and stir with a rubber spatula until just blended. Add the chopped chocolate and stir until combined.

3. Scrape the batter into the prepared baking pan and spread evenly. Scatter the nuts evenly over the batter, if using. Bake until a toothpick inserted in the center comes out with small, gooey clumps of brownie sticking to it, 33 to 38 minutes. Don't overbake or the brownies won't be fudgy. Transfer the baking dish to a rack and let cool completely.

4. Run a knife around the edges of the brownie and then pry it from the pan in one piece. Using a sharp knife, cut the cooled brownie into three equal strips and cut each strip into four equal pieces. Or, use a bench scraper to cut the brownie in the baking pan and then use a spatula to lift out the cut brownies.
—*Abigail Johnson Dodge*

PER BROWNIE: 360 CALORIES | 4g PROTEIN | 45g CARB | 19g TOTAL FAT | 10g SAT FAT | 7g MONO FAT | 5g POLY FAT | 65mg CHOL | 65mg SODIUM | 2g FIBER

chewy brownies

YIELDS SIXTEEN 2-INCH
SQUARES

- 4 oz. (½ cup) unsalted butter; more for the pan
- 4 oz. unsweetened chocolate
- 1½ cups granulated sugar
- Scant ¼ tsp. table salt
- 2 tsp. pure vanilla extract
- 2 large eggs, at room temperature
- 4½ oz. (1 cup) unbleached all-purpose flour
- 2 Tbs. natural unsweetened cocoa (not Dutch-processed)

Added flour helps to give these brownies their chewiness. It's important not to overbake them or they'll dry out.

1. Position a rack in the center of the oven and heat the oven to 350°F.

2. Butter an 8x8-inch pan, line the pan bottom with parchment (or waxed paper), and then butter the parchment.

3. In a double boiler over simmering water, melt the butter and chocolate. Remove the pan from the heat; cool slightly. Stir in the sugar, salt, and vanilla. Mix in the eggs, one at a time, stirring each time until blended. Add the flour and cocoa; beat until incorporated and the mixture is smooth, 30 to 60 seconds.

4. Scrape the batter into the prepared pan and bake until the top is uniformly colored with no indentation and a toothpick inserted in the center comes out almost clean, with a few moist crumbs clinging to it, 35 to 45 minutes. (Use the shorter time for metal pans, the longer for Pyrex pans.) Set the pan on a rack until cool enough to handle. Run a paring knife around the inside edge of the pan and then invert the pan onto a flat surface and peel off the parchment. Flip the baked brownie back onto the rack to cool completely. Cut into squares with a sharp knife. —*Cindy Mitchell*

PER BROWNIE: 200 CALORIES | 3g PROTEIN | 27g CARB | 10g TOTAL FAT | 6g SAT FAT | 3g MONO FAT | 1g POLY FAT | 40mg CHOL | 40mg SODIUM | 1g FIBER

Although it's awfully tempting to cut into a pan of just-baked brownies, hold off. The flavor and texture of each type of brownie will be at its best—and definitely worth waiting for—when completely cool.

brownie cream cheese bites

YIELDS 5 DOZEN BITES

FOR THE BROWNIES

- **4 oz. (½ cup) unsalted butter, cut into 3 pieces**
- **4 oz. unsweetened chocolate, coarsely chopped**
- **4 large eggs, at room temperature**
- **¼ tsp. table salt**
- **2 cups granulated sugar**
- **1 tsp. pure vanilla extract**
- **5¾ oz. (1¼ cups) unbleached all-purpose flour**

FOR THE CREAM CHEESE TOPPING

- **6 oz. cream cheese, at room temperature**
- **3 Tbs. granulated sugar**
- **1 large egg yolk, at room temperature**
- **½ cup semisweet mini chocolate chips**

After baking the first round of these fudgy bites, be sure the tins are completely cool before lining and filling them with the remaining batters. Store these treats at room temperature or freeze in an airtight container, separating the layers with waxed paper.

MAKE THE BROWNIE BATTER

1. Heat the oven to 350°F and line three 1-dozen capacity (five if you have them) mini muffin tins with foil or paper liners.

2. Combine the butter and chocolate in a small heatproof bowl. Set the bowl over simmering water or in a microwave and heat, stirring frequently with a rubber spatula, until the butter and chocolate are melted and smooth. Set aside.

3. Using a stand mixer fitted with the whisk attachment (or in a large bowl with a hand mixer), beat the eggs and salt on medium speed until very foamy, about 2 minutes. Continue beating while gradually adding the sugar. Beat until thick and pale, about 3 minutes. With a large rubber spatula, scrape the chocolate mixture into the eggs, add the vanilla, and fold until the two mixtures are just barely incorporated. Add the flour and continue folding until just incorporated. Scrape the batter into a 1-gallon heavy-duty zip-top bag. Squeeze out as much air as possible and seal.

MAKE THE CREAM CHEESE TOPPING

In a medium bowl, beat the cream cheese and sugar with a wooden spoon until smooth and creamy. Add the egg yolk and mix until blended. Pour in the chips and mix until blended. Scrape into a 1-quart zip-top bag. Squeeze out as much air as possible and seal.

ASSEMBLE AND BAKE

1. Snip off ½ inch from one corner of each bag. Fill each lined muffin cup about two-thirds full with the brownie batter and then top with about 1 teaspoon of the cream cheese mixture.

2. Bake the three trays in the center of the oven until the brownies are puffed and a pick inserted in the brownie comes out just barely clean, about 20 minutes. Let the brownies cool in the trays on racks for 5 minutes before carefully lifting the liners out of the tins and transferring them to racks to cool completely. *—Camilla Leonard*

warm chocolate-nut brownies

- **3 oz. (⅔ cup) unbleached all-purpose flour**
- **⅔ cup granulated sugar**
- **⅔ cup chopped bittersweet or semisweet chocolate or morsels**
- **¾ oz. (¼ cup) natural unsweetened cocoa powder**
- **⅛ tsp. ground cinnamon**
- **¼ tsp. baking powder**
- **¼ tsp. table salt**
- **2 large eggs, lightly beaten**
- **⅓ cup vegetable oil**
- **½ cup chopped nuts (walnuts or pecans)**

Serve these brownies warm with a scoop of ice cream or a dollop of whipped cream.

1. Position a rack in the center of the oven and heat the oven to 350°F. Lightly grease a 9-inch pie plate (preferably Pyrex).

2. In a medium bowl, mix the flour, sugar, chopped chocolate, cocoa, cinnamon, baking powder, and salt with a wooden spoon or rubber spatula until well blended. Add the eggs and oil and mix until blended. Scrape the batter into the pie plate and spread evenly. Sprinkle the chopped nuts over the top.

3. Bake until a pick inserted in the center comes out with some gooey pieces clinging to it, 20 to 25 minutes. Let cool for at least 10 minutes. Cut into 6 to 8 wedges. —*Abigail Johnson Dodge*

PER BROWNIE, BASED ON 8 SERVINGS: 320 CALORIES | 5g PROTEIN | 34g CARB | 21g TOTAL FAT | 5g SAT FAT | 5g MONO FAT | 10g POLY FAT | 55mg CHOL | 110mg SODIUM | 2g FIBER

peppermint brownies

YIELDS ABOUT 30 BROWNIES

- **10** oz. (1¼ cups) unsalted butter; more for the pan
- **10** oz. unsweetened chocolate
- **2** tsp. peppermint tea leaves (from about 2 tea bags)
- **2** cups granulated sugar
- **4** large eggs
- **2** tsp. peppermint extract
- **¼** tsp. kosher salt
- **4½** oz. (1 cup) unbleached all-purpose flour
- **2** oz. semisweet chocolate
- **2** Tbs. light corn syrup
- **2** oz. white chocolate

These brownies only get better after a couple of days, as their texture gets fudgier and their flavor richer. Any herbal peppermint tea or peppermint extract will work in this recipe.

BAKE THE BROWNIES

1. Position a rack in the center of the oven and heat the oven to 350°F. Butter the bottom and sides of a 9x13-inch baking pan, line it with parchment (the paper should extend at least an inch above the long sides to act as handles for getting the brownies out), and butter the paper.

2. Put about 2 inches of water in a small pot and heat to a gentle simmer. In a heatproof bowl set over the water, melt 8 oz. of the butter and 8 oz. of the unsweetened chocolate. Be sure that the water is hot but not boiling and that it doesn't touch the bottom of the bowl. Stir occasionally with a heatproof spatula until the mixture is completely melted and uniform, 6 to 7 minutes. Turn off the heat, but leave the bowl over the water.

3. In a food processor, finely grind the peppermint leaves with the sugar. In a medium bowl, whisk the eggs, peppermint extract, salt, and the peppermint sugar mixture until just combined. Whisk in the melted chocolate mixture (reserve the pot of water for later). Slowly add the flour, gently folding it in with a spatula, until incorporated. Spread the batter into the prepared pan and bake until a pick inserted into the center comes out almost clean (a few bits of batter should cling to the pick), 35 to 40 minutes. Put the pan on a rack to cool to room temperature, about 2 hours. Lift the paper lining to pull the brownies out of the pan. Peel the paper off the brownies and put them on a cutting board.

MAKE THE GLAZE

1. Bring the pot of water back to a gentle simmer. Set a heatproof bowl over the pot and add the semisweet chocolate, corn syrup, and the remaining 2 oz. each butter and unsweetened chocolate. Stir frequently with a heatproof spatula until the mixture is melted and smooth; set aside. Put the white chocolate in a separate heatproof bowl and set it over the water. Stir frequently until it's melted and smooth; remove it from the heat.

2. Spread the chocolate glaze over the cooled brownies in an even layer using a spatula. Drizzle the white chocolate over the glaze in lines. Use a toothpick or a wooden skewer to drag the white chocolate into the glaze (as shown on the facing page). Lift the cutting board and firmly tap it on the counter to settle the glaze.

3. Refrigerate until the glaze is set, at least 20 minutes and up to 12 hours. Cut into 30 bars, about 2 inches square (a knife rinsed in hot water and then dried will cut more cleanly than a cold knife). Keep well covered and serve at room temperature. —*Greg Case*

PER BROWNIE: 220 CALORIES | 3g PROTEIN | 23g CARB | 15g TOTAL FAT | 9g SAT FAT | 4g MONO FAT | 1g POLY FAT | 50mg CHOL | 30mg SODIUM | 2g FIBER

how to create a marbled glaze

Smooth the chocolate glaze in an even layer to the edges. It's fine if some runs over the sides.

Slowly drizzle a stream of white chocolate in an inexact but evenly distributed pattern.

Drag a thin skewer or a toothpick through the glazes in alternating directions to create a marbled look.

bittersweet cocoa brownies

YIELDS 16 BROWNIES

- 2¼ oz. (¾ cup) unsweetened cocoa powder
- 1⅓ cups granulated sugar
- ½ tsp. pure vanilla extract
- ¼ tsp. table salt
- 5 oz. (10 Tbs.) unsalted butter, melted and kept hot
- 2 cold large eggs
- 1½ oz. (⅓ cup) unbleached all-purpose flour
- 1 cup broken walnut or pecan pieces (optional)

For tips on how to bake a flawless batch of brownies, see p. 51.

Brownies made with cocoa powder are softer on the inside than those made with bar chocolate. Use natural cocoa powder to get a tart and lively flavor or use Dutch-processed cocoa powder for a mellower flavor.

1. Heat the oven to 325°F. Line an 8x8-inch baking pan (preferably metal) with foil across the bottom and up two opposite sides of the pan.

2. In a medium bowl, thoroughly mix the cocoa, sugar, vanilla, salt, and hot melted butter with a hand mixer or with vigorous strokes of a whisk. Add the eggs, one at a time, beating until the batter is thick and lightened in color, 1 to 2 minutes. Add the flour and stir with a rubber spatula just until blended. Fold in the nuts, if using.

3. Spread the batter evenly in the prepared pan and bake until the top is puffed and slightly crusted and a toothpick inserted in the center comes out with a little fudge batter clinging to it, 28 to 30 minutes.

4. Let the brownies cool completely in the pan on a rack. Lift the ends of the foil to remove them. Invert the brownies on a tray and peel off the foil. Turn the brownies right side up on a cutting board and cut into squares (wipe the knife between each cut, as the brownies will be soft and sticky). —*Alice Medrich*

cakey brownies

YIELDS SIXTEEN 2-INCH SQUARES

- 2 oz. (¼ cup) unsalted butter, softened at room temperature; more for the pan
- 4 oz. unsweetened chocolate
- ¾ cup granulated sugar
- 1 Tbs. plus 1 tsp. light corn syrup
- 2 large eggs, at room temperature
- 2 tsp. pure vanilla extract
- ¼ cup milk, lukewarm
- 2¼ oz. (½ cup) unbleached all-purpose flour
- ½ tsp. baking powder
- Pinch of table salt

This recipe can be doubled easily; use a 13x9-inch pan and increase the baking time slightly.

These are rich and luscious, with a cakey lightness. Try stenciling with confectioners' sugar.

1. Position a rack in the center of the oven and heat the oven to 350°F. Butter an 8x8-inch pan, line the pan bottom with parchment (or waxed paper), and then butter the parchment.

2. In a double boiler over simmering water, melt the chocolate. Remove the pan from the heat; let cool slightly. In a medium bowl, cream the butter with a fork. Beat in the sugar and corn syrup; be sure there are no lumps in the mixture. Add the eggs, one at a time, whisking thoroughly. Add the vanilla and milk. Whisk until incorporated, about 30 seconds. The batter may appear broken; this is OK. Whisk in the melted chocolate, beating until the batter is smooth and has thickened slightly, 30 to 60 seconds.

3. Stir together the flour, baking powder, and salt so they're well blended; stir the dry ingredients into the chocolate mixture until incorporated. Scrape into the prepared pan and bake until a toothpick inserted in the middle comes out clean with a few moist crumbs clinging to it, 20 to 30 minutes. (Use the shorter time for metal pans, the longer for Pyrex pans.)

4. Set the pan on a rack until cool enough to handle. Run a paring knife around the inside edge of the pan and then invert the pan onto a flat surface and peel off the parchment. Flip the baked brownie back onto the rack to cool completely. Cut into squares with a sharp knife. —*Cindy Mitchell*

PER BROWNIE: 130 CALORIES | 2g PROTEIN | 16g CARB | 8g TOTAL FAT | 4g SAT FAT | 2g MONO FAT | 1g POLY FAT | 35mg CHOL | 40mg SODIUM | 1g FIBER

how to test brownies for doneness

Brownies are underdone when smudges of wet batter cling to the toothpick.

Brownies are just right when traces of moistness and fudgy crumbs cling to the toothpick.

Brownies are overdone when the toothpick comes out perfectly clean.

double-chocolate brownies

YIELDS SIXTEEN 2-INCH-SQUARES

- 5 oz. (10 Tbs.) unsalted butter, softened at room temperature; more for the pan
- 5 oz. bittersweet chocolate
- 2 oz. unsweetened chocolate
- 1 cup granulated sugar
- 2 tsp. pure vanilla extract
- Pinch of table salt
- 2 large eggs, at room temperature
- 1 large egg yolk, at room temperature
- 3 oz. (⅔ cup) unbleached all-purpose flour

Using both bittersweet and unsweetened chocolate gives these brownies a deep, sophisticated chocolate flavor. The consistency is fudgy but not gooey or underdone.

1. Position a rack in the center of the oven and heat the oven to 350°F. Butter an 8x8-inch pan, line the pan bottom with parchment (or waxed paper), and then butter the parchment.

2. In a double boiler over simmering water, melt the butter and both chocolates. Remove the pan from the heat; let cool slightly. Whisk in the sugar and then the vanilla and salt. The mixture will be somewhat grainy; this is fine. Whisk in the eggs and egg yolk, one at a time, stirring each time until blended. Add the flour, beating until thickened and smooth, 30 to 60 seconds.

3. Pour into the prepared pan and bake until a toothpick inserted in the center comes out with moist crumbs (not wet batter) clinging to it, 35 to 45 minutes. Set the pan on a rack until cool enough to handle. Run a paring knife around the inside edge of the pan and then invert the pan onto a flat surface and peel off the parchment. Flip the baked brownie back onto the rack and let cool completely. Cut into squares with a sharp knife. —*Cindy Mitchell*

PER BROWNIE: 210 CALORIES | 3g PROTEIN | 22g CARB | 13g TOTAL FAT | 8g SAT FAT | 3g MONO FAT | 1g POLY FAT | 60mg CHOL | 30mg SODIUM | 1g FIBER

Even with fudgy brownies, you can get neat, uniform squares. Turn them out of the pan and, when they're completely cool, cut them with a sharp knife. Wipe the knife after each pass.

rich cocoa brownies

- 6 oz. (¾ cup) unsalted butter; more for the pan
- 2 oz. (⅔ cup) unsweetened natural or Dutch-processed cocoa
- 1¼ cups granulated sugar
- ¼ tsp. table salt
- 1 tsp. pure vanilla extract
- 3 large eggs
- 2⅔ oz. (⅔ cup) cake flour or 2½ oz. (½ cup) unbleached all-purpose flour
- ½ cup chopped pecans or walnuts (optional)

Use cake flour for a brownie with an ultra-smooth texture, or unbleached all-purpose flour for one with just a hint of crumb.

1. Position a rack in the center of the oven and heat the oven to 350°F. Butter a 9x9-inch square pan. In a 2-quart saucepan, melt the butter, allowing it to get quite hot. Take the pan from the heat and whisk in the cocoa. Let the mixture cool completely.

2. Whisk the sugar, salt, and vanilla into the cooled cocoa mixture. Add all the eggs at once and whisk again to combine. With a rubber spatula, fold in the flour just until incorporated. Fold in the nuts. Spread the batter in the pan and bake until a toothpick inserted in the center comes out moist and gooey but not wet, 18 to 20 minutes. Be careful not to overbake the brownies, as they'll toughen. Allow them to cool completely before cutting.
—Alice Medrich

PER BROWNIE: 180 CALORIES | 2g PROTEIN | 21g CARB | 10g TOTAL FAT | 6g SAT FAT | 3g MONO FAT | 1g POLY FAT | 65mg CHOL | 45mg SODIUM | 1g FIBER

pecan blondies

YIELDS SIXTEEN 2-INCH
SQUARES

- **4 oz. (½ cup) unsalted butter; more for the pan**
- **1½ cups firmly packed dark brown sugar**
- **1 large egg, at room temperature**
- **1 large egg yolk, at room temperature**
- **1½ tsp. pure vanilla extract**
- **5 oz. (1 cup plus 2 Tbs.) unbleached all-purpose flour**
- **Scant ¼ tsp. table salt**
- **2 oz. (¾ cup) pecans, toasted and coarsely chopped**

Blondies have a chewy texture, with rich butterscotch flavor standing in for chocolate. Dark brown sugar will give you an especially flavorful blondie.

1. Position a rack in the center of the oven and heat the oven to 350°F.

2. In a medium saucepan over medium heat, heat the butter and brown sugar, stirring frequently, until the sugar has dissolved. Cook, stirring, about 1 minute longer—the mixture will bubble but should not boil. Set the pan aside to cool for about 10 minutes. Meanwhile, butter an 8x8-inch pan, line the pan with parchment (or waxed paper), and then butter the parchment. Stir the egg, egg yolk, and vanilla into the cooled sugar mixture. Add the flour, salt, and nuts, stirring just until blended.

3. Pour the batter into the prepared pan. Bake until the center is springy when touched (the top may still look doughy) and a toothpick inserted in the center comes out clean (it's fine if there are a few moist crumbs clinging to it), 25 to 35 minutes. (Use the shorter time for metal pans, the longer for Pyrex pans.)

4. Set the pan on a rack until it's cool enough to handle. Run a paring knife around the inside edge of the pan and then invert the pan onto a flat surface and peel off the parchment. Flip the baked brownie back onto the rack to cool completely. Cut into squares with a sharp knife. *—Cindy Mitchell*

PER BLONDIE: 190 CALORIES | 2g PROTEIN | 28g CARB | 9g TOTAL FAT | 4g SAT FAT | 3g MONO FAT | 1g POLY FAT | 40mg CHOL | 40mg SODIUM | 1g FIBER

macadamia double-decker brownie bars

YIELDS 48 BARS

FOR THE BROWNIE LAYER

Nonstick cooking spray

6 oz. (¾ cup) unsalted butter, cut into large chunks

1½ cups granulated sugar

2¼ oz. (¾ cup) unsweetened cocoa powder (natural or Dutch-processed)

¼ tsp. table salt

2 large eggs

1 tsp. pure vanilla extract

3½ oz. (¾ cup) unbleached all-purpose flour

FOR THE MACADAMIA LAYER

½ cup firmly packed light brown sugar

1½ oz. (⅓ cup) unbleached all-purpose flour

⅔ cup light corn syrup

1½ oz. (3 Tbs.) unsalted butter, melted

1½ tsp. pure vanilla extract

2 large eggs

1½ cups roughly chopped salted macadamia nuts

⅓ cup sweetened coconut flakes

These gorgeous two-layer bars have a brownie base topped with a gooey nut-and-coconut-studded topping. Dipping the knife in warm water and wiping it dry between cuts will keep the topping from sticking to the knife.

MAKE THE BROWNIE LAYER

1. Position a rack in the center of the oven and heat the oven to 325°F. Line the bottom and sides of a 9x13-inch baking pan with foil, leaving some overhang on the sides, and spray with cooking spray.

2. In a medium saucepan over medium heat, whisk the butter until melted. Remove the pan from the heat and add the sugar, cocoa powder, and salt. Whisk until well blended, about 1 minute. Add the eggs and vanilla and whisk until smooth. Add the flour and stir with a rubber spatula until blended. Scrape into the prepared pan and spread evenly. Bake until the top is shiny and dry-looking and the brownie springs back very slightly when pressed with a fingertip, about 20 minutes. (The brownie should not be completely baked.) Remove from the oven and put on a rack.

MAKE THE MACADAMIA TOPPING

While the brownie layer is baking, combine the brown sugar and flour in a large bowl. Whisk until well blended, breaking up any large clumps. Add the corn syrup, melted butter, and vanilla. Whisk until blended, about 1 minute. Add the eggs and whisk just until combined, about 30 seconds. (Don't overmix or the batter will be foamy.) Add the nuts and coconut and stir with a rubber spatula until evenly blended.

FINISH BAKING

1. Pour the macadamia topping over the warm, partially baked brownie layer. Using a spatula, carefully spread the mixture into an even layer. Return the pan to the oven and bake until the top is golden brown, 37 to 40 minutes. Transfer the pan to a rack to cool completely.

2. Using the foil as handles, lift the rectangle from the pan and invert onto a work surface. Carefully peel away the foil. Flip right side up. Using a sharp knife, cut into 2-inch squares and then cut each square into triangles.
—Abigail Johnson Dodge

PER BAR: 130 CALORIES | 1g PROTEIN | 16g CARB | 8g TOTAL FAT | 3g SAT FAT | 3.5g MONO FAT | 0g POLY FAT | 25mg CHOL | 35mg SODIUM | 1g FIBER

Make Ahead

After the brownie and macadamia layers have been baked and cooled, the entire pan can be wrapped in plastic wrap, then foil, and frozen for up to 1 month.

chocolate cream cheese brownies

YIELDS ABOUT 48 BARS

FOR THE FILLING

- 4 oz. chopped bittersweet or semisweet chocolate or chocolate chips
- ¼ cup heavy cream
- ½ lb. cream cheese, softened at room temperature
- 1 large egg
- 2 tsp. unbleached all-purpose flour

FOR THE BROWNIE BATTER

- 9 oz. (1 cup plus 2 Tbs.) unsalted butter, softened at room temperature; more for the pan
- 1½ cups granulated sugar
- 5 large eggs
- 1 tsp. pure vanilla extract
- ⅛ tsp. pure almond extract
- 6¾ oz. (1½ cups) unbleached all-purpose flour
- 2¼ oz. (¾ cup) unsweetened cocoa powder
- ¼ tsp. baking powder

FOR THE ICING

- 8 oz. bittersweet or semisweet chocolate, finely chopped

These brownies have a layer of chocolate cream cheese sandwiched between more cakelike layers, with a thin coating of chocolate smoothed on top. The cream cheese adds tang to the brownie, and the finely chopped chocolate makes an instant icing.

MAKE THE FILLING

Slowly melt 2 oz. of the chopped chocolate and cream together in a microwave or a double boiler. Set aside to cool. Using a stand mixer fitted with the paddle attachment (or in a large bowl with a hand mixer), beat the cream cheese and egg until fluffy. Add the cooled chocolate mixture and mix well. Add the flour and the remaining chocolate and mix until incorporated. Chill the filling while you assemble the brownie batter.

MAKE THE BROWNIE BATTER

Position a rack in the center of the oven and heat the oven to 350°F. Butter a 9x13-inch pan (a standard Pyrex baking dish). Using a stand mixer fitted with the paddle attachment (or in a large bowl with a hand mixer), cream the butter and sugar until fluffy. Add the eggs one at a time, making sure that each one is fully incorporated before adding another. Occasionally scrape the bowl. Add the vanilla and almond extracts. Sift together the flour, cocoa, and baking powder and gently blend them into the batter.

ASSEMBLE THE BROWNIES

Using an offset metal spatula, spread half the brownie batter into the prepared pan. Spread the filling over the batter. Spoon the remaining brownie batter over the filling and gently spread it into an even layer. Bake until a knife inserted into the center of the brownies comes out clean, about 35 minutes.

FINISH THE BROWNIES

As soon as you remove the brownies from the oven, sprinkle about three quarters of the chocolate on top. Let sit for about 5 minutes, until the chocolate has melted. Gently spread the soft chocolate into a thin, smooth layer. If it isn't enough chocolate, sprinkle a few more pieces on top and spread again, but be careful not to make the icing too thick. *—Patricia Ann Heyman*

PER BROWNIE: 150 CALORIES | 3g PROTEIN | 14g CARB | 10g TOTAL FAT | 6g SAT FAT | 3g MONO FAT | 0g POLY FAT | 45mg CHOL | 25mg SODIUM | 1g FIBER

Choosing Cream Cheese

When shopping for the cream cheese destined for this dough, or any baked good, go with the brick, not the tub. The cream cheese in a tub is formulated to make it more spreadable than the brick kind. And while that's fine for your toasted bagel, it's usually not good when you're using the cream cheese as an ingredient. Soft cream cheese from a tub won't give you the flakiest baked dough, nor will reduced-fat or fat-free cream cheese.

pumpkin swirl mini cheesecakes

YIELDS 12 MINI CHEESECAKES

Nonstick cooking spray

2 **8-oz. packages cream cheese, softened at room temperature**

⅔ **cup granulated sugar**

1½ **tsp. pure vanilla extract**

Pinch of table salt

2 **large eggs**

⅓ **cup pure solid-pack canned pumpkin**

2¼ **tsp. unbleached all-purpose flour**

½ **tsp. ground cinnamon**

¼ **tsp. ground ginger**

⅛ **tsp. ground nutmeg**

The baked cheesecakes can be refrigerated, covered, for 3 days or frozen for 1 month. Freeze the cooled cheesecakes in the tins in heavy-duty zip-top plastic bags, or remove them from the tins and arrange in airtight containers.

1. Position a rack in the center of the oven and heat the oven to 300°F. Line 12 standard muffin tins (approximately 2¾ inches in diameter) with foil liners and coat lightly with cooking spray.

2. Using a stand mixer fitted with the paddle attachment (or in a large bowl using a hand mixer) beat the cream cheese on medium-high speed until very smooth and fluffy, stopping to scrape down the bowl as necessary, about 4 minutes. Add the sugar, vanilla, and salt, and continue beating until well blended and smooth, scraping down the sides of the bowl frequently, about 1 minute; there should be no lumps. Add the eggs, one at a time, beating on medium speed until just blended. (Don't overbeat once the eggs are added or the cheesecakes will puff and crack during baking.)

3. Transfer ⅔ cup of the batter to a small bowl. Add the pumpkin, flour, cinnamon, ginger, and nutmeg to the small bowl and stir with a wooden spoon until well blended.

4. Portion the plain batter among the muffin cups (about 2 generous tablespoons in each). Then portion the pumpkin batter evenly among the cups (about 1 generous tablespoon in each). Drag the tip of a wooden skewer, toothpick, or paring knife through the two batters in a random, swirly pattern to create a marbled look.

5. Bake until the centers of the cheesecakes barely jiggle when nudged, 15 to 18 minutes. Set the muffin tins on a rack and let cool completely. Cover and refrigerate until very cold, at least 6 hours or up to 3 days.

—Abigail Johnson Dodge

PER SERVING: 190 CALORIES I 4g PROTEIN I 13g CARB I 14g TOTAL FAT I 9g SAT FAT I 4g MONO FAT I 0.5g POLY FAT I 75mg CHOL I 150mg SODIUM I 0g FIBER

blueberry streusel bars with lemon-cream filling

YIELDS 24 BARS

- ½ lb. (1 cup) unsalted butter, softened at room temperature; more for the pan
- 13½ oz. (3 cups) unbleached all-purpose flour
- 1½ cups old-fashioned rolled oats (not quick oats)
- 1⅓ cups packed light brown sugar
- 1 tsp. table salt
- 1 tsp. baking powder
- 1 large egg, separated
- 1 14-oz. can sweetened condensed milk
- ½ cup fresh lemon juice
- 2 tsp. grated lemon zest
- 2½ cups (about 13 oz.) room-temperature blueberries, washed and drained on paper towels

Always a hit at summer picnics, these addictive squares strike the perfect balance between tart and sweet and chewy and crunchy. Be sure to use room-temperature berries. Cold fruit straight from the refrigerator will prevent your dessert from baking evenly.

1. Position a rack in the center of the oven and heat the oven to 350°F. Line a 9x13-inch metal baking pan with foil, leaving a 1-inch overhang on the ends. Lightly butter the bottom and sides of the foil.

2. In a large bowl, combine the flour, oats, sugar, salt, and baking powder. Using your fingers, blend the butter completely into the flour mixture. Transfer 2 cups of crumb mixture to another bowl and reserve for the topping. Blend the egg white into the remaining crumbs and then press the mixture into the bottom of the pan to form a level crust. Tamp it with the bottom of a measuring cup to even it out. Bake the crust until it starts to form a dry top, 10 to 12 minutes.

3. Meanwhile, in a medium bowl, whisk the condensed milk, lemon juice, lemon zest, and egg yolk. Let this mixture stand for 5 minutes; it will begin to thicken.

4. Sprinkle the blueberries evenly over the hot crust and then drop spoonfuls of the lemon mixture over the blueberries. Spread gently with a spatula to distribute a little more evenly, but take care not to crush the berries; it's fine if the lemon mixture isn't perfectly even. Bake until the lemon mixture just begins to form a shiny skin, 7 to 8 minutes.

5. Sprinkle the reserved topping over the lemon-blueberry layer, pressing the streusel between your fingers into small lumps as you sprinkle. Bake until the filling is bubbling at the edges and the topping is brown, 25 to 30 minutes.

6. Let the bars cool in the pan on a rack until just warm, about an hour. Carefully lift them out of the pan using the foil overhang and transfer to a wire rack to cool completely. Remove the foil and cut into 24 bars when cool. The bars may be stored at room temperature for a few hours but otherwise should be kept in the refrigerator. *—Nicole Rees*

PER BAR: 270 CALORIES | 4g PROTEIN | 41g CARB | 10g TOTAL FAT | 6g SAT FAT | 2.5g MONO FAT | 0.5g POLY FAT | 35mg CHOL | 140mg SODIUM | 2g FIBER

Buying and Storing Blueberries

You can judge some fruit with your nose, but not blueberries. Use your eyes first: Blueberries should have a lovely silvery-white bloom over the dark blue. Look for pints free of small, purplish or greenish immature berries, a sign that they were picked before their peak. Then use the "heft" test: Berries should be plump and heavy. The sure-fire way of judging blueberries is to taste a few, because sweetness is variable even within the same pint.

At home, pick through them, discarding any squishy berries that may turn moldy and infect their healthy neighbors. Store the berries in the coldest part of the refrigerator, but not in a drawer, where it's too humid. To keep them dry, don't wash them until you're ready to use them. Fresh-picked blueberries can be kept for up to 2 weeks in an airtight container, although they can lose moisture during the second week and shrink slightly. For baking, this can work in your favor, because the flavor becomes concentrated. After that, it's time to freeze them. Rinse them in a colander, dry thoroughly on paper towels, and then spread them on rimmed baking sheets in a single layer and freeze until solid. Once frozen, they go into plastic storage bags.

lemon cheesecake squares

YIELDS SIXTEEN 2-INCH SQUARES

FOR THE CRUST

9 graham crackers (about 5 oz.)

2 oz. (¼ cup) unsalted butter, melted

FOR THE CHEESECAKE FILLING

1 lb. cream cheese or Neufchâtel (⅓-less-fat cream cheese), softened at room temperature and cut into approximately 1-inch pieces

¾ cup granulated sugar

3 Tbs. fresh lemon juice (from 1 or 2 lemons)

1 Tbs. finely grated lemon zest (from 1 or 2 lemons, preferably using a rasp-style grater)

2 large eggs

FOR THE LEMON CURD

½ cup fresh lemon juice (from 2 or 3 lemons)

½ cup granulated sugar

2 large eggs

1 oz. (2 Tbs.) unsalted butter, cut into pieces

Make the lemon curd while the cheesecake bakes; it pours and spreads best while still warm. When cooking the curd, don't let it come to a boil or the eggs will overcook. These squares need to set up in the refrigerator, so allow at least 5 hours of chilling time before you serve them. You can substitute low-fat cream cheese for regular. The cheesecake itself will be slightly less creamy but still fabulous.

MAKE THE CRUST

1. Cut two 8x16-inch pieces of parchment. Put the strips in an 8x8-inch baking pan (preferably straight-sided) so that they cross each other and the excess hangs over the pan's sides. Push the parchment into the bottom and corners of the pan.

2. Position a rack in the center of the oven and heat the oven to 325°F.

3. Break the graham crackers into a food processor and process until finely ground. Add the melted butter and pulse until the mixture resembles damp sand. Transfer the crumbs to the lined pan and press them firmly and evenly into the pan. Set aside.

MAKE THE CHEESECAKE

1. Rinse, dry, and reassemble the food processor. In the cleaned bowl, combine the cream cheese, sugar, lemon juice, and lemon zest. Process until smooth, about 30 seconds, stopping halfway to scrape the sides of the bowl. Add the eggs and process until the mixture is perfectly smooth and blended, stopping to scrape the sides of the bowl as necessary, about another 20 seconds.

2. Pour the cheesecake mixture into the prepared pan. Bake until the sides are slightly puffed and the center is dry to the touch, about 40 minutes.

MAKE THE LEMON CURD

1. Set a fine strainer over a medium bowl. In another medium bowl, whisk the lemon juice, sugar, and eggs until thoroughly combined and most of the sugar has dissolved.

2. Pour the lemon mixture into a small, nonreactive saucepan. Cook over medium heat, stirring frequently with a wooden spoon or heatproof spatula, until the curd is steaming (but not boiling) and thickened and registers about 175°F on an instant-read thermometer, 3 to 7 minutes.

Packing and Serving Tips

To make packing and serving easier, flatten a paper muffin liner, set a lemon cheesecake square in the center, and fold the sides up. Repeat for the remaining squares, and then pack them in a box or a plastic container. The cheesecake squares need to be kept cool, so refrigerate them or include freezer packs in your carrying bag if you take them to go.

3. Take the curd off the heat, add the butter, and stir until the butter has melted. Pour the curd through the strainer to get rid of any lumps. Set aside but use while still warm to top the cheesecake.

CHILL AND FINISH

1. When the cheesecake comes out of the oven, pour all of the curd onto the cheesecake and use an offset spatula to spread it evenly. Let cool to room temperature and refrigerate for at least 5 hours, preferably overnight. You can refrigerate it uncovered, as no detectable skin forms on the curd.

2. When the cheesecake is thoroughly chilled, carefully lift it out of the pan using the parchment "handles" and onto a cutting board. Slide the parchment out and discard it. Using a large, sharp knife, cut the cheesecake into quarters, and then cut each quarter into four equal squares. To make clean cuts, wipe the knife blade with a damp paper towel between each slice. *—Meg Suzuki*

PER SQUARE: 260 CALORIES | 4g PROTEIN | 24g CARB | 16g TOTAL FAT | 9g SAT FAT | 4.5g MONO FAT | 1G POLY FAT | 95mg CHOL | 160mg SODIUM | 0g FIBER

double dark chocolate thumbprints

YIELDS ABOUT 4 DOZEN COOKIES

FOR THE COOKIES

- **6 oz. (1⅓ cups) unbleached all-purpose flour**
- **½ tsp. table salt**
- **½ tsp. baking powder**
- **¼ tsp. baking soda**
- **4 oz. (½ cup) unsalted butter, softened at room temperature**
- **1⅓ cups granulated sugar**
- **1½ oz. (½ cup) natural, unsweetened cocoa powder, sifted if lumpy**
- **3 large eggs**
- **¾ tsp. pure vanilla extract**
- **3 oz. bittersweet chocolate, melted and cooled slightly**

FOR THE CHOCOLATE FILLING

- **3 oz. bittersweet chocolate, coarsely chopped**
- **2 oz. (¼ cup) unsalted butter, cut into 3 pieces**

These are cookies for true chocoholics. The dough has both cocoa and bittersweet chocolate, and the ganache filling is rich and dark.

MAKE THE COOKIES

1. Position a rack in the center of the oven and heat the oven to 350°F. Line three cookie sheets with parchment or nonstick baking liners.

2. In a medium bowl, whisk the flour, salt, baking powder, and baking soda.

3. In a stand mixer fitted with the paddle attachment (or in a large bowl with a hand mixer), beat the butter, sugar, and cocoa powder on medium speed until well blended, about 2 minutes. Scrape down the bowl and the beater. Add the eggs one at a time, mixing until blended after each addition, about 30 seconds, and adding the vanilla along with the last egg. Continue mixing on medium speed until well blended, about 1 minute. Add the cooled, melted chocolate and mix until just blended, about 30 seconds. Add the flour mixture and mix on low speed until well blended, about 1 minute.

4. Using two tablespoon measures or a mini ice cream scoop, drop tablespoons of dough about 1½ inches apart on the prepared cookie sheets. Bake, one sheet at a time, until the cookies are puffed and the tops are cracked and look dry, 11 to 13 minutes. When the cookies are just out of the oven, use the rounded side of a half-teaspoon measure or the end of a thick-handled wooden spoon to make a small, deep well in the center of each cookie. Let the cookies sit on the cookie sheet for 5 minutes and then transfer them to a rack to cool completely.

MAKE THE FILLING

Melt the chocolate and butter in the microwave or in a medium bowl set in a skillet of barely simmering water, stirring with a rubber spatula until smooth. Remove from the heat and set aside until cool and slightly thickened.

FILL THE COOKIES

Spoon the chocolate mixture into the wells of the cooled cookies. Set aside until the chocolate firms up, about 1 hour. Serve immediately. —*Abigail Johnson Dodge*

PER COOKIE: 90 CALORIES | 1g PROTEIN | 11g CARB | 4.5g TOTAL FAT | 2.5g SAT FAT | 1.5g MONO FAT | 0g POLY FAT | 20mg CHOL | 45mg SODIUM | 1g FIBER

Make Ahead

Store unfilled cookies in an airtight container at room temperature for up to 3 days, or freeze them for up to 1 month before filling. Filled cookies can be stored in an airtight container at room temperature for up to 3 days.

peanut butter and chocolate shortbread bars

YIELDS 4 DOZEN 1½-INCH-SQUARE BARS

FOR THE PEANUT SHORTBREAD CRUST

- 7 oz. (14 Tbs.) unsalted butter, melted and cooled to just warm
- ½ cup granulated sugar
- ½ tsp. table salt
- 9½ oz. (2 cups plus 2 Tbs.) unbleached all-purpose flour
- ½ cup unsalted peanuts, finely chopped

FOR THE PEANUT BUTTER FILLING

- 1 cup creamy peanut butter (not natural but an emulsified variety such as Jif)
- 3 oz. (6 Tbs.) unsalted butter, at room temperature
- 6 oz. (1½ cups) confectioners' sugar
- 1 tsp. pure vanilla extract

FOR THE GANACHE

- 5 oz. good-quality bittersweet chocolate, such as Lindt® Excellence, chopped (about 1 heaping cup)
- ½ cup plus 2 Tbs. heavy cream

Upgrade the classic bar cookie with the buttery tenderness of a shortbread crust. These crowd-pleasing bars are covered with a creamy peanut butter spread and bittersweet chocolate ganache.

MAKE THE PEANUT SHORTBREAD

1. Line a straight-sided 13x9-inch metal baking pan with foil, letting the ends create an overhanging edge for easy removal.

2. In a medium bowl, stir the butter, sugar, and salt. Stir in the flour and peanuts to make a stiff dough. Press the mixture evenly into the bottom of the prepared pan. Prick the dough all over with a fork. Refrigerate the pan for 30 minutes (or freeze for 5 to 7 minutes), until the dough is firm.

3. Meanwhile, position a rack in the center of the oven and heat the oven to 325°F.

4. Bake the dough for 20 minutes, then reduce the oven temperature to 300°F and bake until the crust is golden-brown all over and completely set, 20 to 25 more minutes. Let the crust cool completely before topping.

MAKE THE PEANUT BUTTER FILLING

1. Put the peanut butter and butter in the bowl of a stand mixer fitted with the paddle attachment (or in a large bowl for hand mixing) and beat on medium speed until smooth, about 1 minute. Add about half of the confectioners' sugar to the mixer along with the vanilla and 1 Tbs. hot water. Beat on low speed until combined, then on medium speed until smooth and fluffy, about 1 more minute. Beat in the remaining sugar and mix, about 1 more minute, until the mixture is smooth and thick, like frosting. If the filling seems too stiff, add another 1 Tbs. hot water and beat for another minute.

2. With a knife or metal offset spatula, spread the filling over the fully cooled crust. The filling may not spread smoothly and evenly, but don't worry; the ganache will cover it.

MAKE THE GANACHE

1. Put the chocolate in a small heatproof bowl. In a small saucepan, bring the heavy cream to a boil. Remove from the heat and pour over the chocolate. Let sit for 3 minutes. Stir gently with a rubber spatula until combined and smooth.

2. Spread the ganache over the peanut butter filling with a metal offset spatula to coat evenly. Let the bar sit for at least 3 hours to allow the ganache to set before cutting (or refrigerate for 1 hour).

3. Carefully lift the bar from the pan using the foil sides and transfer them to a cutting board. Separate the foil from the bar by sliding a spatula between them. Cut into 1½-inch-square bars. They will keep at room temperature for 1 week. —*Nicole Rees*

PER BAR: 140 CALORIES | 3g PROTEIN | 26g CARB | 3g TOTAL FAT | 0g SAT FAT | 1g MONO FAT | 1g POLY FAT | 35mg CHOL | 50mg SODIUM | 1g FIBER

caramel turtle bars

**YIELDS ABOUT 4 DOZEN
1½-INCH-SQUARE BARS**

FOR THE CRUST

Nonstick cooking spray, vegetable oil, or melted butter for the pan

7 oz. (14 Tbs.) unsalted butter, melted and cooled to just warm

½ cup packed light brown sugar

½ tsp. table salt

9 oz. (2 cups) unbleached all-purpose flour

FOR THE CARAMEL TOPPING

2 cups pecan halves, toasted and coarsely chopped

1 cup packed light brown sugar

¾ cup heavy cream

4 oz. (½ cup) unsalted butter, cut into chunks

½ cup light corn syrup

¼ tsp. table salt

FOR THE GANACHE

6 Tbs. heavy cream

2 oz. good-quality bittersweet chocolate, finely chopped

To decorate the bars, fill a plastic zip-top baggie with the ganache, snip the tip off a corner, and drizzle the ganache over the caramel bars. Extra ganache can be stored in the refrigerator for up to 5 days.

MAKE THE SHORTBREAD CRUST

1. Line a straight-sided 13x9-inch metal baking pan with foil, letting the ends create an overhanging edge for easy removal. Lightly coat the sides of the foil (not the bottom) with nonstick cooking spray, oil, or melted butter to prevent the caramel from sticking.

2. In a medium bowl, stir the butter, brown sugar, and salt. Stir in the flour to make a stiff dough. Press the mixture evenly into the bottom of the prepared pan. Prick the dough all over with a fork. Refrigerate the pan for 30 minutes (or freeze for 5 to 7 minutes), until the dough is firm.

3. Meanwhile, position a rack in the center of the oven and heat the oven to 325°F.

4. Bake the dough for 20 minutes, and then reduce the oven temperature to 300°F and bake until the crust is golden all over and completely set, about 15 more minutes.

MAKE THE CARAMEL TOPPING

1. Sprinkle the pecans evenly over the crust.

2. In a heavy medium saucepan, bring the brown sugar, cream, butter, corn syrup, and salt to a boil over medium-high heat, stirring until all the ingredients are melted and smooth. Let the mixture continue to boil, without stirring, until a candy thermometer registers 240°F, about 6 more minutes. Turn off the heat and immediately (but carefully) pour the caramel evenly over the prepared crust. Let the bar cool completely, about 2 hours, before garnishing with the ganache.

MAKE THE GANACHE

1. Put the chocolate in a small heatproof bowl. In a small saucepan, bring the heavy cream to a boil. Remove from the heat and pour over the chocolate. Let sit for 3 minutes. Stir gently with a rubber spatula until combined and smooth.

2. Drizzle the ganache decoratively over the caramel bars. Let the ganache set for 30 minutes to an hour. Carefully lift the bar from the pan using the foil sides and transfer them to a cutting board. Separate the foil from the bar by sliding a spatula between them. Cut into 1½-inch-square bars. They will keep at room temperature for 1 week. —*Nicole Rees*

PER BAR: 160 CALORIES | 1g PROTEIN | 15g CARB | 11g TOTAL FAT | 5g SAT FAT | 4g MONO FAT | 1g POLY FAT | 20mg CHOL | 45mg SODIUM | 1g FIBER

cranberry streusel shortbread bars

YIELDS ABOUT THIRTY-FIVE
1¾-INCH-SQUARE BARS

FOR THE CRUST AND STREUSEL

10½ oz. (1 cup plus 5 Tbs.)
unsalted butter, melted and
cooled to just warm

1 cup granulated sugar

¾ tsp. table salt

2 large egg yolks

14¼ oz. (3 cups plus 3 Tbs.)
unbleached all-purpose
flour

FOR THE CRANBERRY FILLING

1 12-oz. bag fresh or frozen
cranberries, picked over,
rinsed, and drained

1 cup granulated sugar

These bars have a tangy cranberry filling that keeps the ultra-rich crust and streusel topping in check. Baking them in the top of the oven helps the streusel brown faster without overbrowning the crust.

MAKE THE CRUST

1. Line a straight-sided 13x9-inch metal baking pan with foil, letting the ends create an overhanging edge for easy removal. In a medium bowl, stir the butter, ¾ cup of the sugar, and the salt. Whisk in the egg yolks. Stir in the flour to make a stiff dough. Transfer about 2 cups of the dough to the prepared pan and press the mixture evenly into the bottom. Prick the dough all over with a fork. Refrigerate the pan for 30 minutes (or freeze for 5 to 7 minutes), until the dough is firm.

2. Meanwhile, position racks in the center rack and upper third of the oven and heat the oven to 325°F.

3. Bake the dough on the center rack until the crust begins to set but does not brown at all on the edges (the center will not be firm yet), about 20 minutes. While the crust bakes, prepare the streusel and the topping.

MAKE THE STREUSEL

With your fingers, combine the remaining ¼ cup granulated sugar with the reserved dough until crumbly. The mixture should hold together when pressed, but readily break into smaller pieces.

MAKE THE CRANBERRY FILLING

1. In a medium saucepan, bring the cranberries, sugar, and ¼ cup water to a boil over high heat. Reduce the heat to medium high and continue to boil until the liquid is reduced to a thick syrup, 5 to 8 minutes. Remove the pan from the heat and let the mixture cool for 5 to 10 minutes—the syrup will continue to thicken as the mixture cools.

2. Spread the cranberry mixture evenly over the hot crust. Scatter the streusel over the cranberries (don't crumble the streusel too much or the texture will be sandy). Increase the oven temperature to 350°F and bake the bar near the top of the oven until the streusel is golden and set, about 25 minutes.

3. Place the pan on a metal rack to cool until the crust is completely firm, at least 1 hour. (For faster cooling, put the bar in the fridge once the pan is no longer piping hot, or even outside in winter.)

4. When the bottom of the pan is cool, carefully lift the bar from the pan using the foil sides and transfer them to a cutting board. Separate the foil from the bars by sliding a spatula between them. Cut into 1¾-inch-square bars. They will keep at room temperature for 1 week. —*Nicole Rees*

PER BAR: 150 CALORIES | 1g PROTEIN | 21g CARB | 7g TOTAL FAT | 4.5g SAT FAT | 2g MONO FAT | 0g POLY FAT | 30mg CHOL | 50mg SODIUM | 1g FIBER

lemon shortbread bars

YIELDS 2 DOZEN 2-INCH-SQUARE BARS

FOR THE CRUST

Nonstick cooking spray, vegetable oil, or melted butter for the pan

7 oz. (14 Tbs.) unsalted butter, melted and cooled to just warm

½ cup granulated sugar

½ tsp. table salt

9½ oz. (2 cups plus 2 Tbs.) unbleached all-purpose flour

FOR THE LEMON TOPPING

4 large eggs

1¼ cups granulated sugar

3 Tbs. unbleached all-purpose flour

⅛ tsp. table salt

¾ cup fresh lemon juice (from 3 to 4 lemons)

1 Tbs. packed, finely grated fresh lemon zest (from 2 lemons, using a rasp-style grater)

1 Tbs. confectioners' sugar

how to turn classic shortbread into bar cookie crust

- Melt the butter and stir it into the sugar and salt for a crust that's rich yet sturdy.

- Chill the dough in the pan so it bakes without puffing or shrinking and has a perfectly crisp texture.

- Fully bake the crust before you add the toppings—it's the key to keeping that crispness.

These bar cookies will keep, refrigerated, for 3 to 4 days. Serve at room temperature.

MAKE THE CRUST

1. Line a straight-sided 13x9-inch metal baking pan with foil, letting the ends create an overhanging edge for easy removal. Lightly coat the sides of the foil (not the bottom) with nonstick cooking spray, oil, or melted butter to prevent the lemon topping from sticking.

2. In a medium bowl, stir the butter, sugar, and salt. Stir in the flour to make a stiff dough. Press the dough evenly into the bottom of the prepared pan. Prick the dough all over with a fork. Refrigerate the pan for 30 minutes (or freeze for 5 to 7 minutes), until the dough is firm.

3. Meanwhile, position a rack in the center of the oven and heat the oven to 325°F.

4. Bake until the crust is golden and set, about 30 minutes. Meanwhile, make the lemon topping.

MAKE THE LEMON TOPPING

1. In a medium bowl, whisk the eggs, sugar, flour, and salt until smooth, about 1 minute. Whisk in the lemon juice and zest.

2. Pour the topping over the hot crust. Return the pan to the oven and increase the heat to 350°F. Bake until the topping is set in the center (it no longer wiggles when the pan is moved) and the edges are golden, 20 to 25 minutes.

3. Set the pan on a metal rack to cool until the crust is completely firm, at least 1 hour. (For faster cooling, put the bar in the fridge once the pan is no longer piping hot, or even outside in winter.) When the bottom of the pan is cool, carefully lift the bars from the pan using the foil sides and transfer them to a cutting board. Separate the foil from the bar by sliding a spatula between them. Sift the confectioners' sugar over the lemon topping. Cut into 2-inch-square bars. —*Nicole Rees*

PER BAR: 170 CALORIES | 2g PROTEIN | 24g CARB | 8g TOTAL FAT | 4.5g SAT FAT | 2g MONO FAT | 0g POLY FAT | 55mg CHOL | 75mg SODIUM | 0g FIBER

chocolate-glazed éclairs

YIELDS ABOUT 1 DOZEN ÉCLAIRS

- **1 cup heavy cream, well chilled**
- **1 Tbs. confectioners' sugar**
- **1 tsp. pure vanilla extract**
- **1 recipe Vanilla Pastry Cream (p. 87)**
- **1 recipe Éclair Pastry Shells (p. 86)**
- **1 recipe Bittersweet Ganache Glaze (p. 87)**

The finished éclairs need to chill for at least 30 minutes, but don't wait longer than 3 hours to serve them.

Most of the components of this pastry-shop classic—the pâte à choux shells, the vanilla pastry cream filling, and the chocolate glaze—can be made well in advance. For the final assembly, all you need to do is lighten the pastry cream with whipped cream, spoon the mixture into the pastry shells, and glaze with chocolate.

1. Combine the cream, confectioners' sugar, and vanilla in a chilled mixing bowl and whisk by hand or with a stand mixer fitted with the whisk attachment until the cream becomes fluffy and forms a soft peak that folds over when you lift the whisk. Be careful not to overwhip the cream or you risk it curdling when you fold it into the custard.

2. Whisk the pastry cream until smooth and then gently whisk in about one-third of the whipped cream to lighten the pastry cream. Scrape the rest of the whipped cream over the mixture and, using the whisk in a folding action, gently blend the two until the mixture is uniform and smooth.

3. Assemble and glaze the éclairs as explained below. —*Carolyn Weil*

PER SERVING: 270 CALORIES | 5g PROTEIN | 19g CARB | 20g TOTAL FAT | 12g SAT FAT | 5g MONO FAT | 1g POLY FAT | 145mg CHOL | 150mg SODIUM | 1g FIBER

continued on p. 86–87 ➤

how to assemble and glaze éclairs

Cut an éclair shell in half lengthwise with a serrated knife. Use your fingers to pinch out the doughy insides of both halves. Use two soup spoons—one to scoop and the other to push the cream off the spoon—to mound the filling into the entire length of the bottom half of the shell, about 2 to 3 Tbs. of filling per shell. Gently place the top half of the éclair shell on the custard and put the assembled éclair on a wire rack set over a rimmed baking sheet. Repeat with the remaining shells.

When all the éclairs are assembled, warm the glaze a little just until it's warm enough to flow off the side of a spoon in a wide, thick ribbon. (If the ganache is too hot, it will run off the éclairs and puddle below on the tray.) Spoon the ganache along the entire length of each éclair top. Put the sheet of glazed éclairs in the refrigerator and chill for at least 30 minutes or up to 3 hours before serving.

continued from p. 84

éclair pastry shells (pâte à choux)

YIELDS ENOUGH DOUGH FOR 12 TO 13 ÉCLAIRS

- 2 oz. (¼ cup) unsalted butter
- ½ tsp. table salt
- 4½ oz. (1 cup) unbleached all-purpose flour
- 3 large eggs

Don't double this recipe because it becomes a struggle to stir the dough in the pan. It's better to make multiple batches of dough if you want to make more éclairs.

1. Position a rack in the center of the oven and heat the oven to 400°F. Cut a sheet of parchment to fit in a heavy-duty 13x18-inch rimmed baking sheet. Using a pencil, draw three sets of two lines spaced 3 inches apart, running the length of the parchment. These will be guidelines for piping the éclair dough. Line the baking sheet with the parchment, penciled side down—you should be able to see the lines through the parchment. If not, draw them darker.

2. In a medium saucepan, bring the butter, salt, and 1 cup water to a boil over medium-high heat. Reduce the heat to medium and add the flour. Using a wooden spoon, stir vigorously to combine. Continue to stir, using a figure-eight motion and smearing the dough against the sides of the pan to cook the flour and work out any lumps, for 2 minutes. The mixture will be thick and look like a firm ball, or balls, of sticky mashed potatoes that pull away from the pan sides. During this process, it's normal for a thin layer of dough to stick to the bottom of the pan and sizzle.

3. Remove the pan from the heat and scrape the dough into a large bowl (for hand mixing) or into the bowl of a stand mixer fitted with the paddle attachment. On low speed, mix until the dough feels merely warm to the touch, not hot, 3 to 5 minutes.

4. With the mixer still on low, beat in the eggs one at a time. After each egg is added, the dough will separate into small lumps and then come back together. After the dough pulls back together, briefly (about 20 seconds) increase the speed to medium low to mix the dough well. Reduce the speed to low before adding the next egg. After the addition of the last egg, scrape the bowl well and beat on medium low for a final 30 seconds.

5. Scrape the dough into a pastry bag fitted with a large star tip. Twist the top of the bag to push the dough toward the tip. Hold the bag at a 60-degree angle and set the tip of the pastry tube on the parchment, right at the top of one of the 3-inch-wide stripes you drew earlier. Squeeze the pastry bag and, using the lines on the parchment as a guide, pipe out 3-inch lengths of dough in a tight zigzag pattern, spacing the éclairs about 1 inch apart.

6. Bake until the shells are puffed, crisp, and thoroughly golden brown, 45 to 50 minutes. If you find that they're baking unevenly, rotate the pan. Remove from the oven, transfer to a rack, and let cool completely, about 15 minutes, before filling or storing.

Make Ahead

Store the shells in an airtight container at room temperature for up to 2 days or freeze them in an airtight plastic freezer bag for up to 6 weeks. To refresh the shells before assembling, arrange them on a baking sheet and warm them in a 350°F oven until dry, firm, and almost crisp, 10 to 15 minutes for room-temperature shells, 15 to 20 minutes for frozen shells. Let cool before using.

vanilla pastry cream

YIELDS ABOUT 1 CUP

- **1** cup whole milk
- **3** large egg yolks
- **¼** cup granulated sugar
- **2** Tbs. cornstarch
- **⅛** tsp. table salt
- **½** tsp. pure vanilla extract

The pastry cream needs to chill for at least 1 hour before use and may be made ahead and refrigerated for up to a day.

1. Warm the milk in a medium saucepan over medium heat until tiny bubbles appear. Meanwhile, in a medium heatproof bowl, whisk the egg yolks and sugar until pale yellow. Add the cornstarch and salt and whisk well. Pour the hot milk into the yolk mixture, ½ cup at a time, whisking constantly. Return the mixture to the saucepan and cook over medium heat, whisking constantly, until it thickens to the consistency of thick pudding, about 2 minutes. (It will look lumpy as it starts to thicken but will smooth out as you continue to whisk.)

2. Remove from the heat and scrape the pastry cream into a large clean metal bowl. Whisk in the vanilla and then lay a sheet of plastic wrap directly on the surface. Refrigerate until thoroughly chilled, about 1 hour.

bittersweet ganache glaze

YIELDS ABOUT ¾ CUP

- **4** oz. bittersweet chocolate (preferably 55% to 63% cacao), chopped
- **½** cup heavy cream
- **1** tsp. light corn syrup

The corn syrup is optional for this recipe but it helps keep the ganache glossy when refrigerated.

STOVETOP DIRECTIONS
In a small saucepan, warm the cream over medium heat until the cream begins to simmer around the edges of the pan. Remove from heat and add the chopped chocolate pieces and the corn syrup. Let stand for 5 to 7 minutes and then stir until smooth.

MICROWAVE DIRECTIONS
In a Pyrex cup, combine the chocolate, cream, and corn syrup. Microwave at 50% power for 30 seconds. Stir to combine. If just a few unmelted chunks of chocolate remain, let the heat of the mixture melt the remaining few chunks. If more than a few chunks remain, microwave at 50% power for another 30 seconds.

Make Ahead

Refrigerate the ganache, tightly covered, for up to 2 weeks. Warm it by placing its bowl in a large bowl of hot tap water and stirring until smooth.

nutty butterscotch and chocolate bars

YIELDS 2 DOZEN
2¼X2-INCH BARS

11¼ oz. (2½ cups) unbleached all-purpose flour

¾ tsp. baking soda

½ tsp. table salt

½ lb. (1 cup) unsalted butter, softened at room temperature; more for the pan

1¾ cups very firmly packed light brown sugar

2 large eggs

1½ tsp. pure vanilla extract

7½ oz. (1¼ cups) semisweet chocolate chips

1¼ oz. (½ cup) sweetened coconut flakes

4½ oz. (1 cup) medium-finely chopped pecans or walnuts

These cookies go by many aliases: blondies, golden brownies, or congo bars. Cover them with plastic and store at room temperature for up to 2 days or freeze for up to a month.

1. Position a rack in the center of the oven and heat the oven to 325°F. Lightly grease the bottom and sides of a 9x13-inch baking pan.

2. In a medium bowl, whisk the flour, baking soda, and salt to blend. In a large bowl, combine the butter and brown sugar. Using a stand mixer fitted with the paddle attachment (or a hand mixer in a large bowl), beat the butter and brown sugar on medium until very well blended and fluffy, about 2 minutes. Add the eggs and vanilla and continue to beat on medium until well blended, about another minute. Add the flour mixture and mix on low until just blended, about 1 minute. Pour in the chocolate chips and coconut; mix on low until combined.

3. Scrape the dough into the prepared pan and spread evenly. Scatter the nuts evenly over the top. Bake until a toothpick inserted in the center comes out almost clean with a few moist crumbs clinging to it, about 40 minutes. Transfer the pan to a rack and let cool completely. Cut into bars, squares, or triangles. *—Abigail Johnson Dodge*

Simple Tools Give a Professional Look

One of the advantages of making bar cookies is that you don't need any fancy equipment. Though not essential, a couple of simple tools will make your bar cookies look more professional.

• Straight-sided 9x13-inch metal pans, such as those made by Parrish® and Doughmakers®, are recommended for baking these cookies. Regular Pyrex pans, with their rounded corners, are fine, but your yield will be smaller because you'll need to trim to get sharp edges.

• Small offset spatulas are great for lifting out squares neatly; especially the short, square 2-inch-wide size. For evenly spreading batters and glazes, a 3- or 4-inch-long offset icing spatula is perfect.

• Parchment is great for lining the bottom of the pan—it makes lifting out the bar cookies much easier.

• A bench scraper is an efficient tool for cutting bar cookies. Its squared-off shape allows you to see just what you're doing and lets you aim straight down for the cleanest cut.

• A ruler helps you measure, so you get an even and consistent yield if you're making multiple batches.

• Toothpicks are helpful for marking off where you'll need to cut.

lemon cornmeal shortbread bars

YIELDS ABOUT FORTY
2½X1-INCH BARS

- **9** oz. (2 cups) unbleached all-purpose flour
- **5** oz. (1 cup) finely ground yellow cornmeal, preferably Quaker®
- **½** tsp. table salt
- **12** oz. (1½ cups) unsalted butter, softened at room temperature; more for the pan
- **7** oz. (2 cups) confectioners' sugar
- **1** Tbs. finely grated lemon zest
- **1** tsp. pure vanilla extract

This shortbread is buttery and fragrant with lemon zest. It's chewier than traditional shortbread, so cornmeal is added for crunch and texture.

1. Position a rack in the center of the oven and heat the oven to 325°F. Lightly grease the sides and bottom of a 9x13-inch baking pan. Line the bottom of the pan with the parchment.

2. In a medium bowl, whisk the flour, cornmeal, and salt to blend. In a large bowl, combine the butter, confectioners' sugar, lemon zest, and vanilla; using a hand mixer or a stand mixer fitted with the paddle attachment, beat on medium-high speed until light and creamy, 3 to 4 minutes. Scrape the bowl. Add the flour mixture and mix on low speed until the dough begins to form moist clumps. Dump the dough into the prepared pan.

3. Using a rubber spatula or lightly floured fingertips, spread the dough into the pan in a smooth, even layer. Dip the tip of a knife or a small metal spatula in flour (to prevent sticking) and score the dough all the way through into bars that measure 1x2½ inches (about 1 inch across the short side and just a smidgen over 2½ inches on the long side). Bake until the tops look dry and golden brown, 35 to 40 minutes. Transfer the pan to a rack. Immediately cut the shortbread into bars with a metal bench scraper or a knife, using the scored lines as a guide (they will have faded a bit during baking). It's important to do this right after the shortbread comes out of the oven; if you wait until it has cooled, it will crumble when you try to cut it. Let the bars cool completely in the pan before removing them with a small, flexible offset spatula.
—*Abigail Johnson Dodge*

Make Ahead

The shortbread dough can be pressed into the pan, scored, covered, and frozen up to a month before thawing and baking. The baked bars will keep, well wrapped, for up to 3 days at room temperature.

Wrapping It Up

For a special gift, give bar cookies in pretty cookie tins, an oversize coffee cup, brightly colored takeout containers, funky flea-market pottery, or in the pan in which you baked them. Or stack them neatly on a cardboard cake round and wrap the whole thing in colorful cellophane. Just use your imagination and, remember, your friends will love the cookies, no matter how they're delivered.

almond cheesecake apple bars

YIELDS SIXTEEN 2½-INCH SQUARES

FOR THE CRUST AND TOPPING

6⅛ oz. (1¼ cups plus 2 Tbs.) unbleached all-purpose flour

¼ tsp. table salt

2 oz. (¼ cup) unsalted butter, well softened

2 oz. (¼ cup) cream cheese, well softened

¼ tsp. pure almond extract

¼ cup plus 2 Tbs. granulated sugar

¼ cup plus 2 Tbs. firmly packed light brown sugar

3 oz. (¾ cup) slivered almonds, coarsely chopped

FOR THE FILLING

4 oz. (½ cup) cream cheese, softened

½ cup granulated sugar

1 large egg, at room temperature

2 tsp. freshly grated lemon zest

1 Tbs. fresh lemon juice

Pinch of table salt

1 lb. (about 2 medium) Braeburn, Gala, or Rome apples, peeled, cored, and cut into ⅛-inch-thick slices (to yield 2½ cups)

Cream cheese and lemon juice give these bars a classic cheese-cake tang and texture.

MAKE THE CRUST AND TOPPING

1. Position a rack in the center of the oven and heat the oven to 350°F. Cut a piece of parchment into a 9x14-inch rectangle. Line a 9x9-inch baking pan with the parchment (it will extend beyond the pan). Butter the parchment and the unlined sides of the pan.

2. Set aside 2 Tbs. of the flour in a small dish. Whisk the remaining 1¼ cups flour and the salt in a small bowl. In a large bowl, beat the butter with an electric mixer on medium speed until smooth. Add the cream cheese and almond extract and beat on medium until smooth, scraping the bowl as needed, about 1 minute. Add ¼ cup each of the granulated and brown sugars and beat on medium speed until blended, scraping as needed. Add the flour-salt mixture and ⅓ cup of the almonds and beat on medium low just until the flour is absorbed and the mixture starts to come together in clumps.

3. Set aside ⅔ cup of the dough in another bowl and press the remaining dough into the prepared pan in a thin but even layer. Prick it all over with a fork. Bake until the crust is golden, especially around the edges, 18 to 20 minutes. Remove from the oven but keep the oven on.

4. While the crust bakes, add the 2 Tbs. reserved flour and the remaining 2 Tbs. each of the granulated and brown sugars to the reserved dough. Mix with your fingertips until well combined and then squeeze the dough together into one clump.

MAKE THE FILLING

1. In a large bowl, beat the cream cheese with an electric mixer on medium speed until smooth. Add the sugar and beat on medium until combined, scraping the bowl as needed. Add the egg and beat until combined, scraping the bowl as needed. Beat in the lemon zest, lemon juice, and salt.

2. Spread the apple slices evenly on the bottom crust and pour the cream cheese filling on top, gently spreading it with a rubber spatula to cover the apples. Crumble the remaining dough on top. The pieces can be fairly large, about the size of a cherry, and the topping needn't completely cover the filling. Sprinkle with the remaining almonds. Bake until the topping and almonds are light golden brown, 45 to 50 minutes. Let the bar cool in the pan until warm, about 30 minutes. Remove from the pan using the parchment sling and set on a wire rack to cool completely. Transfer the bar, still on the parchment, to a cutting board. Slide a long metal spatula between the bar and parchment to separate them, and then slide the parchment out. Cut into 16 bars.
—*Wendy Kalen*

PER BAR: 210 CALORIES | 3g PROTEIN | 30g CARB | 10g TOTAL FAT | 4g SAT FAT | 4g MONO FAT | 1g POLY FAT | 35mg CHOL | 90mg SODIUM | 2g FIBER

gingered lemon bars

- 5 oz. (1 cup plus 2 Tbs.) unbleached all-purpose flour
- 6¼ oz. (1¾ cups plus 1 tsp.) confectioners' sugar
- 1 Tbs. lightly packed finely grated lemon zest
- ½ tsp. plus a tiny pinch of ground ginger
- Pinch of table salt
- 4 oz. (½ cup) chilled unsalted butter, cut into small pieces; more for the pan
- ½ tsp. baking powder
- 3 large eggs, at room temperature
- 6 Tbs. fresh lemon juice

If you're not a ginger lover, feel free to leave it out of these bars— you'll still get a luscious, tart and tangy, sweet lemon bar. To cut the neatest squares, use a flat metal spatula or a bench scraper and cut straight down.

1. Position a rack in the center of the oven and heat the oven to 350°F. Butter an 8x8-inch baking pan.

2. In a medium bowl, whisk 1 cup (4½ oz.) of the flour with ¼ cup of the confectioners' sugar, the lemon zest, ½ tsp. of the ginger, and a pinch of salt. Cut in the butter with a pastry blender or two table knives until the mixture resembles small peas. Knead the dough in the bowl just until it begins to come together. Transfer the dough to the baking pan and, with floured hands, press it evenly over the bottom. Bake until very light golden brown, about 20 minutes. Let cool on a rack while you make the filling.

3. In a small bowl, whisk 1½ cups of the confectioners' sugar, the remaining 2 Tbs. (½ oz.) flour, the baking powder, and a pinch of salt. In a medium bowl, beat the eggs with an electric mixer on high speed until tripled in volume, pale yellow, and very light and fluffy, 3 to 5 minutes (the eggs will hold soft peaks very briefly). Reduce the speed to low, add the sugar and flour mixture, and beat just until blended, scraping the bowl as needed. Add the lemon juice and beat just until blended. Pour the lemon mixture over the warm crust.

4. Bake until the filling is just set in the center, is golden brown on top, and doesn't jiggle when the pan is nudged, 18 to 20 minutes. Let cool completely in the pan on a rack. Just before serving, stir the remaining 1 tsp. confectioners' sugar with the pinch of ginger in a small bowl. Transfer to a small sieve and sift over the lemon filling. Using a bench scraper or a metal spatula, cut into 2-inch squares, slicing straight down (rather than dragging). Store in an airtight container. —*Lori Longbotham*

PER BAR: 140 CALORIES | 2g PROTEIN | 18g CARB | 7g TOTAL FAT | 4g SAT FAT | 2g MONO FAT | 0g POLY FAT | 55mg CHOL | 45mg SODIUM | 0g FIBER

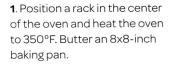

how to get the most out of each lemon you zest

- When grating lemon zest, you want just the thin yellow top coat of the skin. Overzealous grating will result in bitter flavors.
- The lemon's volatile oils are strongest just after zesting, so remove the zest just before using.
- Grate lemon zest over waxed paper to make it easier to gather for measuring.
- Finely grated zest releases more flavor than larger strips.
- If you have more lemons on hand than you can use, grate or peel the zest, juice the lemons, and then freeze the zest and juice separately. Well wrapped, they'll keep for up to 3 months.

ginger bars

YIELDS THIRTY-TWO
3X2-INCH BARS

9 oz. (2 cups) unbleached all-purpose flour, preferably King Arthur®

1 tsp. baking soda

¼ tsp. table salt

2½ tsp. ground ginger

1¼ tsp. ground cinnamon

½ tsp. ground cloves

6½ oz. (13 Tbs.) unsalted butter, softened at room temperature; more for the pan

1⅓ cups granulated sugar

2 Tbs. plus 1½ tsp. molasses

4½ tsp. honey

2 extra-large eggs

Confectioners' sugar, for sprinkling

For information on how to select and store ginger, see p. 199.

These spicy ginger bars are a cross between a gooey blondie and classic gingerbread. The bars' moist, soft texture also makes them great keepers and shippers.

1. Position a rack in the center of the oven and heat the oven to 350°F. Lightly grease a 13x9-inch baking pan. In a medium bowl, whisk the flour with the baking soda, salt, ginger, cinnamon, and cloves until blended.

2. Using a stand mixer with the paddle attachment (or in a large bowl with a hand mixer), beat the butter, sugar, molasses, and honey until creamy and well blended, about 4 minutes. Add the eggs, one at a time, beating after each addition until blended. Add the flour mixture and mix on low speed until just blended.

3. Scrape the batter into the prepared pan and spread evenly. Bake until the edges just begin to pull away from the sides of the pan and a pick inserted in the center comes out almost clean, 23 to 25 minutes. Set the pan on a rack to cool completely. Cut into bars, squares, or triangles. Sift a light coating of confectioners' sugar over the cookies just before serving. Store at room temperature or freeze in an airtight container, separating the layers with waxed paper.
—*Katherine Gibson*

apricot coconut bars

YIELDS SIXTEEN 2-INCH BARS

FOR THE CRUST

5 oz. (1 cup plus 2 Tbs.) unbleached all-purpose flour

2 Tbs. granulated sugar

Pinch table salt

4 oz. (½ cup) cold unsalted butter, cut into ½-inch pieces; more for the pan

FOR THE TOPPING

½ cup packed light brown sugar

1 extra-large egg

2 Tbs. apricot jam

1 Tbs. unbleached all-purpose flour

½ tsp. baking powder

¼ tsp. table salt

¼ tsp. pure almond extract

1 cup firmly packed diced dried apricots (about 6 oz.)

¼ cup sweetened shredded coconut

Bake these bars until the topping is browned around the edges and a pick inserted in the center comes out a bit sticky.

MAKE THE CRUST

Position a rack in the bottom third of the oven and heat the oven to 350°F. Lightly grease an 8x8-inch baking pan and line the bottom with parchment. Combine the flour, sugar, and salt in a food processor. Add the butter pieces and pulse until the mixture resembles moist pebbles. Dump the dough into the prepared pan and press down to form an even layer. Bake until the crust is lightly golden, about 30 minutes. Transfer the pan to a rack and leave the oven set to 350°F.

MAKE THE TOPPING

While the crust is baking, combine the brown sugar, egg, apricot jam, flour, baking powder, salt, and almond extract in a medium bowl. Whisk until blended. Stir in the apricots and coconut. When the crust is baked, scrape the topping into the pan and spread evenly. Continue baking for about 20 minutes. Set the pan on a rack to cool completely before inverting onto a cutting board. Using a warm, thin-bladed knife, trim off the edges and cut into bars. Store at room temperature or freeze in an airtight container, separating the layers with waxed paper. —*Renée Henry*

Tips for Successful Dessert Bars

• Don't overmix the batter. After the flour has been added, mix only to incorporate—too much mixing means tough bars.

• Wait until the very end of the mixing process to add nuts and chocolate; this way, they'll be distributed more evenly throughout the bars.

• Take your time when cutting the bars. Use a serrated knife or a bench knife and wipe it clean between each cut.

chocolate soufflé cookies

**YIELDS ABOUT FORTY
2-INCH COOKIES**

- **6** oz. bittersweet or semisweet chocolate, chopped
- **2** large egg whites, at room temperature
- **⅛** tsp. cream of tartar
- **½** tsp. pure vanilla extract
- **¼** cup granulated sugar
- **¾** cup finely chopped walnuts

These cookies are chocolatey and moist with a light, crisp exterior. They're best eaten on the day they're baked but will last 2 to 3 days if stored in an airtight container.

1. Position racks in the upper and lower thirds of the oven and heat the oven to 350°F. Lightly grease two baking sheets or line them with parchment.

2. Melt the chocolate and set aside. Using a hand or stand mixer, beat the egg whites with the cream of tartar until soft peaks form. With the beaters running, gradually add the vanilla and sugar until the egg whites hold stiff peaks but don't look dry. Pour the nuts and melted chocolate over the whipped whites. Gently fold the mixture with a large rubber spatula, trying not to deflate the egg whites, until the color is just uniform. Immediately drop level measuring teaspoons of the batter onto the baking sheets, leaving at least 1 inch between the cookies. Bake until the cookies are shiny and cracked, 10 to 12 minutes; they should be firm on the outside but still gooey inside when you press them. Slide the parchment liners onto racks or use a metal spatula to transfer the cookies to racks and let cool completely. —*Alice Medrich*

raspberry crumb bars

YIELDS EIGHTEEN 3X2-INCH
BARS

- **9 oz. (2 cups) unbleached all-purpose flour**
- **1¼ cups old-fashioned oats**
- **1 cup packed dark brown sugar**
- **1 tsp. ground cinnamon**
- **½ tsp. table salt**
- **½ lb. (1 cup) chilled unsalted butter, cut into ½-inch cubes**
- **4 oz. (about 1 cup) sliced almonds**
- **1 15¼-oz. jar seedless raspberry fruit spread**

For soft bars, use a small offset spatula to spread the mixture evenly so that the finished bars are uniform. For a thoroughly crisp bar, partially bake the bottom layer before adding the filling and top crumb layer.

1. Position a rack in the center of the oven and heat the oven to 325°F.

2. With an electric mixer, combine the flour, oats, brown sugar, cinnamon, and salt. Mix on low speed until well combined. Add the butter and mix on medium until the butter is mostly blended and the mixture appears moist and begins to pull together, about 3 minutes. Stir in the almonds. Reserve 1½ cups of this crumb mixture and refrigerate. Firmly press the remaining mixture into the bottom of an ungreased 13x9-inch baking pan.

3. Bake until the almonds are just beginning to brown, about 25 minutes. Let cool for about 20 minutes.

4. Spread the fruit spread evenly on top, leaving a ⅛-inch border around the edge of the crust. Crumble the reserved crumb mixture over the top, letting the fruit show through in places.

5. Continue baking until lightly browned and the fruit filling is bubbling all over, including the center of the pan, 35 to 40 minutes. Let cool completely before slicing into 18 bars (or into smaller pieces, if you like). —*Elaine Khosrova*

tuile cookies

YIELDS ABOUT THIRTY
4- TO 4½-INCH ROUNDS

- **¾ cup granulated sugar**
- **3 large egg whites**
- **4 oz. (½ cup) unsalted butter, melted and cooled to room temperature**
- **2¼ oz. (½ cup) unbleached all-purpose flour**
- **1 tsp. pure vanilla extract (or 1 tsp. ground ginger, ½ tsp. ground cinnamon, or ½ tsp. pure almond extract)**

This versatile cookie batter is easy to make and shape, and holds for up to 2 weeks in the refrigerator. You might need to wear sturdy rubber gloves when handling the hot tuiles. The point at which the cookies can be shaped seems to coincide with the point at which they're still a bit too hot to touch.

1. In a medium bowl, whisk the sugar and egg whites until well combined— you're not beating in air and the whites shouldn't be foamy. Add the melted butter and whisk until combined. Add the flour and vanilla (or another extract or spice, if using), and whisk to combine; the mixture should be smooth. Refrigerate the batter for at least 4 hours and up to 2 weeks.

2. Position a rack in the center of the oven and heat the oven to 350°F. Line a very flat, level baking sheet or cookie sheet with a nonstick baking mat (or with parchment sprayed liberally with nonstick cooking spray). To bake and shape the cookies, follow the steps on p. 100. Start off by baking only one or two cookies at a time until you get a feel for the timing—they firm up quickly.
—*Joanne Chang*

PER COOKIE: 60 CALORIES | 1g PROTEIN | 7g CARB | 3g TOTAL FAT | 2g SAT FAT | 1g MONO FAT | 0g POLY FAT | 10mg CHOL | 35mg SODIUM | 0g FIBER

continued on p. 100 ➤

guidelines for shaping tuiles

A freshly baked tuile goes through several stages before it cools to its crisp final state. Immediately out of the oven, it's still too delicate and hot to handle, and if you tried to work with it, it would tear. After 10 to 15 seconds, the cookie cools enough to hold together and bend. It stays pliable for another 15 to 20 seconds—this is your window for manipulating the cookie into a different shape. If you wait too long, the cookie starts to crisp and your shaping attempts will only result in shattered cookies. If that happens, you can put the cookie back on the pan and warm it in the oven for a few seconds until it softens. But with each reheating, the cookie cools and firms faster than before, so reheat twice, at most. Here are some easy shapes to try:

TUILE CONE Roll up a free-form cone or use a mold. To make your own mold, crumple foil and shape it into a cone. Set the cone on the hot cookie with the cone's tip on the edge of the circle. Wrap both sides around the cone so the two edges meet. Hold them together for a few seconds to fuse them as the cookie cools. Remove the foil cone and use it again.

CORKSCREW GARNISH Spread the batter into a rectangle and, after baking, cut it into strips with a pizza cutter. Wrap the strips around the handle of a wooden spoon.

ABSTRACT FORM Cut the hot cookie in half and lay the halves over an object or twist them into any shape you like.

TUILE CIGAR Roll the hot tuile into a tight cylinder and serve as a cookie, or roll it loosely and fill like a cannoli.

continued from p. 98

Ideas for Using Tuiles

Tuiles soften when they're paired with anything moist (like ice cream or lemon curd), so assemble these types of dessert just before serving.

• Make a fruit napoleon: Spoon or pipe pastry cream lightened with whipped cream between flat tuiles and top with fruit.

• Fill a tuile cone with lemon curd and fresh berries.

• Make a hot fudge sundae in a large tuile bowl.

• Garnish a custard or a slice of pie or cake with a tuile corkscrew.

• Fill a small tuile cup with whipped cream and fresh fruit.

• Serve flat tuile cookies with tea or as a light ending to lunch.

• Make a mini tart shell by bending the tuile over the bottom of a clean soda can. Fill with chocolate pudding or ganache and whipped cream. Top with chocolate shavings.

how to bake and shape tuiles

Spoon a small amount of tuile batter on the baking sheet. Spread as evenly and thinly as possible into a circle the size you want (the size won't change much during baking). For a nutty variation, you can sprinkle lightly toasted sliced or chopped almonds on top of the unbaked cookies.

Bake until the cookie is golden brown all over, 9 to 10 minutes. Remove the pan from the oven and immediately start to maneuver a spatula under the edge of the cookie. After 10 seconds or so, it will hold together and can be slid off the sheet with the spatula.

Leave the tuile flat or mold it into a shape. You'll have 15 to 20 seconds to manipulate the cookie.

Any heatproof object can serve as a mold. The tuile will firm up in a minute and should release easily.

Use a new, cool baking sheet for each batch, or let the sheet cool completely (or run it under cool water and dry it well). If the batter is spooned onto a hot pan, it will melt instantly and become unspreadable.

maple-walnut tuiles

YIELDS ABOUT 20 COOKIES

    Nonstick cooking spray (if baking on parchment)

2 **large egg whites**

¼ **cup granulated maple sugar or firmly packed light brown sugar**

    Pinch of table salt

¼ **cup pure maple syrup (preferably Grade B)**

1½ **oz. (3 Tbs.) unsalted butter, melted and cooled slightly**

½ **tsp. pure vanilla extract**

3 **oz. (⅔ cup) unbleached all-purpose flour**

2 **Tbs. finely chopped walnuts**

To give them their curved form, the tuiles are draped over a rolling pin when they're hot from the oven. So measure your rolling pin and figure out how many 4-inch cookies you'll be able to drape over it at once. That's how big your batch of cookies should be. But you don't have to shape them if you don't want to—they're just as delicious flat.

1. Position a rack in the center of the oven and heat the oven to 350°F. Line four cookie sheets with nonstick baking liners or parchment sprayed with cooking spray. If shaping the tuiles, have a rolling pin at the ready.

2. In a medium bowl, combine the egg whites, sugar, and salt. Whisk until blended and a bit foamy, about 1 minute. Add the maple syrup, melted butter, and vanilla and whisk until blended. Add the flour and continue to whisk until smooth and blended.

3. Drop the batter by scant tablespoonfuls onto the prepared cookie sheets, positioning them about 4 inches apart (you should be able to fit four to five to a cookie sheet, but bake only as many as you can drape over your rolling pin, if you plan to shape them). Spread each mound of batter into a 4-inch round with the back of a spoon (use a circular motion to spread the batter outward from the center.)

4. Sprinkle about ¼ tsp. of the walnuts over each cookie. Bake until the cookies are browned around the edges and in spots toward the center, 7 to 9 minutes. The cookies will inevitably be slightly uneven and, therefore, will have a few darker-brown spots. Not to worry—they'll still taste good. Don't underbake or the cookies won't be crisp.

5. Working quickly, move the cookie sheet to a rack. Using a metal spatula, lift off the hot cookies one by one and, if shaping, immediately drape them over the rolling pin. Let cool until set, about 1 minute. Carefully remove the tuiles from the rolling pin and set them on a rack to cool completely. If not shaping, immediately transfer them to a rack. *—Abigail Johnson Dodge*

PER SERVING: 50 CALORIES | 1g PROTEIN | 8g CARB | 2g TOTAL FAT | 1g SAT FAT | 0.5g MONO FAT | 0g POLY FAT | 5mg CHOL | 20mg SODIUM | 0g FIBER

It's worth seeking out granulated maple sugar for this recipe, as it elevates these cookies into something truly special.

raspberry bars

YIELDS ABOUT 48 BARS

13 oz. (1½ cups plus 2 Tbs.) unsalted butter, softened at room temperature; more for the pan

1⅔ cups granulated sugar

2 large eggs

1 lb. (3¾ cups) unbleached all-purpose flour

7½ oz. (1½ cups) chopped, toasted hazelnuts

2 cups raspberry preserves

The better the preserves you use, the better these bars will be. Substitute apricot preserves or even a bitter-orange marmalade in place of raspberry preserves for flavor variation.

1. Position a rack in the center of the oven and heat to 350°F. Butter a 9x13-inch pan. Using a stand mixer fitted with the paddle attachment (or in a large bowl with a hand mixer), cream the butter and sugar until fluffy. Add the eggs one at a time, beating well after each addition. Add the flour and mix just enough to incorporate. Add the nuts and mix a little longer until just blended.

2. Press about two thirds of the mixture into the prepared pan. Wet your hands to keep the dough from sticking while you're pressing it into the pan. Spread with the raspberry preserves and then crumble the remaining dough on top. Bake for about 1 hour, until the top is lightly browned. —*Patricia Ann Heyman*

PER BAR: I 180 CALORIES I 2g PROTEIN I 24g CARB I 9g TOTAL FAT I 4g SAT FAT I 4g MONO FAT I 1g POLY FAT I 25mg CHOL I 10mg SODIUM I 1g FIBER

apricot, pistachio, and chocolate-chip bars

YIELDS EIGHTEEN 3X2-INCH BARS

9 oz. (2 cups) unbleached all-purpose flour

1¼ cups old-fashioned oats

1 cup packed dark brown sugar

½ tsp. ground cinnamon

½ tsp. table salt

½ lb. (1 cup) chilled unsalted butter, cut into ½-inch cubes

4 oz. (about 1 cup) chopped, shelled natural pistachios

½ cup diced dried apricots

½ cup white chocolate or semisweet chocolate morsels

1 15¼-oz. jar apricot preserves

For the best results, allow the bars to cool completely before cutting.

1. Position a rack in the center of the oven and heat the oven to 325°F. With an electric mixer, combine the flour, oats, sugar, cinnamon, and salt; mix on low speed until well combined. Add the butter and mix on medium until the butter is mostly blended and the mixture appears moist and begins to pull together, about 3 minutes. Stir in the pistachios. Reserve 1½ cups of this crumb mixture, stir the dried apricots and chocolate morsels into it, and refrigerate. Firmly press the remaining mixture into the bottom of an ungreased 13x9-inch baking pan.

2. Bake the cookies for 25 minutes. Let cool for about 20 minutes. Spread the apricot preserves evenly on top, leaving a ⅛-inch border around the edge of the crust. Crumble the reserved crumb mixture over the top. Continue baking until lightly browned and the fruit filling is bubbling all over, including the center of the pan, 35 to 40 minutes. Let cool completely before slicing into 18 bars (or into smaller pieces, if you like). —*Elaine Khosrova*

upside-down peanut-butter fig bars

YIELDS EIGHTEEN 3X2-INCH BARS

- **8 oz. (about 1⅔ cups) dried Mission figs**
- **5¾ oz. (1¼ cups) unbleached all-purpose flour**
- **½ tsp. baking powder**
- **½ tsp. baking soda**
- **¼ tsp. table salt**
- **⅔ cup chunky peanut butter**
- **⅔ cup packed light brown sugar**
- **½ cup plus 2 Tbs. granulated sugar**
- **4 oz. (½ cup) unsalted butter, softened at room temperature; more for the pan**
- **1 large egg**
- **⅓ cup tepid water**
- **¼ tsp. ground cinnamon**
- **1 cup granola (without fruit)**

Mission figs have dark purple skin and reddish-brown flesh and are a favorite for cooking. Grown in California, they're widely available in the U.S.

1. Position a rack in the center of the oven and heat the oven to 325°F. Snip off the stem of each fig and cut each into quarters, lengthwise; put the figs in a medium bowl, cover with hot water, and soak for 20 minutes.

2. Meanwhile, butter the bottom of a 13x9-inch baking pan and line with waxed paper. Butter the paper and the sides of the pan. In a small bowl, combine the flour, baking powder, baking soda, and salt. With an electric mixer, beat the peanut butter, brown sugar, ½ cup of the granulated sugar, and the butter until light and fluffy. Beat in the egg and water; scrape down the sides of the bowl. Beat until the mixture looks creamy. Beat in the flour mixture just until combined.

3. Drain the figs well and toss them with the remaining 2 Tbs. sugar and the cinnamon. Arrange the figs, cut side down, in one layer in the lined pan. Sprinkle the granola on top, filling the spaces between the figs.

4. Drop spoonfuls of the dough on top of the figs and then spread it evenly in the pan. Bake until the edges are very lightly browned, 35 to 40 minutes. The edges will be slightly puffed; press them down with a spatula to flatten. Let cool until the pan is warm to the touch. Invert the pan onto a cutting board, remove the pan, and peel off the paper. (If any figs pull away, simply replace them.) Let cool completely before slicing into 18 bars (or into smaller pieces, if you like). —*Elaine Khosrova*

blueberry-hazelnut bars

FOR THE CRUST AND THE TOPPING

Butter or vegetable oil, for
the pan

5 oz. (1 cup) hazelnuts, toasted
and skinned

9 oz. (2 cups) unbleached
all-purpose flour

3½ oz. (1 cup) confectioners'
sugar

2 tsp. baking powder

½ lb. (1 cup) cold unsalted
butter, cut into large cubes

1 large egg

1 large egg yolk

1 tsp. pure vanilla extract

FOR THE FILLING

2 lb. (6 cups) fresh blueberries,
picked over

⅔ cup granulated sugar

⅓ cup cornstarch

2 tsp. fresh lemon juice

½ tsp. ground cinnamon

¼ tsp. table salt

*A rich, nutty pastry sand-
wiches a sweet blueberry
filling. These bars keep for a
day or two, tightly covered
at room temperature. For a
special dessert, warm them
and top them with vanilla
ice cream.*

MAKE THE CRUST AND TOPPING

1. Lightly grease a 9x13-inch baking pan. Line the bottom and sides with a
sheet of parchment, leaving a few inches of paper hanging over the edges of
the two long sides to help remove the finished bars.

2. Roughly chop ½ cup of the hazelnuts; halved or quartered is about right.
Set aside. Put the remaining ½ cup hazelnuts in a food processor and process
until finely ground; put them in a large bowl. Add the flour, confectioners'
sugar, and baking powder and stir with a fork to blend. With a pastry blender
or two knives, cut in the butter until the largest lumps are the size of fat peas.
Lightly beat the egg and yolk and add all but 2 Tbs. of the egg to the butter-
flour mixture. Add the vanilla and gently toss with your fingertips until the mixture clumps together. It should be uniformly blended, moist, and crumbly. If
the dough looks dry and floury, mix in a little more beaten egg. Or you can mix
the dough in a large (11-cup capacity) food processor. Pulse in short bursts to
avoid overworking the dough.

3. Position a rack in the center of the oven and heat the oven to 350°F. Divide
the dough into two portions, one slightly larger than the other. Using floured
fingertips, pat the larger portion into the bottom of the prepared pan, pressing
firmly, and refrigerate for 15 to 20 minutes. Cover the remaining portion with
plastic wrap and refrigerate as well.

4. Remove the pan from the fridge and prick the crust all over with a fork.
Bake until the edges are golden and the pastry is dry and light brown, 20 to
25 minutes. Let cool completely on a wire rack before filling (otherwise, the
bars will get soggy).

MAKE THE FILLING

1. In a large bowl, combine the berries, sugar, cornstarch, lemon juice, cinnamon, and salt. Toss gently to thoroughly coat the berries and then scatter the
filling onto the cooled crust, scraping the bowl well. Spread the berries in an
even layer.

2. Crumble the reserved dough over the berries; it won't cover everything.
Bake for 25 minutes and then sprinkle on the reserved chopped hazelnuts.
Continue baking until the topping is puffed and golden and the filling is bubbling not only near the edges but also close to the center of the pan, another
50 to 60 minutes. Put the pan on a wire rack and let cool completely. Use the
parchment to lift the whole batch out and then cut into bars. A long serrated
knife works well; jiggle it a little through the top layer and then gently push
down to cut through the bottom crust. —*Regan Daley*

PER BITE-SIZE BAR: 120 CALORIES | 2g PROTEIN | 13g CARB | 7g TOTAL FAT | 3g SAT FAT
| 4g MONO FAT | 0g POLY FAT | 20mg CHOL | 30mg SODIUM | 1g FIBER

poppy seed bars

YIELDS ABOUT 48 BARS

FOR THE FILLING

- 1½ cups poppy seeds
- 2 oz. (½ cup) blanched, sliced, and toasted almonds
- 1 Tbs. grated lemon zest
- 1 cup granulated sugar
- ¾ tsp. ground nutmeg
- ⅔ cup milk
- 4 tsp. fresh lemon juice
- 2 oz. (4 Tbs.) unsalted butter

FOR THE BASE AND TOPPING

- 9 oz. (2 cups) unbleached all-purpose flour
- 3½ oz. (1 cup) confectioners' sugar; more for dusting
- 2 tsp. baking powder
- 2 oz. (½ cup) blanched, sliced, and toasted almonds
- ½ lb. (1 cup) cold unsalted butter
- 1 large egg

To freeze these bars, layer them in plastic to keep them from sticking together.

If you love poppy seeds, this confection is for you. When the bars are cool, dust them with confectioners' sugar if you like.

MAKE THE FILLING

Combine the poppy seeds, almonds, and lemon zest in a food processor and pulse until fine. Transfer the mixture to a saucepan and add the remaining ingredients. Cook over medium heat, stirring often, until the mixture boils and thickens to a syrup, about 10 minutes. Remove from the heat and let cool.

MAKE THE BASE

Position a rack in the center of the oven and heat the oven to 350°F. Butter a 9x13-inch pan. Combine the flour, confectioners' sugar, baking powder, and almonds in a food processor. Pulse to blend. Cut the butter into 1-inch pieces and place it on top of the flour mixture. Pulse again until the butter pieces are the size of a pea. With the machine running, add the egg through the feed tube. Pulse until the dough forms a ball. If the blade lifts up, remove the dough and finish mixing by hand.

ASSEMBLE THE BARS

Pat half the dough into the buttered pan, flouring your hands if the dough sticks to them. Pour the cooled filling over the base. Crumble the remaining dough over the filling to create a topping. Bake for 50 to 60 minutes, until the topping is browned. Let the bars cool before you cut them.

—*Patricia Ann Heyman*

PER BAR: 130 CALORIES | 2g PROTEIN | 12g CARB | 8g TOTAL FAT | 3g SAT FAT | 3g MONO FAT | 2g POLY FAT | 20mg CHOL | 25mg SODIUM | 1g FIBER

Poppy Seeds for Dessert

Poppy seeds add not only a delicious flavor, but a sophisticated and striking look to the desserts that feature them. Try these crunchy seeds in the bar cookie above, and then give them a whirl in your next cake, pudding, or slice and bake cookie.

lemon bars

YIELDS SIXTEEN 1½-INCH BARS;
2½ CUPS LEMON CURD

FOR THE SHORTBREAD

- 4 oz. (8 Tbs.) unsalted butter, softened at room temperature
- 2 Tbs. granulated sugar
- 1 Tbs. confectioners' sugar
- ½ tsp. pure vanilla extract
- 2¼ oz. (½ cup) unbleached all-purpose flour
- 2½ oz. (⅔ cup) cake flour
- ¼ tsp. baking powder
- ¼ tsp. table salt

FOR THE LEMON CURD

- 1 cup fresh lemon juice (from 4 to 6 lemons)
- 2 oz. (4 Tbs.) unsalted butter, cut into 2 pieces
- 2 Tbs. heavy cream
- 1 cup granulated sugar
- 4 large eggs
- 2 large egg yolks
- ¼ tsp. table salt
- ¼ tsp. pure vanilla extract

These bars will last several days in the refrigerator in an airtight container but are best when fresh. To help prevent cracks in the topping, let the baked bars cool to room temperature before refrigerating them.

MAKE THE SHORTBREAD

1. In a large bowl, cream the butter and both sugars with a hand mixer on medium speed (or mix by hand with a wooden spoon) until light and fluffy, about 5 minutes. Beat in the vanilla until thoroughly combined, scraping the bowl.

2. In a medium bowl, sift together both flours, the baking powder, and the salt. With the mixer on low speed, slowly blend the dry ingredients into the wet ingredients, scraping the bowl, until the flour is completely blended and the dough is homogenous.

3. Scrape the dough from the bowl onto a sheet of plastic. Wrap well and press down to form a ½-inch-thick square. Refrigerate the dough until it's firm but still pliable, about 20 minutes. Position a rack in the center of the oven and heat the oven to 350°F. Prepare two sheets of parchment or waxed paper, each at least 11x11 inches. If using waxed paper, grease an 8x8-inch metal or glass baking pan with butter.

4. When the dough is firm, unwrap it and put it between the sheets of parchment or paper. Roll the dough to an approximate square, slightly larger than 8x8 inches and about ¼ inch thick. Remove the top sheet of parchment or paper, trim the dough with a dull knife to an 8-inch square, and, if using parchment, put it and the dough into an 8-inch baking pan. If using waxed paper, flip the dough into the greased pan and peel off the paper. Press the dough into the bottom of the pan, letting the excess parchment come up the sides (trim it to about 1 inch above the rim). The dough should be an even thickness all around but it needn't be perfectly smooth. Bake until the shortbread is light golden on top, 25 to 30 minutes; in a glass pan, look for a golden brown color on the bottom. Remove the pan from the oven, but keep the heat set to 350°F as you make the lemon curd.

MAKE THE LEMON CURD

1. In a medium saucepan, heat the lemon juice, butter, and cream to just under a boil; the butter should be melted. Remove from the heat.

2. In a medium bowl, whisk by hand the sugar, eggs, and yolks until combined. Whisk in a bit of the hot liquid and then gradually whisk in a bit more until it's all added. This technique, called tempering, heats the eggs slowly and gently so they don't curdle.

3. Pour the mixture back into the saucepan and heat on medium, stirring constantly with a wooden spoon, scraping the bottom and sides of the pan to keep the eggs from scrambling. Cook until the lemon curd coats the spoon thickly enough to leave a line when you draw your finger through, 5 to 8 minutes. Remove from the heat and strain through a fine sieve. Stir in the salt and vanilla.

Make Ahead

Shortbread dough can be wrapped in plastic and frozen for up 2 months. When you want to make lemon bars (or any other shortbread-based recipe), just let the dough thaw overnight in the refrigerator.

FINISH THE BARS

Pour the curd over the baked shortbread and smooth it evenly with a spatula, if needed. Bake until the curd has set and jiggles like firm Jello®, 15 to 20 minutes. Let cool to room temperature. Gently tug on the parchment on all sides to loosen the bars from the pan. Lift them out and onto a cutting board and refrigerate until the curd has completely set, at least 4 hours. Trim the sides for a cleaner look and cut into 16 pieces. *—Joanne Chang*

PER BAR: 220 CALORIES | 3g PROTEIN | 27g CARB | 12g TOTAL FAT | 7g SAT FAT | 4g MONO FAT | 1g POLY FAT | 110mg CHOL | 95mg SODIUM | 0g FIBER

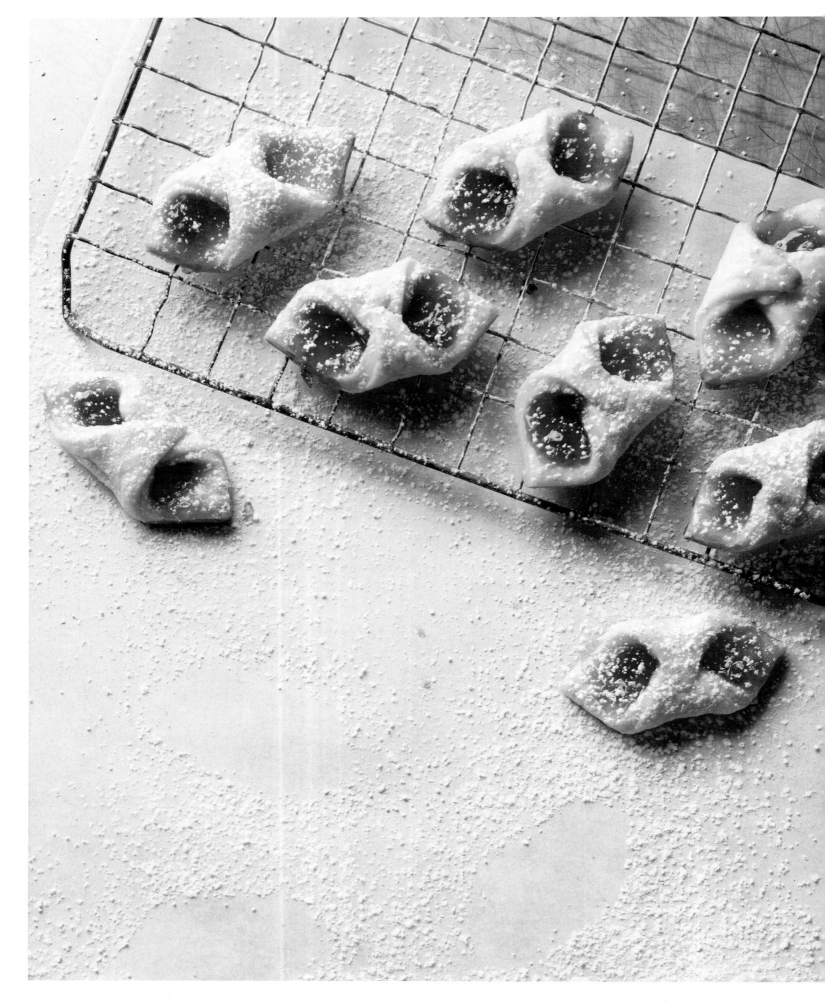

fruit & nut cookies

rugelach

FOR THE DOUGH

10½ oz. (2⅓ cups) unbleached all-purpose flour; more for shaping

¼ cup granulated sugar

½ tsp. table salt

½ lb. (1 cup) cold unsalted butter, cut into 10 pieces

½ lb. cold cream cheese, cut into 10 pieces

FOR THE FILLING

6 Tbs. raspberry or apricot jam

FOR THE TOPPING

1 large egg

¼ cup finely chopped salted pistachios (1¼ oz.)

Make Ahead

> The dough may be refrigerated for up to 3 days or frozen for 1 month before proceeding with the recipe. The rolled logs can be wrapped well and frozen for up to 1 month. Thaw overnight in the refrigerator before proceeding with the recipe.

These buttery, flaky cookies feature a jewel-like filling of jam and a dusting of chopped pistachios. Make a half-batch of dough if your food processor is small.

MAKE THE DOUGH

1. Put the flour, sugar, and salt in a large (11-cup or larger) food processor. Pulse briefly to blend the ingredients. Scatter the butter and cream cheese pieces over the dry ingredients. Pulse until the dough begins to come together in large (about 1-inch) clumps.

2. Portion the dough into four pieces and knead each on a lightly floured surface until smooth. Shape each portion into a flat 6x3-inch rectangle and wrap in plastic. Refrigerate until well chilled, about 1½ hours.

SHAPE AND FILL THE COOKIES

1. Working with one piece of dough at a time, roll the dough on a piece of lightly floured plastic wrap into a rectangle slightly larger than 5x13 inches (if refrigerated overnight, let sit at room temperature until pliable enough to roll). Dust with additional flour as needed. Using a sharp knife, trim off the ragged edges to make a 5x13-inch rectangle.

2. Position the dough with one long edge facing you. Using a metal spatula (offset is best), spread evenly with 1½ Tbs. of the jam. Using the plastic wrap as an aid, roll up the dough jelly roll-style beginning with one long side. Wrap in plastic and refrigerate until firm, at least 1 hour. Repeat with remaining dough and jam.

TOP AND BAKE THE COOKIES

1. Position racks in the upper and lower thirds of the oven and heat the oven to 350°F. Line two cookie sheets with parchment or nonstick baking liners. In a small bowl, mix the egg and 1 Tbs. water with a fork until blended.

2. Unwrap one roll of dough and set it on a cutting board. Using a serrated knife and a ruler, cut the roll into 1¼-inch-wide pieces. Arrange cookies seam side down 1 inch apart on the cookie sheets. Repeat with the remaining rolls. Lightly brush the tops with the egg mixture (you won't need it all) and sprinkle with the chopped pistachios. Bake until the rugelach are golden brown, 28 to 30 minutes, swapping the cookie sheets' positions about halfway through for even baking. Let cool on the sheets for about 20 minutes. Transfer to a rack to cool completely. —*Abigail Johnson Dodge*

PER COOKIE: 100 CALORIES | 1g PROTEIN | 9g CARB | 7g TOTAL FAT | 4g SAT FAT | 2g MONO FAT | 0g POLY FAT | 20mg CHOL | 50mg SODIUM | 0g FIBER

pine nut wedding cookies

YIELDS ABOUT 3 DOZEN COOKIES

- **2** cups pine nuts, toasted
- **10** oz. (2¼ cups) unbleached all-purpose flour
- **½** tsp. table salt
- **½** lb. (1 cup) unsalted butter, softened at room temperature
- **¼** cup granulated sugar
- **1** tsp. pure vanilla extract
- **4** oz. (about 1 cup) confectioners' sugar, sifted

Toasting pine nuts improves their flavor. Either toast them in a skillet on the stovetop, or on a rimmed baking sheet in the oven.

1. In a food processor, pulse the pine nuts and 1 cup of the flour until finely ground. Add the remaining flour and the salt and pulse to blend.

2. With a hand mixer or a stand mixer fitted with the paddle attachment, beat the butter and granulated sugar on medium speed until light and fluffy, about 2 minutes. Add the vanilla and mix on medium until combined, about 15 seconds. Reduce the speed to low and gradually add the dry ingredients, mixing until the dough is just combined. Cover with plastic and refrigerate until firm, about 1 hour.

3. Position racks in the upper and lower thirds of the oven and heat the oven to 350°F. Line two cookie sheets with parchment or nonstick baking liners.

4. Using your palms, roll heaping tablespoonfuls of the dough into 1½-inch balls. Arrange the balls 1 inch apart on the prepared sheets.

5. Bake until golden around the edges and light golden on top, 19 to 21 minutes, rotating and swapping the sheets halfway through for even baking. Transfer the cookies, still on their parchment, to a rack and let cool for 5 to 10 minutes, or until they have firmed up a bit and are cool enough to handle.

6. Put the confectioners' sugar in a small bowl. Gently toss the cookies, a few at a time, in the sugar to coat; let them cool completely on racks. Toss them again in the sugar. *—David Crofton*

PER COOKIE: 130 CALORIES | 2g PROTEIN | 10g CARB | 10g TOTAL FAT | 3.5g SAT FAT | 2.5g MONO FAT | 3g POLY FAT | 15mg CHOL | 35mg SODIUM | 0g FIBER

Make Ahead

These cookies will keep in an airtight container at room temperature for up to 1 week.

The Care and Keeping of Nonstick Baking Liners

If you bake lots of cookies, a couple of nonstick silicone baking liners are handy to have because they're reusable and they reduce the need for parchment. Often referred to generically by the name of the leading brand—Silpat®, they rely on their silicone surface to maintain their nonstick quality, so it's important to treat them with care.

To clean a Silpat, wipe it down with a soft, damp sponge and let it air dry. You may use a diluted solution of mild dishwashing liquid if you like, but remember that an oily feeling on the mat even after cleaning is normal. Silpats are not dishwasher-safe.

Never use knives, scrapers, brushes, or scrubbers on the mats—they will damage the surface.

Store Silpats flat or rolled but not folded. If you store your baking sheets flat, just lay your Silpats in one of them. An empty paper towel tube is another good way to keep them from unrolling.

almond cookie dough

YIELDS 3¾ CUPS (ABOUT
2 LB.) DOUGH, ENOUGH FOR
6 DOZEN COOKIES

½ cup granulated sugar

½ tsp. table salt

4 oz. (¾ cup) whole almonds

12 oz. (1½ cups) unsalted
butter, cut in large chunks
and slightly softened

4 tsp. pure vanilla extract

¼ tsp. pure almond extract

13⅓ oz. (3 cups) bleached
all-purpose flour

One batch of this delicious dough, with very little effort, morphs into three different types of cookies: Chocolate Thumbprints, Hazelnut Almond Crescents, and Almond Sablés.

1. Process the sugar and salt in a food processor until the sugar looks powdery and a little finer, 30 to 60 seconds. Add the almonds and process until they're finely chopped, about 20 seconds. Add the butter and the vanilla and almond extracts. Pulse until the butter is smooth, scraping the bowl as necessary. Add the flour and pulse until a soft dough begins to form around the blade. Transfer the dough to a large bowl and stir briefly with a rubber spatula to be sure it's evenly mixed.

2. Portion the dough into equal thirds. If you have a scale, weigh each third; each should weigh 10½ to 11 oz. Make the variations below and on p. 114 before chilling the dough. —*Alice Medrich*

chocolate thumbprints

YIELDS ABOUT 2 DOZEN
COOKIES

FOR THE COOKIES

One third of a batch (10½ to
11 oz. or 1¼ cups) freshly
made Almond Cookie Dough
(recipe above)

¼ cup coarse sugar, such as
turbinado (also sold as Sugar
in the Raw® in supermarkets),
demerara, or sanding sugar

FOR THE FILLING

2½ oz. bittersweet or semisweet
chocolate, coarsely chopped

5 tsp. unsalted butter

Be sure to fill your thumbprints completely for the most chocolatey flavor in every bite.

1. Scoop up a generous teaspoonful (2 level teaspoons) of the dough and shape it into a 1-inch ball with your hands. Roll the ball in the sugar and set it on a tray lined with waxed paper. Repeat with the rest of the dough, setting the balls slightly apart. Press a thumb or forefinger, dipped in flour, into each ball to create a depression. Cover and refrigerate the cookies for at least 2 hours, but preferably overnight.

2. Remove the cookies from the refrigerator and arrange them 1 inch apart on an ungreased or foil-lined cookie sheet. Position a rack in the center of the oven and heat the oven to 325°F. Let the cookies sit at room temperature while the oven heats. Bake the cookies for 10 minutes. Gently redefine the depressions with your thumb or the tip of a wooden spoon's handle, if necessary. Rotate the sheet and continue to bake until the tops are lightly colored and the bottoms are golden brown, another 8 to 12 minutes. Transfer the cookies to a rack and let cool completely.

3. While the cookies cool, prepare the filling. Put the chocolate and butter in a heatproof bowl set in a wide skillet of almost simmering water, or in the top of a double boiler. (Or microwave on medium power for 1 to 2 minutes, stirring after the first minute.) When the chocolate is almost completely melted, remove the bowl from the heat and stir until completely melted and smooth. Spoon the filling into each depression. If the filling hardens while using, reheat it in the pan of hot water. —*Alice Medrich*

PER COOKIE: 100 CALORIES | 1g PROTEIN | 9g CARB | 7g TOTAL FAT | 3.5g SAT FAT
| 1.5g MONO FAT | 0g POLY FAT | 10mg CHOL | 20mg SODIUM | 1g FIBER

continued on p. 114 ➤

continued from p. 113

hazelnut almond crescents

YIELDS 24 TO 28 COOKIES

One-third of a batch (10½ to 11 oz. or 1¼ cups) freshly made Almond Cookie Dough (recipe p. 113)

4¾ oz. (1 cup) hazelnuts, toasted, skinned, and chopped medium coarsely (for instructions on how to toast and skin hazelnuts, see p. 152)

1 to 2 Tbs. confectioners' sugar; more as needed

You can turn these into double almond crescents by replacing the hazelnuts with the same quantity of whole almonds, toasted and chopped. These cookies taste even better after a day of storage.

1. Use the back of a large spoon (or your hands) to work the hazelnuts into the dough. Shape level measuring tablespoons of dough into fat crescents and put them in a container lined with waxed paper. Cover and refrigerate the cookies for at least 2 hours, but preferably overnight.

2. Position a rack in the center of the oven and heat the oven to 325°F. Arrange the crescents 1 inch apart on an ungreased or foil-lined cookie sheet. Let the cookies sit at room temperature while the oven heats. Bake the cookies until the tops are lightly colored and the bottoms are golden brown, 20 to 22 minutes, rotating the sheet from front to back halfway through for even baking. Let the cookies cool on the sheet for about 5 minutes and then sift the confectioners' sugar over them. Transfer to a rack and let cool completely. Sift more confectioners' sugar over the cookies before serving if necessary. —*Alice Medrich*

PER COOKIE, BASED ON 28 SERVINGS: 90 CALORIES | 1g PROTEIN | 6g CARB | 7g TOTAL FAT | 2.5g SAT FAT | 3.5g MONO FAT | 0.5g POLY FAT | 10mg CHOL | 15mg SODIUM | 1g FIBER

almond sablés

YIELDS ABOUT 2 DOZEN COOKIES

One-third of a batch (10½ to 11 oz. or 1¼ cups) freshly made Almond Cookie Dough (recipe p. 113)

1½ Tbs. granulated sugar

¼ cup turbinado sugar (also sold as Sugar in the Raw in supermarkets)

Of the three different cookies you can make with the versatile Almond Dough, this is the easiest: the dough is simply sliced and rolled in raw sugar for a crunchy, crumbly cookie that's not too sweet.

1. Use the back of a large spoon or a rubber spatula to mash the 1½ Tbs. granulated sugar into the dough until it's evenly dispersed. On a lightly floured surface, shape the dough into a log about 6 inches long and 1¾ inches in diameter. Wrap the log in waxed paper or foil. Refrigerate for at least 2 hours, but preferably overnight.

2. Put the turbinado sugar on a flat surface such as a tray or clean countertop. Roll the log of dough in the sugar, pressing so the sugar adheres. Cut the log into ¼-inch slices and arrange them at least 1 inch apart on an ungreased or foil-lined cookie sheet.

3. Position a rack in the center of the oven and heat the oven to 350°F. Let the cookies sit at room temperature while the oven heats. Bake until the edges are golden brown, 12 to 15 minutes, rotating the pan from front to back about halfway through for even baking. Let the cookies sit on the sheet for a minute or two before transferring them to a rack with a metal spatula. Let cool completely before storing airtight. —*Alice Medrich*

PER COOKIE, BASED ON 24 SERVINGS: 80 CALORIES | 1g PROTEIN | 8g CARB | 4.5g TOTAL FAT | 2.5g SAT FAT | 1.5g MONO FAT | 0g POLY FAT | 10mg CHOL | 15mg SODIUM | 0g FIBER

honey-nut bars

YIELDS 16 BAR COOKIES

FOR THE CRUST

Nonstick cooking spray

½   cup whole blanched almonds, toasted

½   cup granulated sugar

11¼ oz. (2½ cups) unbleached all-purpose flour

½   tsp. baking powder

½   tsp. table salt

6   oz. (¾ cup) cold unsalted butter, cut into ½-inch pieces

1   large egg, lightly beaten

FOR THE TOPPING

¾   cup packed light brown sugar

3   oz. (6 Tbs.) unsalted butter

⅓   cup clover honey

½   tsp. table salt

2   Tbs. heavy cream

3   cups whole unsalted mixed nuts, toasted

Some flavor combinations bring out the best in one other. Honey and nuts are one of those perfect flavor marriages. Add some light brown sugar, and you've got this sweet, salty, crunchy bar that could become your new go-to cookie.

MAKE THE CRUST

1. Position a rack in the center of the oven and heat the oven to 350°F. Spray a 9x13-inch baking pan with cooking spray and line the bottom with parchment.

2. In a food processor, finely grind the almonds and sugar. Add the flour, baking powder, and salt and pulse to blend. Add the butter and pulse until it's the size of small peas, 5 to 6 one-second pulses. Add the egg and pulse just until the dough begins to gather into large clumps.

3. With your fingertips, press the dough into the bottom of the prepared pan and about 1 inch up the sides to form a ¼-inch-thick crust. Using the tines of a fork, prick the crust evenly all over.

4. Bake until light golden brown on the edges and the center looks dry, 15 to 20 minutes. Let the crust cool on a rack.

MAKE THE TOPPING

1. Bring the sugar, butter, honey, and salt to a boil in a medium saucepan over medium-high heat, stirring often. Slowly and carefully add the cream and return to a boil. Remove from the heat and carefully add the nuts, stirring to coat. Pour the nut mixture over the crust and spread evenly with a spatula. Tilt the pan to help spread the liquid to the edges and corners. Bake until the topping has just started to bubble slowly in the center, about 20 minutes. Let cool on a wire rack for 10 minutes and then run a knife around the inside edge of the pan to loosen the crust from the sides. Let the bars cool completely.

2. Invert the pan onto a flat surface and peel off the parchment. Reinvert onto a cutting board and cut into 16 bars with a sharp knife.

—*David Crofton*

PER BAR: 460 CALORIES | 8g PROTEIN | 45g CARB | 30g TOTAL FAT | 11g SAT FAT | 13g MONO FAT | 4g POLY FAT | 50mg CHOL | 170mg SODIUM | 3g FIBER

Make Ahead

These cookies will keep in an airtight container at room temperature for 3 to 5 days.

bowtie cookies with apricot preserves

YIELDS ABOUT 70 COOKIES

- ½ **lb. cream cheese, softened at room temperature**
- ½ **lb. (1 cup) unsalted butter, softened at room temperature**
- 11¼ **oz. (2½ cups) unbleached all-purpose flour, sifted; more for rolling**
- 1 **12-oz. jar good-quality apricot preserves (about ¾ cup)**
- 1 **large egg, beaten**

  Confectioners' sugar, for dusting

These are the perfect cookies to make if you want to get a head start on holiday baking. You can freeze them, in freezer bags, for up to 3 months.

1. Using a stand mixer fitted with the paddle attachment, beat the cream cheese and butter on medium-high speed until light and fluffy, about 3 minutes. Scrape the bowl and paddle. With the mixer on low, gradually mix in the flour until a shaggy dough forms. Turn out onto a lightly floured work surface and knead it gently to form a ball. Portion the dough into thirds, wrap each in plastic or waxed paper, and flatten into squares. Refrigerate for at least 4 hours or overnight.

2. Position a rack in the center of the oven and heat the oven to 400°F. Line three cookie sheets with parchment. Remove one piece of dough from the refrigerator and roll it out on a lightly floured surface into a ⅛-inch-thick rectangle. Using a sharp knife or a pizza cutter, trim the rough edges of the dough so the sides are straight, and then cut into 2-inch squares. Spoon about ½ tsp. of the preserves onto the center of each square. Fold one corner into the center, dab with the beaten egg, and then bring the opposite corner into the center and pinch firmly together to seal the corners. With a thin spatula, transfer the cookie to the cookie sheet. Repeat the process with the remaining dough.

3. Bake the cookies one sheet at a time until golden and very lightly browned and puffed, 10 to 12 minutes. Transfer to a rack to cool completely and then dust with confectioners' sugar. —*Debbie Reid*

PER COOKIE: 70 CALORIES | 1g PROTEIN | 7g CARB | 4g TOTAL FAT | 2.5g SAT FAT | 1g MONO FAT | 0g POLY FAT | 15mg CHOL | 15mg SODIUM | 0g FIBER

nutty caramel thumbprints

YIELDS ABOUT 2 DOZEN COOKIES

FOR THE COOKIES

- ½ lb. (1 cup) unsalted butter, softened at room temperature
- 2 oz. (⅔ cup) confectioners' sugar
- 1½ tsp. pure vanilla extract
- ½ tsp. table salt
- 10 oz. (2¼ cups) unbleached all-purpose flour

FOR THE CARAMEL FILLING

- 22 small caramels (6 oz.), such as Kraft® brand
- 3 Tbs. heavy cream
- 1½ oz. (⅓ cup) finely chopped pecans, lightly toasted

Make Ahead

Baked, unfilled cookies can be frozen for 1 month or stored at room temperature for 5 days. Layer them between parchment or waxed paper in an airtight container. You can fill the cookies up to 3 days ahead. Arrange them on a sheet pan in a single layer and cover tightly with plastic (don't let it touch the caramel tops). Store at room temperature.

This cookie recipe uses a great shortcut: use melted store-bought caramels as a filling for the thumbprints. Look for individually wrapped caramels in the candy aisle of the supermarket.

MAKE THE COOKIES

1. Position a rack in the center of the oven and heat the oven to 350°F. Line two cookie sheets with parchment or nonstick baking liners.

2. In a stand mixer fitted with a paddle attachment (or in a large bowl with a hand mixer), beat the butter, confectioners' sugar, vanilla, and salt on medium speed until well blended and smooth, about 3 minutes. Scrape the bowl and beater. Add the flour and mix on low speed until a soft dough forms, about 1 minute.

3. Using two teaspoon measures, scoop up about 2 tsp. of dough at a time, and using your palms, roll into smooth balls that are 1 to 1¼ inches in diameter. Arrange them about 1½ inches apart on the prepared cookie sheets. Using the back of a ½-tsp. measure, press down into the middle of each mound to make a well that is almost as deep as the dough ball. (If the edges crack or break open, it's best to reroll and try again—the finished cookie will look better and hold the caramel without leaking).

4. Bake one sheet at a time until the tops of the cookies look dry and the edges are golden brown, 15 to 20 minutes. Let the cookies cool on the cookie sheet for 5 minutes and then transfer them to a rack to cool completely.

MAKE THE CARAMEL FILLING

1. In a small saucepan, combine the unwrapped caramels and heavy cream. Set the pan over very low heat and cook, stirring constantly, until the caramels have melted and the mixture is smooth, 4 to 6 minutes.

2. Arrange the cooled cookies on a cookie sheet or jelly roll pan. Using a small spoon or spatula, drizzle the warm caramel into each indentation, filling to the rim. Scatter the nuts over the caramel and press them in lightly. Let cool completely before storing or serving. *—Abigail Johnson Dodge*

PER COOKIE: 170 CALORIES | 2g PROTEIN | 17g CARB | 10g TOTAL FAT | 6g SAT FAT | 3g MONO FAT | 1g POLY FAT | 25mg CHOL | 70mg SODIUM | 0g FIBER

giant cranberry oatmeal cookies

YIELDS 16 TO 18 BIG, CHEWY COOKIES

- 6 oz. (¾ cup) unsalted butter, softened at room temperature
- ½ cup granulated sugar
- ½ cup packed light brown sugar
- 1 large egg, at room temperature
- 1 Tbs. light corn syrup
- 1 tsp. pure vanilla extract
- 6¾ oz. (1½ cups) unbleached all-purpose flour
- 1 oz. (¼ cup) cake flour
- 1 tsp. baking soda
- ½ tsp. table salt
- ½ cup sweetened dried cranberries
- ½ cup rolled oats (old-fashioned, not quick cooking)
- ½ cup pecan pieces (or coarsely chopped pecan halves), lightly toasted
- ½ cup sweetened coconut flakes, lightly toasted
- 3½ oz. white chocolate, coarsely chopped

Make Ahead

These cookies will keep for 3 or 4 days at room temperature or for several weeks in the freezer.

If you're not a fan of white chocolate, you can omit it from this recipe and double the amount of dried cranberries instead.

1. Position two racks near the center of the oven and heat the oven to 325°F. Line three baking sheets with parchment.

2. Using a stand mixer fitted with the paddle attachment (or in a large bowl with a hand mixer), beat the butter and both sugars at medium speed until light and fluffy, about 2 minutes. Scrape the bowl. Add the egg, corn syrup, and vanilla; beat for 1 minute on medium speed. Mix in half the all-purpose flour on low speed until thoroughly combined, 30 seconds to 1 minute. Scrape the bowl. Briefly mix in the remaining half of the all-purpose flour. Sprinkle the cake flour, baking soda, and salt into the bowl and beat on low speed until well blended, 30 seconds to 1 minute. With a wooden spoon or a rubber spatula, stir in the cranberries, oats, pecans, coconut, and white chocolate.

3. Using your fingertips, shape 2-ounce pieces of dough (about a scant ¼ cup) into 2-inch diameter disks that are ½ inch thick. Space them at least 2 inches apart on the parchment-lined sheets. Bake until the cookies' edges and bottoms are golden and the centers feel dry on the surface but still soft inside, 15 to 16 minutes. When baking two pans of cookies at once, switch the position of the pans halfway through for even browning. Let the cookies cool on the baking sheets for at least 1 minute before transferring them to a rack to cool completely. *—Jill Silverman Hough*

PER COOKIE, BASED ON 18 COOKIES: 250 CALORIES | 3g PROTEIN | 30g CARB | 13g TOTAL FAT | 7g SAT FAT | 3.5g MONO FAT | 1g POLY FAT | 35mg CHOL | 150mg SODIUM | 1g FIBER

Dried Cranberries: Sweetened vs. Unsweetened

Even if you generally prefer to buy dried fruit that hasn't been sweetened, cranberries should be the exception. Unsweetened cranberries are remarkably dry, astringent, sour, and even bitter. Fortunately, most producers lightly sweeten the berries during the drying process; it helps keep them tender and tasty but doesn't mask their pleasing tartness.

maple-walnut butter cookies

YIELDS ABOUT THIRTY
2-INCH-SQUARE COOKIES

- 4¾ oz. (1 cup plus 1 Tbs.) unbleached all-purpose flour
- ¼ tsp. baking powder
- ¼ tsp. table salt
- 4 oz. (½ cup) unsalted butter, softened at room temperature
- ½ cup finely granulated maple sugar
- 2 Tbs. firmly packed light brown sugar
- 1 large egg
- 3 oz. (about ⅔ cup) coarsely chopped walnuts

Make Ahead

This dough can be kept, well wrapped, in the freezer for up to 3 weeks.

Granulated maple sugar is made by heating maple syrup and stirring it as it cools. It delivers a richly flavored sweetness to these buttery squares.

SEVERAL HOURS OR THE DAY BEFORE BAKING

1. In a medium bowl, sift together the flour, baking powder, and salt. With an electric mixer, beat the butter and both sugars until creamy and well blended, about 5 minutes. Beat in the egg, scrape down the sides of the bowl, and beat again until blended. Add the flour mixture, beating just until combined, and then mix in the nuts.

2. Transfer the soft dough to the center of a 12-inch-long piece of plastic wrap. Cover with the wrap and shape the dough into an 8-inch-long squared-off log. (It may be hard to square off the sides completely when the dough is soft; after chilling, the dough is easier to model.) Refrigerate for at least 3 hours or overnight.

BAKE THE COOKIES

Position a rack in the center of the oven and heat the oven to 350°F. Line two cookie sheets with parchment. Cut the firm dough crosswise into ¼-inch-thick slices. Arrange the slices about an inch apart on the sheets. Bake the cookies, one sheet at a time, until the edges just begin to brown, 12 to 14 minutes. Let cool on the cookie sheet for 5 minutes; transfer to a rack to cool completely. —*Elaine Khosrova*

PER COOKIE: 80 CALORIES I 1g PROTEIN I 7g CARB I 5g TOTAL FAT I 2g SAT FAT I 1g MONO FAT I 1.5g POLY FAT I 15mg CHOL I 25mg SODIUM I 0g FIBER

cinnamon currant oatmeal lace cookies

YIELDS ABOUT 28 COOKIES

- **2 oz. (¼ cup) unsalted butter**
- **½ cup packed light brown sugar**
- **2 Tbs. whipping cream**
- **½ tsp. pure vanilla extract**
- **½ tsp. ground cinnamon**
- **Pinch of table salt**
- **1⅛ oz. (¼ cup) unbleached all-purpose flour**
- **1½ oz. (½ cup) old-fashioned oatmeal (not quick cooking)**
- **½ cup currants**

These cookies, made with brown sugar, have a slightly softer texture than those made with granulated sugar. Currants are great for their flavor and also for their small size—they don't need chopping. But you can use chopped raisins or chopped dried cranberries instead.

1. Position racks in the center and upper third of the oven and heat the oven to 350°F. Line two baking sheets with nonstick liners or parchment. Line a wire rack with paper towels.

2. In a medium saucepan, heat the butter, brown sugar, and cream over low heat, stirring often, until the butter melts and the brown sugar dissolves. Increase the heat to medium high and, stirring constantly, bring the mixture just to a boil. Remove the pot from the heat and stir in the vanilla extract, cinnamon, and salt. Stir in the flour until incorporated and then stir in the oatmeal and currants. Drop the batter by the teaspoon 3 inches apart on the baking sheets, about ½ dozen cookies per baking sheet.

3. Bake the cookies until evenly light brown, about 10 minutes total. About 6 minutes into baking, switch the sheets from top to bottom and back to front to promote even baking. Remove the cookies from the oven and let them cool for a few minutes on the baking sheets, until they're firm. Use a wide spatula to transfer them to the rack to cool completely. Bake off the remaining cookies; the batter will have firmed up a bit, but that's fine. —*Elinor Klivans*

PER COOKIE: 50 CALORIES | 1g PROTEIN | 8g CARB | 2g TOTAL FAT | 1.5g SAT FAT | 0.5g MONO FAT | 0g POLY FAT | 5mg CHOL | 15mg SODIUM | 0G FIBER

fig bars
with thyme

YIELDS TWENTY-FIVE
1½-INCH SQUARES

FOR THE PASTRY

2 oz. (½ cup) walnuts

¼ cup plus 2 Tbs. granulated sugar

6¾ oz. (1½ cups) unbleached all-purpose flour

½ cup packed light brown sugar

½ tsp. table salt

½ tsp. baking powder

4 oz. (½ cup) cold unsalted butter, cut into small pieces

1 large egg yolk

1 tsp. pure vanilla extract

FOR THE JAM

2 lb. very ripe figs, stems removed, unpeeled

¼ cup granulated sugar

7 to 8 large sprigs fresh thyme

Finely grated zest of 1 lemon

1 to 2 Tbs. fresh lemon juice; more or less to taste

This fig jam keeps for weeks, so if you like, make it well ahead of time. Try to use lemon thyme, if possible. These bars are good with a dollop of whipped cream.

MAKE THE PASTRY
Position a rack in the center of the oven and heat the oven to 350°F. In a food processor, grind the walnuts with 2 Tbs. of the granulated sugar until fine; remove and set aside. Put the flour, the remaining ¼ cup granulated sugar, the brown sugar, salt, and baking powder in the food processor; process until blended. Add the butter; process until the mixture looks crumbly. Add the egg yolk and vanilla and pulse until the mixture is wet and clumping, about 40 seconds (it won't form a ball). Pack two-thirds of the dough into an ungreased 8x8-inch baking dish; set aside the other third. Bake until the dough is lightly browned and keeps a slight indentation when you press it lightly, about 30 minutes.

MAKE THE JAM
While the crust is baking, coarsely chop the figs. Put them in a nonreactive skillet with the sugar and thyme and cook over medium-high heat, stirring occasionally, until the juices have reduced and the fruit is tender and thick, about 20 minutes. Discard the thyme sprigs. Stir in the lemon zest, add the lemon juice to taste, and set aside. (If not using right away, refrigerate in a closed container.)

ASSEMBLE THE FIG BARS
In a bowl, crumble together the remaining dough with the reserved walnut and sugar mixture. Gently spread the fig jam on top of the baked crust and sprinkle the dough mixture over the filling. The top will look crumbly. Bake until browned on top, about 40 minutes. Let cool completely before cutting into 1½-inch squares. —*Deborah Madison*

PER SQUARE: 140 CALORIES | 2g PROTEIN | 23g CARB | 5g TOTAL FAT | 2.5g SAT FAT | 1.5g MONO FAT | 1g POLY FAT | 20mg CHOL | 90mg SODIUM | 2g FIBER

prune-apricot frangipane tart bars

YIELDS THIRTY 1²/₃X3-INCH BARS

FOR THE FRUIT AND FRANGIPANE FILLING

- ½ cup fresh orange juice
- 1 cup plus 2 Tbs. granulated sugar
- 8 dried prunes, pitted and quartered
- 8 dried apricots, quartered
- 8 oz. (2¼ cups) sliced un-blanched almonds
- 4 large eggs
- ½ lb. (1 cup) unsalted butter, softened at room temperature
- 1 Tbs. dark rum
- ½ tsp. pure vanilla extract
- ½ tsp. almond extract

FOR THE TART CRUST

- 9 oz. (2 cups) unbleached all-purpose flour
- ½ cup granulated sugar
- ⅛ tsp. table salt
- 6 oz. (¾ cup) cold unsalted butter, diced
- 1 large egg, lightly beaten

Part tart, part cookie, this treat is always moist and tender. For the richest-tasting frangipane, the freshest almonds are essential, of course—they should taste crunchy and sweet. You'll grind the nuts to a fine meal, staying clear of grinding them all the way to nut butter. Grinding the nuts is a snap with a food processor.

SIMMER THE FRUIT

In a small saucepan, combine the orange juice and 2 Tbs. of the sugar. Bring to a boil and cook until the liquid is reduced by almost one-third, about 3 minutes. Reduce the heat; add the prunes and apricots, keeping each to one side of the pan (they'll be easier to fish out this way). Simmer for about 3 minutes, stirring occasionally. Remove from the heat and set aside.

MAKE THE FRANGIPANE

In a food processor, blend the almonds with the remaining 1 cup sugar to a cornmeal consistency. Add the eggs, butter, rum, vanilla extract, and almond extract; process until creamy and set aside.

MAKE THE TART CRUST

1. Position a rack in the lower third of the oven and heat the oven to 350°F. In a food processor, briefly blend the flour, sugar, and salt. Add the butter; pulse until the mixture resembles cornmeal. Add the egg and process just until the dough comes together into a ball. Pat the dough into a 6x4-inch rectangle. On a lightly floured surface, roll the dough into a rectangle that's about 9x12 inches.

2. Drape the dough around the pin and transfer to an ungreased 10x15-inch rimmed baking sheet or two 9-inch round tart pans. Press the dough so it just fits the bottom of the pan (it's all right if the dough cracks). Bake until light golden, 10 to 13 minutes. (The crust will look set and won't be shiny on top.) Let the pan cool on a wire rack.

3. Pour the frangipane onto the baked crust, spreading it evenly over the dough. Score a shallow centerline to divide the tart in half. Remove the fruit from the juice (you don't need to pat it dry; the juices will dry during baking). Arrange half the tart with dried apricots and half with dried prunes in five rows of six pieces each, gently pressing the pieces into the filling. Bake until the top is light golden and springs back when lightly pressed, 25 to 30 minutes.
—Flo Braker

PER BAR: 240 CALORIES | 4g PROTEIN | 22g CARB | 16g TOTAL FAT | 7g SAT FAT | 6g MONO FAT | 2g POLY FAT | 65mg CHOL | 20mg SODIUM | 1g FIBER

When making the frangipane, use blanched or unblanched almonds, depending on the look you want. Blanched almonds produce an ivory-colored frangipane; unblanched almonds give the frangipane a golden color. It's fine to use whole or slivered almonds, as long as you're careful not to grind them too long. Sliced almonds are easier to measure exactly. (They're the thin, flat ovals, as compared to slivered almonds, which are like thick matchsticks.) Sliced almonds are easier to grind, too.

What is Frangipane?

Frangipane, also called almond cream, is a classic almond pastry filling usually made with equal proportions by weight of ground almonds, butter, sugar, and eggs. Sometimes flour is added for body. According to the *Larousse Gastronomique*, frangipane is named for an Italian count named Frangipani. In the 16th century, he developed an almond perfume that Parisian pastry makers used to flavor almond pastry filling.

pecan-chocolate squares

YIELDS SIXTEEN 2½-INCH
SQUARES

FOR THE COOKIE BASE

- 6 oz. (¾ cup) cold unsalted butter, cut into ½-inch pieces
- 9 oz. (2 cups) unbleached all-purpose flour
- ½ cup packed light brown sugar
- 2 tsp. ground cinnamon
- ½ tsp. table salt
- 2 oz. finely grated bittersweet chocolate

FOR THE PECAN TOPPING

- 10 oz. (3 cups) pecans, toasted
- 4 oz. (½ cup) unsalted butter
- 1 cup firmly packed dark brown sugar
- ⅓ cup honey
- 2 Tbs. heavy cream
- ½ tsp. table salt

In a nod to Mexican chocolate, the cookie layer of this bar is spiced with cinnamon and then coated in a thin layer of chocolate.

MAKE THE COOKIE BASE

Position a rack in the center of the oven and heat the oven to 350°F. Put the butter in a food processor, along with the flour, light brown sugar, cinnamon, and salt. Pulse until the mixture is well combined (about 20 pulses). Scatter the dough into a 9x9-inch baking pan and press it evenly over the bottom. (Wipe out the processor bowl but don't bother washing it.) Bake the base until firm and lightly browned, about 25 minutes. When the cookie base comes out of the oven, sprinkle the grated chocolate evenly over the top. (Don't turn off the oven.) Set the pan aside.

MAKE THE PECAN TOPPING

As the cookie base bakes, pulse the pecans in the food processor until coarsely chopped. In a medium-size heavy saucepan, melt the butter. Stir in the dark brown sugar, honey, cream, and salt. Simmer for 1 minute, stirring occasionally. Stir in the pecans. Pour the pecan mixture over the chocolate-sprinkled cookie base, spreading evenly. Bake until much of the filling is bubbling (not just the edges), 16 to 18 minutes. Let cool completely in the pan. When ready to serve, cut into 16 squares. —*Paula Disbrowe & David Norman*

PER SQUARE: 430 CALORIES | 4g PROTEIN | 43g CARB | 30g TOTAL FAT | 11g SAT FAT | 11g MONO FAT | 5g POLY FAT | 40mg CHOL | 160mg SODIUM | 3g FIBER

Make Ahead

Tightly covered, these bars will keep for about 5 days.

chocolate-glazed chocolate-hazelnut cookies

YIELDS 6 TO 7 DOZEN 2¾- TO 3-INCH COOKIES

FOR THE COOKIES

5	oz. (1 cup) whole hazelnuts, toasted
1½	tsp. instant espresso powder
3	oz. bittersweet or semisweet chocolate (not unsweetened), broken up or coarsely chopped
5⅓	oz. (⅔ cup) unsalted butter, slightly softened
¾	cup granulated sugar
1⅛	oz. (⅓ cup) unsweetened Dutch-processed cocoa powder
1	large egg
1½	tsp. pure vanilla extract
¼	tsp. table salt
8¼	oz. (1¾ cups) unbleached all-purpose flour
	Butter or nonstick spray for the baking sheets

FOR THE GLAZE

16	oz. bittersweet or semisweet chocolate (not unsweetened), broken up or coarsely chopped
1	Tbs. corn oil or other flavorless vegetable oil

The cookies will keep, refrigerated, for up to 5 days. Remove them from the refrigerator about 10 minutes before serving; if the cookies stand unrefrigerated for longer than about an hour, the chocolate surface may begin to dull.

MAKE THE COOKIES

1. In a food processor, process the hazelnuts and espresso powder until they're ground to the consistency of a nut butter, 2 to 3 minutes.

2. Melt the chocolate in a microwave or on the stove. Set aside to cool until warm.

3. In a large bowl, beat the butter, sugar, cocoa powder, and hazelnut mixture with a stand mixer (use the paddle attachment) or a hand-held mixer on medium speed until very well blended and fluffy, 1½ to 2 minutes; scrape the bowl as needed. Add the egg, vanilla, and salt; beat until completely blended and smooth, about 1½ minutes. On low speed, mix in half of the flour and then the melted chocolate just until evenly incorporated. Mix or stir in by hand the remaining flour until evenly incorporated. Set aside for 10 minutes; the dough will firm up slightly.

4. Cut the dough into thirds. Set each third between sheets of parchment or waxed paper. Roll out each portion to ⅛ inch thick; check the underside and smooth any wrinkles. Stack the rolled pieces (paper still attached) on a tray. Refrigerate until firm, about 45 minutes, or for several hours (or freeze for about 20 minutes to speed chilling).

5. Position a rack in the center of the oven and heat the oven to 350°F. Butter several large baking sheets or coat with nonstick spray. Working with one piece of dough at a time and keeping the remainder chilled, gently peel away and then replace the top sheet of paper. Flip the dough over. Peel off and discard the second sheet of paper. Cut out the cookies using a 2½ - to 2¾-inch fluted round, oval, or other cutter. (If the dough softens too much to handle easily, transfer the paper and cookies to a tray and refrigerate until firm again.) Using a spatula, carefully transfer the cookies to the baking sheets, arranging them about 1½ inches apart. Reroll the dough scraps. Continue cutting out the cookies until all dough is used; refrigerate as necessary if it becomes too soft to handle.

6. Bake the cookies one sheet at a time (keep the rest refrigerated) until they feel dry and almost firm when pressed in the center, 7 to 10 minutes. Let cool on the sheets for 3 or 4 minutes before transferring to racks to cool completely. Prepare the cookies for glazing by freezing them for at least 20 minutes or up to several hours. (You can also freeze the cookies at this point, tightly wrapped, for up to 2 months.) To glaze the cookies, follow the directions in the sidebar on the facing page.

MAKE THE GLAZE

1. Line several small trays or baking sheets with aluminum foil. Combine the chocolate and oil in a medium metal bowl. Set the bowl over a saucepan containing about an inch of barely simmering water and stir with a spatula until melted. Turn off the burner under the saucepan but leave the bowl over the hot water to keep the chocolate warm; stir the chocolate occasionally. (Replace the water in the pan with hot water as it cools off during the dipping process, but be careful not to splash water into the chocolate.)

2. Working with only about five or six cookies at a time (keep the remainder frozen), glaze them by dipping in the chocolate glaze as directed below.
—*Nancy Baggett*

to glaze, just tilt, dip, and scrape

With the bowl tipped so that the chocolate pools on one side, hold a cookie vertically and dip until half is submerged in the chocolate. Lift the cookie out and shake off excess chocolate. Gently scrape the bottom of the cookie against the side of the bowl to remove excess chocolate from the bottom surface.

Arrange the dipped cookies on the foil-lined sheets, spacing them slightly apart. When a pan is full, refrigerate it for 30 minutes so the chocolate can firm up. Then peel the cookies from the foil, pack them in airtight containers, and return them to the refrigerator.

Chocolate and Hazelnuts

Throughout Europe, chocolate and hazelnuts are a classic pair. The combination appears frequently in Italian cakes, in various frozen desserts called semifreddo, and in a hazelnut-chocolate confection known as gianduia. Gianduia originated in Italy, but it's enormously popular throughout Switzerland, Germany, and Austria as well, turning up in an array of bonbons, truffles, and other candies. The Swiss, Germans, and Austrians also use chocolate and chopped hazelnuts or ground hazelnuts in all sorts of tortes, puddings, pastries, and cookies.

lemon-lime butter wafers

YIELDS ABOUT 8 DOZEN
2¼-INCH COOKIES

- **10** oz. (2¼ cups) unbleached all-purpose flour
- **½** tsp. table salt
- **½** lb. (1 cup) unsalted butter, softened at room temperature
- **1** Tbs. finely grated lemon zest (from about 1 large lemon)
- **1** Tbs. finely grated lime zest (from about 1 large lime)
- **1¼** cups granulated sugar
- **1** Tbs. fresh lemon juice
- **1** Tbs. fresh lime juice
- **1** tsp. pure vanilla extract

Make Ahead

Logs of slice-and-bake cookie dough can be stored in the refrigerator for up to 3 days. For longer storage, put the logs in airtight, zip-top bags and freeze for up to 3 months. To thaw the logs, put them in the refrigerator overnight. Any unused dough may be frozen again. Store baked, cooled cookies, layered between sheets of waxed paper in airtight containers, for up to a week, or freeze for up to 3 months.

Before mixing the dough, be sure the butter is softened at room temperature but still firm; butter that's too soft will make dough that's harder to shape into logs.

MIX THE DOUGH

Sift the flour and salt into a medium bowl. In the bowl of a stand mixer fitted with the paddle attachment (or in a large bowl with a hand mixer), beat the butter and both zests on medium low until well blended, about 2 minutes. Add 1 cup of the sugar in a steady stream and mix for another 2 minutes until well blended. Blend in the lemon juice, lime juice, and vanilla. Reduce the speed to low and add the flour mixture in two additions, mixing just until blended.

SHAPE THE DOUGH

Have ready two 15-inch sheets of plastic wrap. Put the remaining ¼ cup sugar in a long, shallow pan (like a 7x11-inch Pyrex dish). Shape one half of the dough into a log about 10 inches long and roll gently in the sugar to thoroughly coat. Position the log on a sheet of plastic, centering it on the long edge closest to you. Roll tightly, twisting the ends of the plastic firmly to seal. With your hands on either end of the log, push it firmly toward the center to compact the dough. The finished log should be about 9 inches long and 1½ inches thick. Repeat with the remaining dough. Refrigerate the logs until firm enough to slice, about 2½ hours, or freeze for up to 3 months.

BAKE THE COOKIES

1. Position a rack in the center of the oven and heat the oven to 375°F. Line two rimmed baking sheets with parchment.

2. Working with one log at a time, use a sharp, thin-bladed knife to cut ⅛-inch thick rounds. Set the rounds 1 inch apart on the baking sheets and bake one sheet at a time until lightly browned around the edges, about 10 minutes, rotating the sheet as needed for even browning. Let cool on the pan for about 5 minutes before transferring the cookies to racks with a thin-bladed spatula.

—*Carole Walter*

glazed maple-pecan cookies

YIELDS ABOUT 6 DOZEN 2-INCH COOKIES

FOR THE DOUGH

11¼ oz. (2½ cups) unbleached all-purpose flour

½ tsp. table salt

¼ tsp. baking soda

¾ cup granulated sugar

¼ cup very firmly packed, very fresh dark brown sugar

1½ tsp. maple flavoring (available in supermarkets)

6 oz. (¾ cup) unsalted butter, slightly softened

1 large egg, at room temperature

¼ cup pure maple syrup

1 tsp. pure vanilla extract

8 oz. (2 cups) toasted pecans, coarsely chopped

FOR THE GLAZE

¾ cup sifted confectioners' sugar

¼ cup pure maple syrup, warmed

Hot water as needed for thinning

how to cut even slices

To cut even slices of cookie dough, lay a ruler alongside the log of dough. Use your sharpest thin-bladed knife and a continuous slicing motion if the log is uncoated. If it's coated with nuts or other garnishes, use a small, serrated knife and a gentle sawing motion for the cleanest cut.

After baking, these crunchy cookies are brushed with a thin, delicious layer of maple glaze for an extra dose of sweetness.

MIX THE DOUGH

1. Sift together the flour, salt, and baking soda. In a food processor, pulse both sugars to blend and then add the maple flavoring. Pulse five or six times and then process for 15 seconds. Scrape the bowl to be sure all of the flavoring has been incorporated.

2. Using a stand mixer fitted with the paddle attachment (or in a large bowl with a hand mixer), cream the butter on medium-low speed until very smooth, about 2 minutes. Add the sugar mixture in three additions. Mix until lightened in color, about another 3 minutes. Add the egg and then the maple syrup and vanilla, mixing just until blended. Scrape the bowl as needed. Reduce the mixer speed to low. Mix in the dry ingredients in three additions, and then add the pecans and mix just until blended.

SHAPE THE DOUGH

Have ready three 15-inch sheets of plastic wrap. Portion the dough into three equal pieces and roll each piece back and forth until it forms a log about 10 inches long. (You needn't flour the rolling surface.) Position each log on a sheet of plastic wrap, centering it at the edge closest to you. Roll tightly, twisting the ends firmly to seal. With your hands on either end, push the log firmly toward the center to compact the dough. The finished log should measure about 9 inches long and about 1½ inches thick. Refrigerate the logs until firm enough to slice, 2 to 3 hours, or freeze for up to 3 months.

BAKE THE COOKIES

1. Position racks in the upper and lower thirds of the oven and heat the oven to 350°F. Line two rimmed baking sheets with parchment. Working with one log at a time, use a tomato knife or other small serrated knife to cut the dough into ¼-inch rounds using a gentle sawing motion. Set the rounds 1 inch apart on the prepared pans and bake until the cookies are lightly browned, about 18 minutes, rotating the pans as needed for even browning.

2. Meanwhile, whisk the confectioners' sugar and maple syrup in a separate bowl until smooth and pourable to make the glaze.

3. Remove the sheets from the oven and let rest on the baking sheets for 2 minutes. While the cookies are still hot, use a pastry brush to brush a thin layer of the glaze on top of each cookie. (If the glaze becomes too thick as it stands, thin it with a few drops of hot water.) Transfer the cookies to a rack; the glaze will become firm within minutes. —*Carole Walter*

Make Ahead

Store the cookies, layered between sheets of waxed paper, in an airtight container for up to a week, or freeze for up to 3 months.

oatmeal-cranberry cookies

YIELDS ABOUT 6 DOZEN
2¼-INCH COOKIES

- ⅓ **cup orange juice**
- ½ **cup dried cranberries**
- 1¾ **cups old-fashioned oatmeal**
- 5¾ **oz. (1¼ cups) unbleached all-purpose flour**
- 1 **tsp. ground cinnamon**
- ½ **tsp. baking soda**
- ½ **tsp. table salt**
- 6 **oz. (¾ cup) unsalted butter, slightly firm**
- 1 **tsp. finely grated orange zest**
- ¾ **cup very firmly packed, very fresh dark brown sugar**
- ¼ **cup granulated sugar**
- 1 **large egg**
- 1½ **tsp. pure vanilla extract**

storing dried cranberries

Store unopened packages of dried cranberries in a cool, dry place. An open container of dried cranberries stores best in the refrigerator with low humidity, and should be used within 12 months after opening.

A hint of orange zest and flecks of cranberry give classic oatmeal cookies a festive new twist. Logs of dough can be frozen for up to 3 months. Store baked, cooled cookies between sheets of waxed paper in an airtight container for up to a week, or freeze for up to 3 months.

MIX THE DOUGH

1. In a small saucepan, heat the orange juice until very hot. Add the cranberries; let steep off the heat until softened, about 15 minutes. Drain the cranberries, pat dry on paper towels, and coarsely chop into ¼-inch pieces.

2. Put the oatmeal in a food processor and pulse 8 to 10 times to just break up the oatmeal. Remove ½ cup and transfer to a long shallow pan (like a 7x11-inch Pyrex dish). Add the flour, cinnamon, baking soda, and salt to the food processor and pulse with the remaining oatmeal 8 to 10 times just to blend the ingredients. Don't overprocess; the oatmeal should remain coarse.

3. Using a stand mixer fitted with the paddle attachment (or in a large bowl with a hand mixer), beat the butter and orange zest on medium-low until well blended, about 2 minutes. Add both sugars and mix for another 2 minutes. Blend in the egg and vanilla, scraping the bowl as needed. Reduce the mixer speed to low. Add half of the dry ingredients, then the cranberries, and then the remaining dry ingredients. Mix just until combined.

SHAPE THE DOUGH

Have ready six 15-inch sheets of plastic wrap. Portion the dough into thirds. Drop spoonfuls of dough onto three of the sheets and use the plastic to roll and shape the dough into logs about 8 inches long. Refrigerate the dough to firm it slightly, about 30 minutes. When chilled, roll one log at a time in the reserved oatmeal. Reroll each log tightly in a clean sheet of plastic wrap, twisting the ends firmly to seal. With your hands at either end of the log, push firmly toward the center to compact the log so it measures about 7 inches long and 1½ inches thick. Refrigerate the logs until firm enough to slice (they must be very well chilled), about 4 hours.

BAKE THE COOKIES

Position racks in the upper and lower thirds of the oven and heat the oven to 350°F. Line two rimmed baking sheets with parchment. Working with one log at a time, use a tomato knife or other small serrated knife to slice the dough into ¼-inch-thick rounds, using a gentle sawing motion. Set the rounds 1 inch apart on the prepared pans. Bake the cookies until set on top and lightly browned around the edges, about 15 minutes, rotating the pans as needed for even browning. Let cool on the sheets for about 5 minutes before transferring the cookies to racks. —*Carole Walter*

pecan thumbprint cookies

14¼ oz. (3 cups plus 2 Tbs.) unbleached all-purpose flour

½ tsp. table salt

¾ lb. (1½ cups) unsalted butter, softened at room temperature

6 oz. (1½ cups) pecans, toasted and finely ground in a food processor

3 oz. (1 cup) confectioners' sugar

2 tsp. pure vanilla extract

½ to ¾ cup red raspberry preserves with seeds

If there are kids nearby, get them to help make these cookies. They'll love poking the balls of dough to make the pocket for the jam.

1. Position a rack in the center of the oven and heat the oven to 350°F. In a medium bowl, whisk the flour and salt to blend. Using a stand mixer with the paddle attachment (or in a large bowl with a hand mixer), beat the butter and pecans on medium speed until very soft and light, about 3 minutes. Beat in the confectioners' sugar and vanilla until thoroughly combined, about 1 minute. Scrape the bowl with a rubber spatula. With the mixer on low speed, slowly blend in the flour mixture until totally incorporated, about 30 seconds.

2. Using your hands, roll the dough into 1- to 1¼-inch balls and set them about 2 inches apart on ungreased cookie sheets. Press your thumb into the middle of each dough ball to create a well for the preserves. Stir the preserves to loosen and then spoon about ½ tsp. into the middle of each dough ball. Bake until the cookies are golden brown, about 20 minutes. Let the cookies cool on the sheet for 1 minute before transferring them to a rack to cool.
—*Joanne Chang*

Make Ahead

These cookies can be stored in an airtight container for 3 to 4 days.

macadamia lace cookies

**YIELDS ABOUT FIFTY-TWO
3-INCH COOKIES**

- **4 oz. (½ cup) unsalted butter, cut into 5 pieces**
- **4½ oz. (1 cup) finely chopped lightly salted macadamia nuts**
- **1 cup granulated sugar**
- **1 large egg, lightly beaten**
- **1 tsp. vanilla bean paste or pure vanilla extract**
- **½ tsp. table salt**

Be sure to drop the batter at least 3 inches apart on the baking sheet; this buttery dough spreads a lot.

The combination of rich macadamia nuts and browned butter gives these pretty, delicate cookies an intense flavor. The recipe calls for vanilla bean paste (a combination of vanilla extract and vanilla seeds), but vanilla extract works well, too.

1. Position a rack in the center of the oven and heat the oven to 350°F. Line two or three large baking sheets with nonstick baking liners or parchment.

2. In a small saucepan over medium heat, melt the butter. Continue cooking it just until the butter solids at the bottom of the pan turn deep golden brown (not black), 5 to 7 minutes. Watch the butter carefully. Immediately remove the pan from the heat and pour the butter into a small bowl, scraping the pan to get all the solids. Let cool slightly, about 5 minutes.

3. Combine the chopped nuts, sugar, egg, vanilla, and salt in a medium bowl. Stir until blended. Slowly add the browned butter and continue stirring until blended.

4. Drop the batter by slightly heaping teaspoonfuls about 3 inches apart on the prepared baking sheets. Bake one sheet at a time until the cookies are golden brown, 6 to 8 minutes. Let the cookies cool on the sheets on racks for 5 minutes before transferring them to racks to cool completely. Repeat with the remaining batter after the sheets have cooled. Store at room temperature or freeze in an airtight container, separating the cookie layers with waxed paper.
—*Denise Pierce*

raspberry diamonds

FOR THE COOKIES

11¼	oz. (2½ cups) unbleached all-purpose flour
¼	tsp. cream of tartar
⅛	tsp. table salt
½	lb. (1 cup) unsalted butter, softened at room temperature
½	cup granulated sugar
2	Tbs. confectioners' sugar
1	large egg, at room temperature
½	tsp. pure vanilla extract
¼	tsp. pure almond extract
6	Tbs. seedless raspberry jam

FOR THE ALMOND GLAZE

3½	oz. (1 cup) sifted confectioners' sugar
	Pinch of table salt
1	Tbs. plus 1 tsp. water
¼	tsp. pure almond extract

These pretty cookies are tender and buttery. For best results, store the cookies without the glaze. (After a day, the glaze will begin to absorb the raspberry color.)

MAKE THE COOKIES

1. In a medium bowl, whisk the flour with the cream of tartar and salt until well blended. Using a stand mixer fitted with the paddle attachment (or in a large bowl with a hand mixer), beat the butter, sugar, and confectioners' sugar in a large bowl on medium speed until light and fluffy, about 4 minutes, scraping the bowl as needed. Add the egg, vanilla, and almond extract and beat until blended. Add the flour mixture and mix on low speed until just blended.

2. On a lightly floured surface, portion the dough into six equal pieces. If the dough is very soft, wrap each portion in plastic and refrigerate until firmer, about 1 hour.

3. Position a rack in the center of the oven, heat the oven to 350°F, and have ready two large ungreased baking sheets (or line them with nonstick baking liners). If the dough is in the refrigerator, remove it and unwrap it. Using your hands or a rolling pin (or both), shape each piece into a flat 12x1½-inch strip about ¼ inch thick, dusting with flour if needed. Transfer the strips to the sheets, spacing them about 3 inches apart.

4. Using the end of a knife handle dipped lightly in flour, make an indentation down the middle of each strip (this will widen the strip to about 1¾ inches and make a depression about halfway down into the strip). Spread 1 Tbs. of the jam evenly down the indentation of each strip.

5. Bake one sheet at a time until the cookie strips are lightly browned on the bottom and edges, about 20 minutes. Let the strips cool on the sheets on racks for 5 minutes before carefully transferring them to racks to cool completely (a long offset metal spatula is good for this). Before glazing, set the rack over a baking sheet or a sheet of waxed paper. If you plan to freeze these cookies, do it before glazing.

GLAZE THE COOKIES

In a small bowl, mix the confectioners' sugar with the salt, water, and almond extract. The glaze should be thick enough to hold its shape when drizzled; add more confectioners' sugar or water if needed. Using the tines of a fork, drizzle the glaze over the tops of the cooled cookies. (Or transfer the glaze to a sturdy zip-top plastic bag, snip off a tiny bit of one corner of the bag, and drizzle.) Leave the cookies on the rack until the glaze is set, about 30 minutes, and then transfer to a cutting board. With a serrated knife, cut each bar on the diagonal into 1-inch-thick diamond shapes. Store at room temperature or freeze (unglazed) in an airtight container, separating the cookie layers with waxed paper. —*Maxine Henderson*

orange chocolate-chip cookies

YIELDS ABOUT THIRTY-TWO
2½-INCH COOKIES

- **9 oz. (2 cups) unbleached all-purpose flour**
- **½ tsp. baking soda**
- **½ tsp. table salt**
- **4 oz. (½ cup) unsalted butter, softened at room temperature**
- **¼ cup whole-milk ricotta, at room temperature**
- **1 cup granulated sugar**
- **1 tsp. finely grated orange zest**
- **1 tsp. pure vanilla extract**
- **1 large egg, at room temperature**
- **4½ oz. (¾ cup) chocolate chips**

These cookies are nicknamed "cannoli" cookies after the Italian dessert, because they're enriched with whole-milk ricotta and scented with grated orange zest. For a special treat, look for fresh ricotta sold in Italian groceries; though it's highly perishable, these smaller-batch ricottas have a much more complex flavor than the mass-produced versions.

1. In a medium bowl, whisk the flour with the baking soda and salt until well blended.

2. Using a stand mixer fitted with the paddle attachment (or in a large bowl with a hand mixer), beat the butter and ricotta on medium-high speed until light and fluffy, about 2 minutes. Add the sugar, orange zest, and vanilla; beat until blended, about 3 minutes. Scrape the bowl. On medium speed, add the egg and beat until blended. Add the flour mixture and mix on low speed until almost completely blended. Pour in the chocolate chips and continue mixing until just incorporated. Scrape the dough from the sides of the bowl, cover with plastic, and refrigerate until slightly firmer, about 30 minutes.

3. Position a rack in the center of the oven and heat the oven to 350°F. Line large baking sheets with nonstick baking liners or parchment. Drop the batter by rounded tablespoons about 2 inches apart on the prepared baking sheets. Bake one sheet at a time until the cookies are light golden, about 15 minutes. Let the cookies cool on the sheets on racks for 5 minutes before transferring them to racks to cool completely. Store at room temperature or freeze in an airtight container, separating the cookie layers with waxed paper.

—Judi Terrell Linden

chocolate cherry coconut macaroons

YIELDS ABOUT 20 MACAROONS

YIELDS ABOUT 20 MACAROONS

- 1¾ cups sweetened shredded coconut
- ⅔ cup cream of coconut, such as Coco Lopez® (not coconut milk)
- ⅓ cup unsweetened cocoa powder, preferably Dutch-processed
- 2 large egg whites
- 1 tsp. pure vanilla extract
- Pinch of table salt
- 3 oz. (½ cup) dried cherries (preferably tart ones), coarsely chopped

A cross between a cookie and a chocolate truffle, these macaroons are moist and fudgy inside.

1. Heat the oven to 325°F. Spread 1½ cups of the shredded coconut on a rimmed baking sheet. Bake, stirring frequently, until some of the shreds begin to turn a light golden brown, 8 to 10 minutes (you're not so much toasting the coconut as you are drying it). Let cool. Turn off the oven.

2. In a medium bowl, whisk the cream of coconut, cocoa, egg whites, vanilla, and salt until well combined. Stir in the dried cherries and the 1½ cups of coconut. Cover and refrigerate until thoroughly chilled and firm, at least 2 hours and up to 24 hours.

3. About 20 minutes before you plan to bake the macaroons, position a rack in the center of the oven and heat the oven to 325°F. Line a heavy baking sheet with parchment. With damp hands, shape slightly heaping tablespoons of the batter into balls. Arrange on the baking sheet about 2 inches apart (they should all fit on one sheet). Top each macaroon with a pinch of the remaining untoasted coconut. Bake until the outsides are no longer sticky but the insides still feel somewhat soft when poked with a finger and the coconut topping is golden brown, about 20 minutes. Let the macaroons cool for 3 minutes on the baking sheet before transferring them to a rack to let cool completely.
—*Jennifer Armentrout*

Cocoa Powder: Regular vs. Dutch-processed

Some recipes call for unsweetened regular, or "natural," cocoa powder while others call for Dutch-processed cocoa. Regular cocoa is intense and full flavored; it's also somewhat acidic. Dutch-processed cocoa (also called Dutched or European-style) is treated with an alkali to neutralize its acidity. The treatment process, invented by a Dutchman in 1828, smooths and mellows the cocoa's flavor and darkens its color. The two types of cocoa aren't necessarily interchangeable because the leavening agents in recipes are typically balanced against the specific pH of the cocoa. (That is, baking soda, which is alkaline, is generally paired with natural cocoa to neutralize its acidity; baking powder is paired with Dutched cocoa because both ingredients are essentially neutral already.) Dutch-processed cocoa isn't as widely available as natural cocoa, but some supermarkets do carry both.

pistachio meringues with toasted coconut

YIELDS ABOUT 40 KISSES

- **3 oz. (¾ cup) confectioners' sugar**
- **½ cup superfine sugar**
- **Pinch of table salt**
- **4 large egg whites, at room temperature**
- **½ tsp. cream of tartar**
- **¼ tsp. pure vanilla extract**
- **⅓ cup unsalted shelled pistachios, chopped medium fine**
- **⅓ cup shredded unsweetened coconut, lightly toasted**
- **3 Tbs. finely chopped pistachios, for garnish (optional)**

If you can't find superfine sugar, pulse granulated sugar in a food processor to a fine grind; measure after grinding. If you don't have a pastry bag, simply spoon the meringues into free-form shapes. Pistachios and coconut are a great flavor combination, but feel free to substitute with other additions. Fold in any ground nut, or even tiny chocolate morsels, if you like. Don't try to make meringues on a very humid day. The humidity can prevent them from ever getting crisp.

1. Position racks in the upper and lower thirds of the oven and heat the oven to 175°F. Line a large heavy baking sheet with parchment. Sift together the confectioners' sugar, superfine sugar, and salt.

2. Using a stand mixer fitted with the whisk attachment (or in a large bowl with a hand mixer), beat the egg whites and cream of tartar. Begin mixing on medium-low speed until frothy. Increase the speed to medium high and beat until the whites form soft peaks. Continue beating while gradually sprinkling in the sifted sugars. When all the sugar is added, increase the speed to high and whip until firm, glossy peaks form. Add the vanilla and the ⅓ cup pistachios and beat just until blended, about 10 seconds.

3. Spoon about half of the meringue into a large pastry bag fitted with a large (#8) star tip. Pipe shapes as you like (for kisses, about 1½ inches wide and about 2 inches from tip to base) onto the prepared baking sheet, about ½ inch apart. If the tip gets clogged with a nut, use the back of a small knife or spoon to pry open the points of the star tip slightly and the nut will wiggle out. Sprinkle the toasted coconut over the meringues, along with a dusting of pistachios, if you like.

4. Bake the meringues until dried and crisp but not browned, about 3 hours. Turn off the oven (leave the door shut) and let the meringues sit in the oven for about 1 hour. Remove them from the oven and gently lift the meringues off the parchment. Serve immediately or store in an airtight container for up to a month. —*Abigail Johnson Dodge*

how to make meringues

Add a little cream of tartar to your egg whites before you begin mixing. It will strengthen the whites and help to maintain the structure of your meringues.

When the whites are very foamy—almost at the stage where they form soft, floppy peaks—begin adding the sugar gradually. Turn up the speed on the mixer as you add the sugar.

Since the sugar helps stabilize the egg whites, this is one time when you don't have to be cautious about beating—you want to whip the mixture until glossy, firm peaks form. At this point, stir in the vanilla and the chopped nuts.

Fit a pastry bag with a wide star tip. Twist the bag slightly just over the tip and stuff the twist into the tip. Fold the bag over one hand and spoon the meringue into it with a rubber spatula. Fill the bag about halfway and twist it shut. Untwist the part over the tip and squeeze out some meringue to remove any air bubbles.

With one hand, hold the bag perpendicular to the pan and squeeze gently from the top of the bag. Use your other hand to guide the tip. Lift the bag straight up while releasing pressure to let a peak form.

Simple Steps for Successful Meringues

Before you start, remember two important things. First, your bowl and beater should be impeccably clean. Any speck of grease will keep the egg whites from expanding properly. A quick rinse with a little white vinegar and some water will do the trick. Be sure to dry the equipment well. Second, your ingredients should be at room temperature to get the best volume out of your meringue. Since it's easier to separate whites from yolks when they're cold, go ahead and separate your eggs straight out of the refrigerator. Then let your whites warm to room temperature in a bowl, or put the bowl over warm water to speed the process.

orange poppy seed cookies

**YIELDS ABOUT 3 DOZEN
2½-INCH COOKIES**

- 5¾ oz. (1¼ cups) unbleached all-purpose flour
- 1 Tbs. poppy seeds
- ¼ tsp. baking powder
- ¼ tsp. table salt
- 4 oz. (½ cup) unsalted butter, softened at room temperature
- ¾ cup granulated sugar
- 1 large egg
- 1 Tbs. fresh orange juice
- 1 Tbs. packed finely grated orange zest (from about 1½ large oranges)
- 1 tsp. finely grated lemon zest

Make Ahead

This dough can be kept frozen, well wrapped, for several weeks.

For chewier cookies, line your cookie sheets with parchment. On greased sheets, the cookies will spread a bit more and be slightly crisper.

SEVERAL HOURS OR THE DAY BEFORE BAKING

1. In a small bowl, whisk the flour, poppy seeds, baking powder, and salt. Using a stand mixer fitted with the paddle attachment (or in a large bowl using a hand mixer), beat the butter and sugar until light and fluffy. Add the egg, orange juice, orange zest, and lemon zest; beat until blended, scraping the bowl. Add the flour mixture, beating on low just until combined. Scrape the soft dough onto a large piece of plastic wrap (about 13 inches long), wrap, and freeze for 30 minutes.

2. Unwrap the dough and knead it briefly on a floured surface to remove any air pockets. Wrap the dough in plastic again; roll and gently pull opposite ends of the wrapped dough to create a 9-inch-long log. Freeze the log for 1 hour or refrigerate for several hours until very firm.

BAKE THE COOKIES

Position a rack in the center of the oven and heat the oven to 350°F. Lightly grease two or three baking sheets or cover them with parchment. Unwrap the log and roll it briefly on a lightly floured surface to remove the wrinkles on the dough's surface and to make the log more evenly round. Slice the log crosswise into ³⁄₁₆-inch-thick rounds. Set the rounds 1 inch apart on the cookie sheets. Bake the cookies one sheet at a time until the edges are lightly browned, 12 to 14 minutes. Let cool for 5 minutes on the sheets; transfer to a wire rack to cool completely. —*Elaine Khosrova*

orange-hazelnut olive oil cookies

YIELDS ABOUT 6 DOZEN COOKIES

- **2** cups toasted and skinned hazelnuts (for instructions on how to toast and skin hazelnuts, see p. 152)
- **10** oz. (2¼ cups) unbleached all-purpose flour
- **1** tsp. baking powder
- **¼** tsp. table salt
- **¾** cup plus 2 Tbs. granulated sugar
- **½** cup extra-virgin olive oil
- **2** large eggs

   Finely grated zest of 2 medium oranges (about 1½ packed Tbs.)
- **1** tsp. pure vanilla extract

Reminiscent of biscotti in texture, these not-too-sweet cookies are a perfect dipper for after-dinner coffee. Unbaked logs of dough may be frozen for up to a month. Baked cookies will keep in an airtight container at room temperature for up to a week.

1. Finely grind the hazelnuts in a food processor. In a medium bowl, whisk the hazelnuts, flour, baking powder, and salt to blend. Using a stand mixer fitted with the paddle attachment (or in a large bowl with a hand mixer), beat the sugar, oil, eggs, zest, and vanilla on low speed until the sugar is moistened, about 15 seconds. Increase the speed to high and mix until well combined, about 15 seconds more (the sugar will not be dissolved at this point). Add the dry ingredients and mix on low speed until the dough has just pulled together, 30 to 60 seconds.

2. Divide the dough in two. Pile one half of the dough onto a piece of parchment. Using the parchment to help shape the dough, form it into a log 11 inches long and 2 inches in diameter. Wrap the parchment around the log and twist the ends to secure. Repeat with the remaining dough. Chill in the freezer until firm, about 1 hour.

3. Position racks in the upper and lower thirds of the oven and heat the oven to 350°F. Line four cookie sheets with parchment or nonstick baking liners.

4. Unwrap one log of dough at a time and cut the dough into ¼-inch slices; set them 1 inch apart on the prepared sheets. Bake two sheets at a time until light golden on the bottoms and around the edges, about 10 minutes, rotating and swapping the sheets halfway through for even baking. Let cool completely on racks. —*David Crofton*

PER COOKIE: 60 CALORIES | 1g PROTEIN | 6g CARB | 4g TOTAL FAT | 0g SAT FAT | 3g MONO FAT | 0g POLY FAT | 5mg CHOL | 15mg SODIUM | 0g FIBER

lime nut buttons

YIELDS ABOUT THIRTY
1½-INCH COOKIES

- **4½ oz. (1 cup) unbleached all-purpose flour**
- **¼ tsp. table salt**
- **½ cup confectioners' sugar; more for coating**
- **⅓ cup coarsely chopped pecans**
- **¼ cup sweetened shredded coconut**
- **4 oz. (½ cup) unsalted butter, softened at room temperature**
- **2 tsp. finely grated lime zest**
- **1 tsp. pure vanilla extract**

When shaping, work with half the dough at a time, keeping the remainder chilled. Shape the cookies identically so that they bake within the same time.

SEVERAL HOURS BEFORE BAKING

In a small bowl, combine the flour and salt. In a food processor, combine the confectioners' sugar, pecans, and coconut. Process until the pecans are finely ground. In a large bowl with an electric mixer, beat the butter on medium speed until creamy. Add the pecan mixture and beat until well blended. Beat in the lime zest and vanilla. Scrape the bowl and add the flour mixture, beating just until combined. Remove the dough from the bowl, wrap in plastic, and chill until firm, about 3 hours.

BAKE THE COOKIES

Position a rack in the center of the oven and heat the oven to 350°F. Measure the dough into heaping teaspoon-size pieces and roll each piece between your palms to form a ball. Put the balls 1½ inches apart on ungreased cookie sheets; bake one sheet at a time until the edges of the cookies barely begin to brown, 12 to 14 minutes. Let cool on the sheets for 3 to 4 minutes and then roll in confectioners' sugar while still very warm. Repeat rolling to create a delicate, powdery coating. —*Elaine Khosrova*

chocolate-raspberry truffles

YIELDS ABOUT 60 TRUFFLES

- **1 cup fresh raspberries**
- **1 lb. semisweet or bittersweet chocolate, finely chopped**
- **1½ cups heavy cream**
- **Small pinch of table salt**
- **1 cup unsweetened Dutch-processed cocoa powder**

Use the best-quality chocolate you can find. When warmed, the chocolate mixture doubles as a delicious sauce for ice cream. For more information on making truffles, see p. 39.

1. Pass the berries through a food mill fitted with a fine disk or force them through a fine sieve, mashing with a wooden spoon, into a medium bowl. This will make about ½ cup purée; set it aside and discard the contents of the strainer.

2. Put the chopped chocolate in a medium bowl. In a small saucepan, heat the cream just until boiling. Pour the hot cream over the chopped chocolate; whisk to blend. Stir in the raspberry purée and the salt. Refrigerate the mixture until completely chilled, about 1 hour.

3. Pour the cocoa powder onto a plate. With a melon baller or spoon, scoop the chocolate and shape it into 1-inch balls. If the truffles are very soft, put them on a baking sheet and refrigerate briefly to firm. Roll the shaped truffles in the cocoa, coating them thoroughly. If sealed and refrigerated, they'll keep for about a week. —*Michelle Polzine*

raspberry linzer cookies

**YIELDS ABOUT TWENTY
2½-INCH SANDWICH COOKIES**

2 ½   oz. (½ cup) sliced almonds

2 ½   oz. (½ cup) coarsely chopped
      hazelnuts

9 ½   oz. (2 cups plus 1 Tbs.)
      unbleached all-purpose flour;
      more for rolling

  ¾   cup granulated sugar

  2   tsp. lemon zest

  ½   tsp. baking powder

  ½   tsp. table salt

  ½   tsp. ground cinnamon

  ¼   tsp. ground cloves

  7   oz. (14 Tbs.) chilled unsalted
      butter

  1   large egg

  ½   cup raspberry preserves

      Confectioners' sugar

*The little window in this nut-flavored
cookie reveals a delicious fruit filling.
Just before serving, sift confectioners'
sugar lightly over the cookies.*

SEVERAL HOURS BEFORE BAKING

In a food processor, process the
almonds and hazelnuts with ½ cup of the
flour until finely textured but not powdered.
Add the remaining flour, granulated sugar, lemon zest,
baking powder, salt, cinnamon, and cloves. Pulse to combine. Cut the butter
into ½-inch cubes and add to the flour mixture; pulse until the mixture looks
like coarse meal. Don't overprocess. Transfer to a large bowl. Whisk together
the egg and 1 Tbs. cold water; sprinkle over the flour mixture and toss gently
to combine. The dough should hold together when pinched. (If it seems dry,
sprinkle on a bit more water.) Gather the dough into two balls and knead briefly
just to blend. Wrap in plastic and chill until firm, 2 to 3 hours.

BAKE THE COOKIES

Position a rack in the center of the oven and heat the oven to 325°F. Line
several cookie sheets with parchment. Generously flour a work surface. Roll
one ball of the dough ³⁄₁₆ inch thick. (Keep the rest in the refrigerator, and if the
dough warms up to the point of being sticky while you're working with it, return
it to the refrigerator.) Cut out as many 2½-inch rounds as possible, rerolling
the scraps to make more rounds. Arrange on the cookie sheets about ¾ inch
apart. Cut 1¼-inch holes in the center of half the rounds. Reroll these center
scraps to make more cookies. Bake the cookies one sheet at a time until the
edges are lightly browned, about 15 minutes. Let cool on the sheets. Repeat
with the remaining dough.

ASSEMBLE THE COOKIES

Spread a heaping ½ tsp. preserves on the underside of the whole cookie
rounds. Top with the doughnut-shaped cookies, bottom sides against the
preserves. —*Elaine Khosrova*

coconut macaroons

YIELDS 4 DOZEN COOKIES

- ¾ cup egg whites (from about 5 large eggs)
- 1½ cups plus 1 Tbs. granulated sugar
- 12 oz. unsweetened coconut, finely shredded

The coconut toasts as the macaroons bake, making the outside irresistibly crisp while the interior stays moist. To make perfectly round macaroons, use a small ice cream scoop and bake them right after they're shaped.

1. Position racks in the center and upper third of the oven and heat the oven to 350°F. Line two heavy baking sheets with parchment.

2. In a large bowl, thoroughly whisk the egg whites and sugar. Work the coconut into the egg mixture by hand or with a wooden spoon until completely incorporated. Scoop the coconut mixture onto the pans in packed, level tablespoons or with a ½-ounce ice cream scoop. These cookies don't spread so they can be spaced fairly close together.

3. Bake until the cookies are an even golden color and look dry (not at all sticky or wet looking), about 25 minutes. Halfway through baking, switch the pans from top to bottom and rotate them from back to front for even baking.

—Kay Cabrera

PER COOKIE: 50 CALORIES | 1g PROTEIN | 8g CARB | 2.5g TOTAL FAT | 2g SAT FAT | 0g MONO FAT | 0g POLY FAT | 0mg CHOL | 10mg SODIUM | 1g FIBER

chocolate-drizzled Florentines

YIELDS ABOUT SIXTY
1¼-INCH COOKIES

FOR THE DOUGH

14	oz. (1¾ cups) unsalted butter, softened at room temperature
1½	tsp. finely chopped lemon zest
¾	cup granulated sugar
½	tsp. table salt
1	large egg
1	tsp. pure vanilla extract
1	lb. 5 oz. (4⅔ cups) unbleached all-purpose flour

FOR THE TOPPING

1¾	cups granulated sugar
2	Tbs. light corn syrup
¾	cup water
7	oz. (14 Tbs.) unsalted butter
¾	cup honey
1	cup heavy cream
2	tsp. finely grated orange zest
17	oz. (4 cups) sliced blanched almonds, lightly toasted
¾	cup chopped candied citrus peel (optional)
6	oz. semisweet chocolate, melted and kept warm

For best results, you'll need a candy thermometer for this recipe. Chopped candied citrus peel is an excellent addition. To make candied citrus peel, see the recipe on p. 183.

MAKE THE DOUGH

1. With an electric mixer, combine the butter, zest, sugar, and salt and beat with the paddle until light and fluffy. Add the egg and beat it in well. In three additions, stir in the flour until blended. Spread the dough out, about an inch thick, on a baking sheet, cover with plastic wrap, and chill until firm. You can refrigerate the dough, wrapped well, for up to a week.

2. Lightly grease a half sheet pan (a sided pan that measures 11½ x 16½ inches). Line the pan with parchment.

3. Roll the chilled dough between pieces of 16½ x 24½-inch parchment into a rectangle until it's between ⅛ and ¼ inch thick. Remove the top piece of parchment and flip the dough into the prepared half sheet pan so that it fits along the bottom and up the sides completely. If the dough cracks a bit, just press it back together. Press it into the sides of the pan; don't leave any gaps. Cut off any excess dough by running a rolling pin along the edges of the pan. Chill until firm.

4. Position a rack in the center of the oven and heat the oven to 350°F. Line the dough with foil or parchment and weight it with dried beans or pie weights. Bake until the edges are golden, about 20 minutes. Remove the weights and the foil or parchment and continue to bake until completely set, about another 10 minutes. Let cool before topping.

MAKE THE TOPPING

In a large heavy saucepan, combine the sugar, corn syrup, and water and bring to a boil. Cook until the mixture becomes amber in color (approximately 350°F to 360°F on a candy thermometer). Immediately remove from the heat. Carefully add the butter and honey, return to the heat, and stir until dissolved. Bring the mixture back to a boil and carefully add the heavy cream and zest (the mixture will bubble up and may splatter). Boil the mixture until it reaches 250°F on a candy thermometer. Remove from the heat and stir in the almonds (and candied citrus peel, if using). Quickly pour the mixture into the baked cookie shell before it cools. Spread the nut mixture evenly with a lightly greased spatula.

BAKE AND FINISH THE COOKIES

1. Bake until the topping begins to bubble, 18 to 20 minutes. Let cool completely in the pan. Cut along the edge of the pan to loosen the edges. Turn the Florentines out, upside down, onto a clean cutting surface. Line two clean baking sheets with parchment.

2. Cut through these thick, chewy cookies in two stages to avoid cracking the crust. First, score the ragged edges of the cookie crust with a bread knife, cutting through the crust completely (see the sidebar on page 148). With a large chef's knife, cut through the filling to cut off the ragged edges completely. Next, score 1¼-inch-wide horizontal bands from top to bottom (again deeply, through the crust but not through the filling). To make the diamonds, score

continued on p. 148 ▶

continued from p. 146

1¼-inch strips starting at the top left corner and dividing that corner into two 45-degree angles. Continue scoring at this width and this angle until all the cookies are scored. Follow the scoring lines with the chef's knife, using steady force to cut through the thick nut filling.

3. Turn each Florentine over and set on the clean sheet pans. Fill a pastry bag with a tiny tip, a heavy plastic bag with a corner cut off, or a paper cone with the melted chocolate (or use a fork dipped in the chocolate) and drizzle it on the diamonds. The cookies are best at room temperature but can be refrigerated if the kitchen is too warm for the chocolate to set. —*Melissa Murphy*

PER COOKIE: 230 CALORIES | 3g PROTEIN | 23g CARB | 15g TOTAL FAT | 7g SAT FAT | 6g MONO FAT | 1g POLY FAT | 30mg CHOL | 25mg SODIUM | 1g FIBER

how to cut Florentines

Careful scoring keeps the cookie crust intact. First, use a large serrated knife to cut through just the cookie layer.

Next, use a large chef's knife and a good amount of pressure to cut through the nut topping. The cookies cut best at room temperature.

coconut sablés

YIELDS ABOUT 80 COOKIES

- 2½ oz. (⅔ cup) **finely ground almonds**
- 2½ oz. (1 cup) **unsweetened shredded coconut**
- 10 oz. (2¼ cups) **unbleached all-purpose flour**
- 10 oz. (1¼ cups) **unsalted butter, softened at room temperature**
- 5 oz. (1⅓ cups) **confectioners' sugar**
- ½ tsp. **table salt**
- 1 **large egg, at room temperature**

Make Ahead

> **You can roll out sheets of this dough and freeze them, well wrapped, for several weeks. The dough is rolled out so thinly that you can cut it out and bake it straight from the freezer.**

No matter how many times you reroll the scraps, these cookies always come out tender and delicate. The recipe calls for unsweetened coconut, which can be found at health food stores.

1. In a medium bowl, blend the ground almonds, coconut, and flour; set aside. Using a stand mixer fitted with the paddle attachment (or in a large bowl with a hand mixer), beat the butter on medium speed until soft and creamy. Add the confectioners' sugar and salt; mix on medium-low speed until thoroughly combined, about 5 minutes, scraping the bowl as needed. Reduce the speed to low and add the egg; mix until incorporated. Add the flour mixture. As soon as the dough comes together, stop the mixer.

2. Portion the dough into three equal pieces. Roll each piece between two sheets of parchment to about ⅛ inch thick. Transfer the dough, still between the parchment, to baking sheets and chill in the freezer for about 30 minutes.

3. Position a rack in the center of the oven and heat the oven to 375°F. Line a baking sheet with parchment.

4. When the dough is quite firm, remove it from the freezer and peel off the top sheet of parchment and stamp out shapes with a cookie cutter (or whatever shape you like, though shapes with skinny parts will brown unevenly). Lay the cookies ½ inch apart on the baking sheet. Reroll the scraps, chilling first if necessary.

5. Bake until the cookies are light golden around the edges, 8 to 10 minutes, rotating the sheet halfway through. Let stand on the baking sheet until cool enough to handle (about 10 minutes) and then transfer the cookies to a rack to cool completely. Repeat with the remaining dough. —*Joanne Chang*

PER COOKIE: 60 CALORIES | 1g PROTEIN | 5g CARB | 4g TOTAL FAT | 2.5g SAT FAT | 1G MONO FAT | 0g POLY FAT | 10mg CHOL | 15mg SODIUM | 0g FIBER

toasted almond thins

YIELDS ABOUT 12 DOZEN
COOKIES

- **9 oz. (2¼ cups) slivered almonds, toasted**
- **4½ oz. (1¼ cups) cake flour**
- **4½ oz. (1 cup) unbleached all-purpose flour**
- **½ lb. (1 cup) unsalted butter, softened at room temperature**
- **10 oz. (2⅔ cups) confectioners' sugar**
- **¾ tsp. table salt**
- **1 large egg, at room temperature**

If the dough starts to get too soft as you cut the cookies, stick it in the freezer to firm it up.

1. Blend the almonds and both flours in a small bowl; set aside. Using a stand mixer fitted with the paddle attachment (or in a large bowl using a hand mixer), beat the butter on medium speed until soft and creamy. Add the confectioners' sugar and salt; mix on medium-low speed until thoroughly combined, about 5 minutes, scraping the bowl as needed. Reduce the speed to low and add the egg; mix until blended. Add the flour mixture. As soon as the dough comes together, stop the mixer.

2. Scrape the dough onto a large sheet of plastic wrap. Using the wrap to help shape the dough, gently press it into a rectangle that's about 4½ x 8 inches and about 1½ inches thick. Wrap the dough in plastic and refrigerate until it's firm enough to slice, at least 3 hours.

3. Position a rack in the center of the oven and heat the oven to 400°F. Line a baking sheet with parchment.

4. Unwrap the dough, trim the edges, and slice it into three 1½-inch-square logs. With a sharp knife, slice each log into square cookies between ⅛ and ¼ inch thick. Lay the squares ½ inch apart on the baking sheet.

5. Bake until lightly browned around the edges, about 8 minutes, rotating the sheet halfway through for even baking. Let stand on the baking sheet until cool enough to handle (about 10 minutes) and then transfer the cookies to a rack to cool completely. Repeat with the remaining dough. —*Joanne Chang*

PER COOKIE: 35 CALORIES | 1g PROTEIN | 4g CARB | 2.5g TOTAL FAT | 1g SAT FAT | 1g MONO FAT | 0.5g POLY FAT | 5mg CHOL | 15mg SODIUM | 0g FIBER

lime zest wafers

YIELDS ABOUT 100 COOKIES

½ lb. (1 cup) unsalted butter, softened at room temperature

1 cup granulated sugar

½ tsp. pure vanilla extract

4 egg whites, at room temperature

4½ oz. (1 cup) unbleached all-purpose flour, sifted after measuring

⅛ tsp. table salt

1 tsp. finely grated lime zest

These somewhat delicate cookies hold up well during travel due to their uniform size: just pack them in a sleeve and surround it with bubble wrap.

1. Cream the butter and sugar with a mixer or a wooden spoon until well blended. Add the vanilla extract. Mix in the egg whites just until incorporated. Gradually add the flour and salt and mix just until absorbed. Stir in the lime zest.

2. Position a rack in the center of the oven and heat the oven to 350°F. Spray baking sheets with vegetable spray or lightly brush them with vegetable oil. Use a ½-tsp. measure to drop the batter onto the baking sheets. Leave a few inches between cookies because they spread.

3. Bake the cookies one sheet at a time until the edges are lightly browned, about 10 minutes. Immediately transfer the cookies from the baking sheet to a rack to cool. (If the wafers become brittle before you have removed them from the baking sheet, slide the sheet back into the oven for 30 seconds to soften them.) *—Margery K. Friedman*

lemon snow drops

YIELDS ABOUT 3 DOZEN COOKIES

FOR THE DOUGH

½ lb. (1 cup) unsalted butter, softened at room temperature

2½ oz. (⅖ cup) confectioners' sugar

2½ tsp. grated lemon zest

2 tsp. fresh lemon juice

Pinch of table salt

12 oz. (2⅔ cups) unbleached all-purpose flour

FOR ROLLING

1 cup confectioners' sugar

These cookies stay fresh for up to a week; reroll them in confectioners' sugar before serving.

1. Position a rack in the center of the oven and heat the oven to 325°F. Line baking sheets with parchment or leave them ungreased.

2. Beat the butter and sugar with a wooden spoon or a mixer until creamy. Add the lemon zest, lemon juice, and salt; mix until combined. Add the flour; mix until just blended. Shape the dough into 1-inch balls and set them 1 inch apart on the baking sheets.

3. Bake the cookies one sheet at a time until they are light golden and give slightly when pressed, 18 to 20 minutes. Let the cookies cool slightly on the baking sheet; while still warm, roll them in confectioners' sugar. Transfer to a rack to cool completely. *—Abigail Johnson Dodge*

hazelnut toffee squares

YIELDS ABOUT 6 DOZEN SQUARES

- ½ lb. (1 cup) unsalted butter, softened at room temperature; more for the pan
- 1 cup firmly packed dark brown sugar
- 1 large egg yolk
- 1 tsp. pure vanilla extract
- ¼ tsp. table salt
- 9 oz. (2 cups) unbleached all-purpose flour
- 10 oz. bittersweet chocolate, chopped
- ¼ cup milk
- 3½ oz. (1 cup) chopped hazelnuts, toasted

One batch will make a lot of cookies. Be sure to let the chocolate set before you cut them.

1. Position a rack in the center of the oven and heat the oven to 350°F. Lightly butter a 13x9-inch baking pan.

2. With a wooden spoon or a mixer, cream the butter and brown sugar until smooth and no lumps remain. Add the egg yolk, vanilla, and salt; beat until well blended. Add the flour and mix until the dough begins to come together (if you're using an electric mixer, set it on low speed). Pat the dough into the pan.

3. Bake until the dough begins to pull away from the sides of the pan and keeps a slight indentation when pressed lightly, 26 to 28 minutes. Meanwhile, melt the chocolate and the milk in a double boiler, stirring as little as possible to prevent separating. Pour the warm ganache over the warm baked cookie crust and spread it evenly. Sprinkle with the nuts and let cool completely until the chocolate has set, about 4 hours. Cut into 1½-inch squares.
   —*Abigail Johnson Dodge*

PER COOKIE: 80 CALORIES | 1g PROTEIN | 8g CARB | 5g TOTAL FAT | 2.5g SAT FAT | 1.5g MONO FAT | 0.5g POLY FAT | 10mg CHOL | 10mg SODIUM | 0g FIBER

How to Toast and Skin Hazelnuts

The skin of a hazelnut is bitter, and that's why many recipes call for skinning the nuts. Here are two ways to skin them yourself. (For both methods, let the nuts cool completely before using or before storing in a sealed container in the freezer for up to 3 months.)

THE TOASTING METHOD

Spread the nuts in a single layer on a baking sheet and toast in a 375°F oven until the skins are mostly split and the nuts are light golden brown (the skins will look darker) and fragrant, about 10 minutes. Don't overtoast or the nuts will become bitter. Wrap the hot nuts in a clean dishtowel and let them sit for 5 to 10 minutes. Then vigorously rub the nuts against themselves in the towel to remove most of the skins. Try to get at least half of the skins off. This may take a lot of rubbing, so be persistent.

Pros: The nuts get toasted and skinned all in one step; uses the oven (which might be heating anyway for whatever you'll be making with the nuts) rather than dirtying a saucepan.

Cons: Almost impossible to get the nuts completely skinned; stains a dishtowel (so don't use one you really care about).

THE BLANCHING METHOD

For every ½ cup of hazelnuts, bring 1½ cups water to a boil. Add 2 Tbs. baking soda and the nuts; boil for 3 minutes—expect the water to turn black and watch out for boilovers. Run a nut under cold water and see if the skin slips off easily. If not, boil the nuts a little longer until the skins slip off. Cool the nuts under cold running water, slip off the skins, blot dry, and then toast in a 375°F oven.

Pros: Completely skins the nuts.

Cons: Each nut must be skinned individually (which is easy but time-consuming if you're skinning a lot of nuts); nuts must be toasted in a separate step; nuts won't be as crisp as with the toasting method.

hazelnut linzer thumbprints

YIELDS ABOUT 4 DOZEN
COOKIES

- 5 oz. (about 1 cup) hazelnuts, toasted and cooled
- 10 oz. (2¼ cups) unbleached all-purpose flour; more as needed
- ½ cup granulated sugar
- 1 tsp. baking powder
- 1 tsp. ground cinnamon
- ¼ tsp. table salt
- ½ lb. (1 cup) unsalted butter, cut into ½-inch cubes
- 2 large eggs, separated
- 1 tsp. pure vanilla extract
- 1 Tbs. finely grated lemon zest
- 1 cup raspberry preserves
- 3½ oz. (about ¾ cup) hazelnuts, toasted and hand chopped medium-fine, for rolling
- Confectioners' sugar, for dusting

Hazelnuts give the classic thumbprint cookie a sophisticated texture and flavor. These cookies are simply decorated with confectioners' sugar. After applying, dip your finger in water and tap the center of each cookie so that the jam shines through.

1. In a food processor, process the 5 ounces hazelnuts with ½ cup of the flour until fine-textured but not powdered. Add the remaining flour, sugar, baking powder, cinnamon, and salt. Pulse to combine. With your fingers, toss the butter in the flour to coat it, being careful to avoid the blade. Pulse until the mixture looks like cornmeal. Add the 2 egg yolks (reserve the whites), the vanilla, and the lemon zest and pulse until the dough just begins to hold together. Cover the dough with plastic and refrigerate until firm.

2. Position racks in the upper and lower thirds of the oven and heat the oven to 350°F. Line two cookie sheets with parchment.

3. Lightly beat the reserved egg whites. Shape the dough into 1-inch balls. Roll each ball in the beaten egg whites and then in the chopped 3½ ounces hazelnuts (lightly flour your hands, if necessary). Arrange the balls 1½ inches apart on the prepared cookie sheets. Flatten them slightly with your palm.

4. Press your thumb (floured if necessary) into the center of each cookie to create an indentation. If the dough splits apart, gently press it back together. Fill each cookie with about ½ tsp. of the preserves.

5. Bake until the cookies are lightly browned, about 20 minutes. Let them cool on the cookie sheets on a rack. When cool, lightly sift the confectioners' sugar over the cookies. *—Melissa Murphy*

PER COOKIE: 120 CALORIES | 2g PROTEIN | 12g CARB | 7g TOTAL FAT | 3g SAT FAT | 4g MONO FAT | 0g POLY FAT | 20mg CHOL | 25mg SODIUM | 1g FIBER

cocoa walnut butter cookies

YIELDS ABOUT 30 COOKIES

4½ oz. (1 cup) unbleached all-purpose flour

½ cup unsweetened natural or Dutch-processed cocoa powder

½ tsp. baking soda

¼ tsp. baking powder

¼ tsp. table salt

3 oz. (6 Tbs.) unsalted butter, softened at room temperature

1 oz. (2 Tbs.) vegetable shortening

½ cup packed brown sugar, sifted free of lumps

½ cup granulated sugar

1 large egg

1 tsp. pure vanilla extract

About 4 oz. (¾ cup) chopped walnuts

Underbake these brownie-like cookies slightly and you'll get cookies that are crisp outside and chewy inside.

1. Position racks in the upper and lower thirds of the oven and heat it to 350°F. Line two baking sheets with parchment or foil. In a medium bowl, combine the flour, cocoa, baking soda, baking powder, and salt. Mix thoroughly with a wire whisk. Set aside.

2. Using a stand mixer fitted with the paddle attachment (or in a large bowl with a hand mixer), beat the butter and shortening on medium speed until creamy. Add the sugars, beating until well combined. Beat in the egg and vanilla. Turn the mixer to low speed and mix in the flour mixture just until incorporated. Mix in the nuts.

3. Drop heaping teaspoonfuls of batter about 1½ inches apart on the prepared baking sheets. Bake for 10 to 12 minutes. (After 5 minutes, swap the position of the baking sheets and rotate them 180 degrees for even baking.) The cookies will puff up and then settle down slightly when done. With a metal spatula, transfer the cookies to a rack to cool completely. —*Alice Medrich*

PER COOKIE: 100 CALORIES | 1g PROTEIN | 12g CARB | 5g TOTAL FAT | 2g SAT FAT | 2g MONO FAT | 1g POLY FAT | 15mg CHOL | 45mg SODIUM | 1g FIBER

chocolate-nut wafers

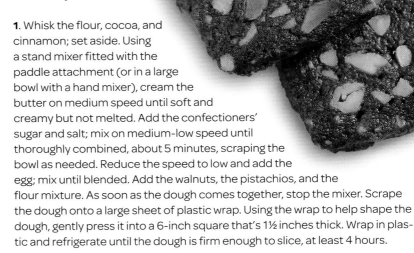

YIELDS ABOUT 12 DOZEN COOKIES

- **9** oz. (2 cups) unbleached all-purpose flour
- **2** oz. (½ cup) unsweetened natural (not Dutch-processed) cocoa powder
- **½** tsp. ground cinnamon
- **½** lb. (1 cup) unsalted butter, softened at room temperature
- **10** oz. (2⅔ cups) confectioners' sugar
- **¾** tsp. table salt
- **1** large egg, at room temperature
- **8** oz. (scant 2 cups) chopped walnuts
- **4** oz. (scant 1 cup) chopped pistachios

Aside from great flavor, pistachios add eye-catching color to these chocolatey cookies.

1. Whisk the flour, cocoa, and cinnamon; set aside. Using a stand mixer fitted with the paddle attachment (or in a large bowl with a hand mixer), cream the butter on medium speed until soft and creamy but not melted. Add the confectioners' sugar and salt; mix on medium-low speed until thoroughly combined, about 5 minutes, scraping the bowl as needed. Reduce the speed to low and add the egg; mix until blended. Add the walnuts, the pistachios, and the flour mixture. As soon as the dough comes together, stop the mixer. Scrape the dough onto a large sheet of plastic wrap. Using the wrap to help shape the dough, gently press it into a 6-inch square that's 1½ inches thick. Wrap in plastic and refrigerate until the dough is firm enough to slice, at least 4 hours.

2. Position a rack in the center of the oven and heat the oven to 400°F. Line a baking sheet with parchment. Unwrap the dough, trim the edges, and slice the square into four 1½-inch square logs. With a sharp knife, slice each log into square cookies between ⅛ and ¼ inch thick. Lay the squares ½ inch apart on the prepared baking sheet. Bake one sheet at a time until the tops look dry and the nuts look golden, 8 to 10 minutes, rotating the sheet halfway through for even baking. Let the cookies sit on the baking sheet until cool enough to handle (about 10 minutes) and then transfer them to a rack to cool completely. Repeat with the remaining dough. —*Joanne Chang*

PER COOKIE: 35 CALORIES | 1g PROTEIN | 4g CARB | 2.5g TOTAL FAT | 1g SAT FAT | 1g MONO FAT | 0.5g POLY FAT | 5mg CHOL | 15mg SODIUM | 0g FIBER

rosemary and pine nut cookies

YIELDS ABOUT 30 COOKIES

- **6¾** oz. (1½ cups) unbleached all-purpose flour
- **½** tsp. baking soda
- **¼** tsp. table salt
- **¾** cup granulated sugar
- **1½** tsp. chopped fresh rosemary
- **½** cup pine nuts, toasted
- **6** oz. (¾ cup) unsalted butter, softened at room temperature
- **1** large egg
- **½** tsp. pure vanilla extract

Make Ahead

These cookies can be stored in an airtight container for up to 5 days.

These buttery crisps are like shortbread cookies with Italian flair. The fresh rosemary adds a wonderful fragrance and flavor, while the toasted pine nuts both enrich the cookie dough and serve as a pretty decoration on top.

1. In a medium bowl, combine the flour, baking soda, and salt until well blended, and set aside. In a food processor, pulse the sugar and rosemary until the rosemary is finely chopped. Transfer to a stand mixer fitted with the paddle attachment. Put all but 2 Tbs. of the pine nuts in the food processor and process until finely chopped.

2. Add the butter to the sugar mixture and beat on medium speed until fluffy, about 2 minutes. Reduce the speed to low and add the egg and vanilla; beat until thoroughly combined. Add the chopped pine nuts and then the flour mixture and mix until the dough absorbs the flour and starts to come together. Turn the dough out onto a large piece of plastic and shape it into a log about 2 inches thick and 11 inches long. Refrigerate until firm, 1 to 2 hours.

3. Position a rack in the center of the oven and heat the oven to 350°F. Cut the dough into disks between ¼ and ½ inch thick (about 30 cookies). Sprinkle the cookies with the whole pine nuts and gently press in place so they adhere. Arrange on three baking sheets, spaced about 1½ inches apart.

4. Bake the cookies one sheet at a time until they're set and the sides are lightly brown, 10 to 12 minutes. Let cool on the sheet for 10 minutes. Using a spatula, transfer the cookies to a rack and let cool to room temperature, about 1 hour. —*Tony Rosenfeld*

PER COOKIE: 100 CALORIES | 1g PROTEIN | 10g CARB | 6g TOTAL FAT | 3g SAT FAT | 1.5g MONO FAT | 1g POLY FAT | 20mg CHOL | 45mg SODIUM | 0g FIBER

3 Ways to Toast Pine Nuts

Heat releases and intensifies the rich flavor of pine nuts, which is why many recipes call for toasted nuts. There are three ways to go about toasting the nuts, each with its own pros and cons:

IN THE OVEN
Spread the nuts on a baking sheet and bake at 375°F, stirring occasionally, until golden brown, 5 to 10 minutes.

Pro: The color of oven-toasted nuts is evenly golden.

Con: You have to heat the oven. We tend to use this method only if we're heating the oven for other reasons, too.

IN A TOASTER OVEN
Spread the nuts on the baking sheet that came with the toaster oven and bake at 325°F, stirring frequently, until golden brown, 3 to 5 minutes.

Pro: Produces results similar to those from a conventional oven, but a toaster oven heats up much faster and is more energy efficient.

Con: Closer proximity to the heating elements in a toaster oven increases the risk of burning the nuts, hence the need for more frequent stirring and a lower baking temperature.

IN A SKILLET
Put the nuts in a dry skillet and cook over medium-low heat, stirring frequently, until golden in spots, about 3 minutes.

Pro: The quickest and most convenient method.

Con: The nuts develop spotty, uneven color and burn more easily than with the two oven methods.

pine nut and chocolate caramel bars

YIELDS 24 BARS

FOR THE CRUST

½	lb. (1 cup) unsalted butter, softened at room temperature, cut into 6 pieces
⅔	cup granulated sugar
1	Tbs. finely grated orange zest
¼	tsp. kosher salt
11¼	oz. (2½ cups) unbleached all-purpose flour
5	oz. bittersweet chocolate, chopped

FOR THE TOPPING

1¼	cups granulated sugar
¾	cup heavy cream
1½	oz. (3 Tbs.) unsalted butter, cut into 6 pieces
¼	tsp. kosher salt
1½	cups pine nuts

Pine nuts are delicious but spoil quickly. Taste a few before using; if they're bitter, it's time to toss them and buy a fresh batch.

MAKE THE CRUST

1. Position a rack in the center of the oven and heat the oven to 350°F. Line a straight-sided 13x9-inch metal baking pan with a large piece of heavy-duty foil, leaving a 2-inch overhang on two sides.

2. Using a stand mixer fitted with the paddle attachment (or in a large bowl with a hand mixer), beat the butter, sugar, orange zest, and salt on medium-high speed until light and fluffy, 1 to 3 minutes. Scrape the bowl. On low speed, mix in the flour until the dough is uniformly sandy, 1 to 2 minutes. Transfer the dough to the prepared pan and press evenly into the bottom. Bake until lightly golden, about 20 minutes. Let the crust cool completely on a wire rack.

3. Melt the chocolate in a medium heatproof bowl set in a skillet of barely simmering water, stirring frequently, until smooth (be careful not to get any water in the chocolate). With a small offset spatula, spread all but about 2 Tbs. of the melted chocolate evenly over the cooled crust. Return the bowl with the remaining chocolate to the skillet of warm water and set aside off the heat to keep warm.

MAKE THE TOPPING

Put 3 Tbs. water in a heavy-duty 3-quart saucepan. Pour the sugar in the center of the pan and pat it down with a spatula just until evenly moistened. Cook over medium-high heat without stirring until the syrup turns amber, 6 to 8 minutes; swirl the pan as the sugar caramelizes to help it cook evenly. Slowly whisk in the cream (be careful—it will bubble vigorously and produce a lot of steam). Whisk in the butter and salt and boil until the butter is combined, 1 minute more.

ASSEMBLE THE BARS

Pour the caramel evenly over the crust. Sprinkle the pine nuts over the caramel. Bake until the caramel is bubbling all over and jiggles only slightly in the center when the pan is nudged, 24 to 26 minutes. If necessary, reheat the remaining chocolate until fluid. With a spoon, drizzle the chocolate over the top. Let cool completely before cutting into squares.
—*Samantha Seneviratne*

PER BAR: 310 CALORIES | 3g PROTEIN | 31g CARB | 20g TOTAL FAT | 9g SAT FAT | 5g MONO FAT | 3.5g POLY FAT | 35mg CHOL | 35mg SODIUM | 1g FIBER

almond-pistachio macaroons

YIELDS 32 MACAROONS

- **18 oz. (2 cups) almond paste**
- **7 oz. (1 cup) granulated sugar**
- **7 oz. (2 cups) sifted confectioners' sugar**
- **½ cup (3 to 4 large) egg whites**
- **2 tsp. rose water or pure vanilla extract**
- **⅛ tsp. table salt**
- **4 oz. (1 cup) unsalted, undyed chopped pistachios**

These flourless macaroons stay fresher longer than cookies made with flour. In a tin or wrapped in plastic, they remain delicious for weeks.

1. Rip the almond paste into pieces (about ¼ cup each) and put them in the bowl of a heavy-duty mixer fitted with a paddle. (Don't use a food processor; the batter is too heavy.) Add the granulated sugar. Quickly turn the mixer on and off a few times to draw the sugar into the almond paste so it doesn't fly out of the bowl. Work on a low speed until the mixture forms coarse, even crumbs. Don't allow the mixture to go beyond this point to a paste, because it will be difficult to incorporate the confectioners' sugar. Turn off the mixer and add the confectioners' sugar. Mix on a low speed for 1 minute and then on medium speed for 1 to 2 minutes until the mixture is very smooth and begins to compact itself around the sides of the bowl or when pinched. Scrape the sides and bottom of the bowl.

2. Add the egg whites, rose water or vanilla, and salt. Mix on a medium speed until combined, but still moist and tacky. Scrape the sides and bottom of the bowl and paddle. Turn the mixer to medium-high speed until the mixture is light in texture and almost white in color, 2 minutes or longer. Reduce to a low speed, add half of the pistachios, and mix until combined.

3. Position a rack in the center of the oven and heat the oven to 325°F. Line two or three cookie sheets with parchment. Use a #40 (1½-inch) ice cream scoop to portion the batter onto the prepared sheets, leaving room between one another. (No scoop? Use a heaping tablespoon instead.) Sprinkle each macaroon with some of the remaining pistachios and press down slightly so that the nuts stick. Some will fall off, but you can save them after baking and use them for the next batch, or have a toasted pistachio treat.

4. Bake the macaroons one sheet at a time until they're puffed and light and still feel a little soft but not wet, 25 to 28 minutes. The bottoms should be very light brown, not dark. Transfer the sheet to a rack and let the macaroons cool completely before moving. Carefully peel the macaroons from the parchment and store at room temperature in an airtight container. —*Jane Spector Davis*

What is Almond Paste?

Almond paste, often mistaken for marzipan, is a firm paste of almonds and sugar finely ground between heavy-duty rollers. Almond paste is often used in cake batters, pastry fillings, or mixed with hot sugar syrup to be shaped into marzipan.

biscotti & shortbread

biscotti rustica

FOR THE DOUGH

- ½ cup dried currants
- ½ cup golden raisins
- 2 Tbs. brandy
- Finely grated zest of 1 lemon (to yield about 1 Tbs.)
- ½ oz. (1 Tbs.) crystallized ginger, chopped
- 15¾ oz. (3½ cups) unbleached all-purpose flour; more as needed
- 2 cups granulated sugar
- ¼ cup yellow cornmeal
- 1 Tbs. baking powder
- ¼ tsp. kosher salt
- 3 large eggs
- 3 large egg yolks
- 1 tsp. pure vanilla extract
- ¾ cup pine nuts, toasted until golden

FOR THE GLAZE

- 1 egg white, lightly beaten
- 1 Tbs. turbinado sugar (also sold as Sugar in the Raw in supermarkets)

vary the size and yield as you please

The width of a log of biscotti dough will determine the length of your finished biscotti, and you can vary this according to your preference. (The thinner the slices, the bigger the yield, of course.) You can cut them as thin as ¼ inch and reduce the baking time slightly.

Biscotti start as logs of dough that get baked until they're firm. After the first bake, the logs get sliced into cookies, which are then baked a second time. If stored airtight, the biscotti will keep for about 2 weeks.

MIX THE DOUGH

In a small bowl, combine the currants, raisins, brandy, lemon zest, and ginger and let stand for 20 minutes. Using a stand mixer fitted with the paddle attachment (or in a large bowl with a hand mixer), combine the flour, granulated sugar, cornmeal, baking powder, and salt. In a small bowl, whisk the eggs, egg yolks, and vanilla. With the mixer on low speed, add the egg mixture to the dry ingredients until just combined and the dough looks crumbly. Take care not to overmix. Add the fruit mixture and the pine nuts, mixing just until the dough comes together (bring the dough together with your hands if it's a bit stiff). Let the dough rest for 15 to 30 minutes before shaping.

SHAPE THE DOUGH AND DO THE INITIAL BAKING

Position racks in the center and upper third of the oven and heat the oven to 350°F. Line a large baking sheet with parchment. Cut the dough in half. Using as little flour as possible on the work surface, roll each half into a log that's 16 inches long and 2 inches wide, working out the air pockets as you go. (If you're working ahead, wrap the logs in plastic and refrigerate them overnight). Transfer the logs to the baking sheet, setting them about 3 inches apart and patting the sides to smooth and straighten. Brush the tops and sides with the beaten egg white and sprinkle with the turbinado sugar. Bake on the center rack until golden brown and firm in the center, 30 to 35 minutes, rotating the sheet to ensure even baking. Set the sheet on a rack until the logs are cool enough to handle and so the dough won't compress when you cut it, about 30 minutes.

SLICE THE BAKED LOAF AND BAKE A SECOND TIME

Reduce the oven temperature to 300°F. Line two large baking sheets with parchment. With a serrated knife, saw the logs into ½-inch-thick slices, cutting on the diagonal so each slice is about 6 inches long. Lay the slices flat on the baking sheets. Bake for about 15 minutes, rotating the sheets and switching their positions as needed for even baking. Turn the biscotti over. Bake until both sides are a rich golden brown, another 10 to 15 minutes. Set the baking sheets on racks, letting the cookies cool and crisp completely on the sheets.
—*Kathleen Weber*

PER COOKIE: 140 CALORIES | 3g PROTEIN | 26g CARB | 3g TOTAL FAT | 0g SAT FAT | 1g MONO FAT | 1g POLY FAT | 35mg CHOL | 50mg SODIUM | 1g FIBER

honey shortbread

YIELDS 12 COOKIES

Nonstick cooking spray

7½ oz. (1⅔ cups) unbleached all-purpose flour

⅓ cup granulated sugar

6 oz. (¾ cup) cold unsalted butter, cut into 1-inch pieces

3 Tbs. honey

1 tsp. kosher salt

You'll need a tart pan with a removable bottom for this recipe. The main difference between a tart pan and a pie pan is the shape and depth of the sides. A tart pan has straight sides (some fluted, some not) that turn out neat, more "professional" looking pastries than slope-sided pie pans. Most tart pans are made of metal and have a removable bottom, allowing you to slip off the outer ring without marring the beautiful crust.

Make Ahead

These cookies will keep in an airtight container at room temperature for 1 week.

1. Spray a 9½-inch tart pan with removable bottom with cooking spray.

2. In a food processor, briefly pulse the flour and sugar. Add the butter and pulse until incorporated and the mixture is sandy and uniform. Press the dough evenly into the prepared pan with your fingers. There will be some loose crumbs around the edges, but most of the dough should be solid and compact. Refrigerate until chilled, at least 30 minutes.

3. Position a rack in the center of the oven and heat the oven to 350°F. Using the tines of a fork, prick the dough evenly all over. Bake the shortbread until golden in the center, 40 to 45 minutes.

4. Heat the honey in the microwave until warm and liquid but not boiling, about 10 seconds. Pour the honey over the shortbread and spread with a pastry brush over the entire surface. Sprinkle the salt evenly over the honey. Return the pan to the oven and bake for 3 minutes more.

5. Transfer the pan to a rack and let the shortbread cool slightly, about 15 minutes. While still warm, remove the tart pan ring and cut the shortbread into 12 wedges with a sharp knife. Let cool completely before serving or storing.
—*David Crofton*

PER COOKIE: 200 CALORIES | 2g PROTEIN | 23g CARB | 12g TOTAL FAT | 7g SAT FAT | 3g MONO FAT | 0.5g POLY FAT | 30mg CHOL | 95mg SODIUM | 0g FIBER

pistachio-cranberry biscotti straws

YIELDS ABOUT 2½ DOZEN
BISCOTTI

5¾ oz. (1¼ cups) unbleached
all-purpose flour

½ cup granulated sugar

1 tsp. baking powder

¼ tsp. table salt

¾ cup (3½ oz.) unsalted
pistachio nuts, shelled

½ cup (2½ oz.) sweetened
dried cranberries

1 large egg

1 large egg white

1 Tbs. finely grated orange zest
(from about 2 oranges)

1 Tbs. fresh orange juice

¾ tsp. pure vanilla extract

Biscotti are great cookie candidates for packing—they're sturdy enough to travel well and arrive at their destination as delicious and fragrant as the day you baked them.

1. Position a rack in the center of the oven and heat the oven to 325°F. Line a large cookie sheet with parchment or a nonstick baking liner.

2. Using a stand mixer fitted with the paddle attachment (or in a large bowl with a hand mixer), mix the flour, sugar, baking powder, and salt on low speed until well blended. On low speed (or with a wooden spoon if mixing by hand), briefly mix in the nuts and cranberries.

3. In a small bowl or a 1-cup glass measure, whisk together the egg, egg white, orange zest, orange juice, and vanilla. With the mixer on low speed, slowly pour in the egg mixture (or mix in with the spoon). Continue mixing until well blended and a sticky, moist dough forms, 1 to 2 minutes. Dump the dough onto the prepared cookie sheet. Using slightly damp hands, shape the dough into a 7x11½-inch rectangle. Press and shape the dough as evenly as possible.

4. Bake until the rectangle is golden brown on top and slightly darker brown around the edges, about 25 minutes. Transfer the cookie sheet to a rack to cool until it can be easily handled, about 10 minutes.

5. Transfer the biscotti to a cutting board; use a spatula to loosen it from the parchment if necessary. Using a serrated knife, cut the biscotti crosswise into slices about ⅓ inch thick. (Use a gentle sawing motion to break through the crust. After that, a firm push down on the knife is all that's needed.) Discard the parchment, return the slices to the cookie sheet, and arrange them with a cut side down. (It's all right if they touch because they don't spread.)

6. Bake until the biscotti are light golden brown and feel dry, about 14 minutes. Transfer the baking sheet to a rack and let the biscotti cool completely; they'll crisp as they cool. —*Abigail Johnson Dodge*

PER STRAW: 60 CALORIES | 2g PROTEIN | 10g CARB | 1.5g TOTAL FAT | 0g SAT FAT | 1g MONO FAT | 0g POLY FAT | 5mg CHOL | 35mg SODIUM | 1g FIBER

Make Ahead

The cooled biscotti can be frozen for up to 6 weeks or stored at room temperature for up to 3 weeks, layered between sheets of parchment or waxed paper in an airtight container.

nutty chocolate shortbread wedges

YIELDS 12 OR 16 WEDGES

FOR THE SHORTBREAD

- 4 oz. (½ cup) unsalted butter, softened at room temperature; more for the pan
- ½ cup granulated sugar
- ¾ oz. (¼ cup) unsweetened cocoa powder, preferably Dutch-processed
- ¼ tsp. table salt
- 1 large egg yolk
- ½ tsp. pure vanilla extract
- 4½ oz. (1 cup) unbleached all-purpose flour

FOR THE GLAZE

- 3 oz. bittersweet or semisweet chocolate, coarsely chopped
- 1 oz. (2 Tbs.) unsalted butter, cut into two pieces
- 2 oz. (½ cup) coarsely chopped pecans or walnuts, toasted and cooled, or chopped pistachios

This is a nontraditional shortbread because it contains an egg yolk, which gives the shortbread a softer, less sandy texture. Use pistachios, pecans, or walnuts—whichever is your favorite—for these nutty cookies.

MAKE THE SHORTBREAD

1. Position a rack in the center of the oven and heat the oven to 350°F. Lightly butter the bottom and sides of a 9½-inch fluted tart pan with a removable bottom.

2. In a medium bowl, combine the butter, sugar, cocoa, and salt. Beat with an electric mixer on medium speed until well blended. Scrape the bowl. Add the egg yolk and vanilla and continue beating on medium speed until just combined. Add the flour and mix on low speed, scraping the bowl as needed, until the dough begins to clump together, about 1 minute. Scrape the dough into the prepared pan, scattering the pieces of dough evenly. Using your fingertips (lightly floured, if necessary), pat the dough onto the bottom (not up the sides) of the prepared pan to create an even layer. Bake until the top no longer looks wet and the dough just barely begins to pull away slightly from the sides of the pan, about 25 minutes.

SHORTLY BEFORE THE SHORTBREAD IS DONE, MAKE THE GLAZE

Melt the chocolate and butter on the stove or in a microwave. Stir until smooth. When the shortbread is done, transfer the pan to a rack. Pour the warm glaze over the shortbread and, using an offset spatula, spread the glaze evenly to within ½ inch of the edge. Scatter the nuts evenly over the glaze and gently press them in. Let cool completely until the glaze is set. Remove the shortbread from the tart pan and cut it into 12 or 16 wedges. Serve at room temperature. *—Abigail Johnson Dodge*

PER COOKIE, BASED ON 16 SERVINGS: 180 CALORIES | 2g PROTEIN | 16g CARB | 13g TOTAL FAT | 6g SAT FAT | 4g MONO FAT | 1.5g POLY FAT | 30mg CHOL | 40mg SODIUM | 1g FIBER

gingerbread biscotti

YIELDS ABOUT 24 BISCOTTI

- **10** oz. (2¼ cups) unbleached all-purpose flour; more as needed
- **1¼** cups packed dark brown sugar
- **2** tsp. ground ginger
- **1¼** tsp. baking powder
- **1** tsp. ground cinnamon
- **½** tsp. table salt
- **¼** tsp. ground nutmeg
- **¼** tsp. baking soda
- **4** oz. (1 cup) pecans, coarsely chopped
- **4** oz. (½ cup) lightly packed dried apricots, coarsely chopped
- **¼** cup molasses
- **2** large eggs
- **2** tsp. finely grated orange zest (from about 1 medium navel orange)

Biscotti are very forgiving, and you can bake these to your taste: chewy, crunchy, or somewhere in between. In this recipe, nutmeg and cinnamon bring out the best of dried ginger's warm, earthy flavor.

1. Position a rack in the center of the oven and heat the oven to 350°F. Line a large cookie sheet with parchment.

2. In a stand mixer fitted with the paddle attachment, combine the flour, brown sugar, ginger, baking powder, cinnamon, salt, nutmeg, and baking soda on medium-low speed until well blended. On low speed, briefly mix in the pecans and apricots. In a measuring cup, lightly whisk the molasses, eggs, and orange zest. With the mixer on low, slowly pour in the egg mixture. Continue mixing until the dough is well blended and comes together in large, moist clumps, 1 to 2 minutes.

3. Dump the dough onto an unfloured work surface. Divide into two equal piles (about 1 lb. each). Shape each pile into a log that's 10 inches long and about 1½ inches in diameter, lightly flouring your hands as needed (the dough is a bit sticky).

4. Position the logs on the lined cookie sheet about 4 inches apart. Bake until the tops are cracked and spring back slightly when gently pressed, 30 to 35 minutes. Transfer the sheet to a rack and let cool until the logs are cool enough to handle, about 10 minutes.

5. Carefully peel the biscotti logs from the parchment and transfer to a cutting board. Using a serrated knife, saw each log into diagonal slices ¾ inch wide. Return the slices to the cookie sheet (no need for fresh parchment) and arrange them cut side down. It's all right if they touch because they won't spread.

6. Bake until the biscotti are dried to your taste, about 10 minutes (for slightly moist and chewy) to 20 minutes (for super-dry and crunchy). Put the cookie sheet on a rack and let the biscotti cool completely. The biscotti will still give slightly when pressed, but will harden as they cool. When cool, store in airtight containers. —*Abigail Johnson Dodge*

PER COOKIE, BASED ON 24 SERVINGS: 150 CALORIES | 2g PROTEIN | 26g CARB | 4g TOTAL FAT | 0g SAT FAT | 2g MONO FAT | 1g POLY FAT | 20mg CHOL | 95mg SODIUM | 1g FIBER

triple-orange pecan biscotti

YIELDS ABOUT 60 BISCOTTI

12 oz. (2⅔ cups) unbleached all-purpose flour; more as needed

1½ cups granulated sugar

2 tsp. baking powder

¾ tsp. table salt

Finely grated zest of 2 oranges (to yield a scant ¼ cup lightly packed)

4½ oz. (1 cup) coarsely chopped pecans

3 large eggs, at room temperature

5 Tbs. olive oil

2 Tbs. fresh orange juice

1 Tbs. orange liqueur, such as Grand Marnier®

Orange zest, juice, and liqueur flavor these cookies. They smell divine as they bake and are delicious dunked into a cup of hot tea.

1. Position racks in the center and upper third of the oven and heat the oven to 350°F. Line two large baking sheets with parchment.

2. In a large bowl, whisk the flour with the sugar, baking powder, and salt to combine. Put a bit of the flour mixture in a small bowl, add the orange zest, and rub the zest into the flour to keep it from clumping. Stir the coated zest and the pecans into the rest of the flour mixture.

3. In a small bowl, whisk the eggs with the olive oil, orange juice, and liqueur until well blended. Pour into the center of the flour mixture. Stir with a wooden spoon until the dough is blended. The dough will be very sticky.

4. Dump the dough onto a heavily floured work surface and portion into six equal pieces. Roll each piece into a log that's 12 inches long, dusting with flour along the way to keep the dough from sticking. Set the logs about 3 inches apart on the prepared baking sheets and then press gently to flatten each log so that it's 1½ to 2 inches wide.

5. Bake until the logs are golden and the tops are fairly firm near the center, 22 to 25 minutes, rotating the sheets and switching their positions after 10 minutes to ensure even baking. Set the sheets on racks until the logs are cool enough to handle, 20 to 30 minutes. Leave the oven set to 350°F.

6. Transfer the logs to a cutting board and, using a serrated knife, saw them on a sharp diagonal into slices ½ inch thick. Arrange the slices on the baking sheets, laying them flat with a cut side down. Return the baking sheets to the oven and bake the biscotti for about 6 minutes. Turn the biscotti over, rotate the baking sheets and switch their positions, and bake until the biscotti are golden, another 8 to 10 minutes. Let cool on the sheets on racks for 5 minutes before transferring them to racks to cool completely (the biscotti won't get crisp until then). Store at room temperature or freeze in an airtight container, separating the cookie layers with waxed paper. *—Susan Betz*

dried cherry and almond biscotti with white chocolate

YIELDS ABOUT 3 DOZEN BISCOTTI

- 11¼ oz. (2½ cups) unbleached all-purpose flour; more as needed
- 1 cup granulated sugar
- 1¾ tsp. baking powder
- ¾ tsp. table salt
- 9 oz. (1¾ cups) dried cherries
- 3 oz. (¾ cup) slivered almonds, toasted
- 3 large eggs
- 3 Tbs. kirsch or brandy
- ½ tsp. pure almond extract
- 14 to 16 oz. white chocolate, chopped

Cherries jubilee—sweet cherries in a spiked syrup over vanilla ice cream—is reinterpreted as biscotti, with dried cherries, toasted almonds, and white chocolate.

1. Position a rack in the center of the oven and heat the oven to 350°F. Line a large cookie sheet with parchment or a nonstick baking liner.

2. In a stand mixer fitted with the paddle attachment, combine the flour, sugar, baking powder, and salt on medium-low speed until well blended. On low speed, mix in the cherries and almonds. In a small bowl, whisk the eggs, kirsch, and almond extract. Slowly pour in the egg mixture. Mix until the dough comes together in large, moist clumps, about 1 minute.

3. Turn the dough out onto a lightly floured surface and knead to incorporate any remaining dry ingredients. Divide into two equal piles. Shape each pile into a log 10 inches long and about 4 inches wide, lightly flouring your hands as needed (the dough will be sticky).

4. Position the logs on the cookie sheet about 4 inches apart. Bake until the tops are cracked and spring back slightly when pressed, 32 to 36 minutes. Transfer the sheet to a rack and leave until the logs are cool enough to handle, about 10 minutes. Reduce the oven temperature to 300°F.

5. Carefully peel the logs from the parchment and transfer to a cutting board. Using a serrated knife, cut each log on a sharp angle into ½-inch-thick slices. Return the slices to the cookie sheet and arrange them cut side down. It's fine if they touch because they won't spread.

6. Bake until the biscotti are dried to your taste, 10 minutes (for slightly moist) to 20 minutes (for super-dry and crunchy), turning them over halfway through baking. Transfer the cookie sheet to a rack and let the biscotti cool completely. They will still give slightly when pressed but will harden as they cool.

7. When the biscotti are cool, melt the white chocolate in a microwave or in a heatproof bowl set in a skillet of barely simmering water. Dip one end of each biscotti in the chocolate and place on a baking sheet lined with fresh parchment until set, about 30 minutes.

—Abigail Johnson Dodge

PER COOKIE: 160 CALORIES | 3g PROTEIN | 23g CARB | 6g TOTAL FAT | 2.5g SAT FAT | 1g MONO FAT | 0g POLY FAT | 20mg CHOL | 85mg SODIUM | 1g FIBER

almond biscotti

YIELDS ABOUT 3 DOZEN
BISCOTTI

7 oz. (1⅓ cups) whole almonds, skin on

12¼ oz. (2¾ cups) unbleached all-purpose flour; more as needed

1⅔ cups granulated sugar

½ tsp. table salt

1 tsp. baking powder

1 tsp. aniseed

Finely grated zest of 1 lemon, 1 lime, and 1 orange

3 large eggs

3 egg yolks

1 tsp. pure vanilla extract

This basic almond biscotti is easily varied; see the sidebar below for ideas.

1. Position racks in the center and upper third of the oven and heat the oven to 350°F. Toast the almonds on a baking sheet for 10 to 15 minutes, until they emit a nutty aroma but haven't turned dark brown inside. Let cool.

2. Using a stand mixer fitted with the paddle attachment (or in a large bowl with a hand mixer), combine the flour, sugar, salt, baking powder, aniseed, and grated zests on medium-low speed. In a separate bowl, lightly beat together the eggs, egg yolks, and vanilla extract with a whisk. With the mixer running, pour the egg mixture into the mixing bowl. When the egg mixture is almost completely incorporated, reduce the speed to low, add the almonds and mix just until the dough comes together. Do not overmix.

3. Dump the dough on a lightly floured surface. Portion the dough into thirds and, with floured hands, roll each piece into a log about 10 inches long and 2 inches in diameter. Set the logs 4 inches apart on parchment-lined baking sheets.

4. Bake the logs at 350°F for about 45 minutes, until they're light brown but still soft. Remove the baking sheet from the oven and reduce the oven temperature to 300°F. Let the logs cool on the baking sheet for at least 10 minutes before slicing. Cut the logs on a slight diagonal into ¾-inch-thick biscotti. Arrange the biscotti flat on the baking sheet and dry them in the oven for 10 to 15 minutes, until the biscotti offer resistance when pressed, but the cut side hasn't begun to darken. Transfer the biscotti to a rack to cool. Store them at room temperature in airtight containers, or wrap them well and put them in the freezer. —*Emily Luchetti*

Make Your Own Biscotti Variations

There are endless varieties of biscotti. Changing a couple of ingredients can change the whole character of the cookie. For example, the amount and type of citrus zest (orange, lemon, or lime) can be altered, and the type of nuts can be changed as well. Macadamia nuts, almonds, and hazelnuts all taste great in biscotti, and each nut gives a very different taste. Don't be stingy with the nuts; they're one of the key flavors in biscotti. Too many nuts, however, can cause problems. You need more dough than nuts or the biscotti won't hold together. As a rule, use about 2½ ounces (about ½ cup) of nuts for every cup of flour. Always toast nuts first to keep them from getting soggy when combined with the dough, and also to bring out their flavor. Start with whole nuts because many of them get cut when the biscotti are sliced.

You can play with spices, too. Aniseed is a traditional choice for biscotti; cinnamon and ginger are other popular additions. Keep in mind the strength of the spice when adding it to a recipe. For example, ginger is stronger than cinnamon and should be added in smaller quantities. Nuts and spices can be teamed up to make interesting and varied combinations. Chopped dried fruit is a good addition to biscotti, adding a slightly chewy texture as well as fruit flavor. Finally, biscotti can be coated in dark, milk, or white chocolate.

classic shortbread cookies

YIELDS ABOUT 4 DOZEN
1½X2-INCH BARS

½ **lb. (1 cup) cold unsalted butter, cut into ½-inch pieces**

½ **cup granulated sugar**

½ **tsp. table salt**

10 **oz. (2¼ cups) unbleached all-purpose flour; more as needed**

Make Ahead

The cookies stay fresh for 10 to 14 days at room temperature, or for at least a month when frozen. If you're going to freeze them, be sure to wrap them well in plastic and store them in an airtight container.

Shortbread cookies are rich and buttery, sturdy, and keep for a couple of weeks. They're also among the simplest cookies to make. All you need are four ingredients: butter, sugar, flour, and salt.

1. Using a stand mixer fitted with the paddle attachment (or in a large bowl with a hand mixer), combine the butter, sugar, and salt on low speed until the butter combines with the sugar but isn't perfectly smooth, 1 to 2 minutes. Add the flour and mix on low speed, scraping the bowl frequently, until the dough has just about pulled together, about 3 minutes; don't overmix.

2. On a lightly floured surface, roll the dough to about ¼ inch thick. Aim for a uniform thickness to ensure even baking.

3. Cut the dough into bars or squares with a sharp knife or, using cookie cutters, cut out shapes as close to one another as possible. Press the scraps together, roll them out, and cut out more cookies. If the dough becomes sticky, refrigerate it briefly. Arrange the cookies on two parchment-lined baking sheets and refrigerate until chilled, at least 20 minutes.

4. Position racks in the upper and lower thirds of the oven and heat the oven to 300°F. Bake the cookies until golden on the bottom and edges and pale to golden on top, 30 minutes to 1 hour. (After 15 minutes, swap the position of the baking sheets and rotate them 180 degrees for even baking.) If the cookies are done before 30 minutes, reduce the oven temperature to 275°F for the remaining batches; if they take longer than 1 hour, increase the temperature to 325°F. *—Carolyn Weil*

Secrets to Shortbread Success

Use cold butter and don't overmix the dough. Start with butter that's refrigerator-cold to prevent the dough from warming up too fast, which would make it greasy and difficult to roll. If the dough does get soft or sticky as you're rolling or cutting it, put it in the refrigerator for 10 or 15 minutes to chill the butter.

When you beat the butter and sugar, only mix until combined. The butter should get smoother and lose its chunkiness, but it shouldn't look light or fluffy. Similarly, when you add the flour, beat until the dough just comes together. It's fully mixed when the small pebbles of dough combine and clump around the beater.

Be space-efficient when cutting out shapes. Using a cookie cutter or a knife, cut shapes as close to one another as possible to minimize scraps. You can press the scraps together and reroll them, but after the third round of rolling, the cookies come out a bit tougher.

Keep your eye on the cookies, not on the clock. These cookies get their sweet flavor from a low oven temperature (300°F) and a long baking time, which produce a complex caramelization of sugar and butter. How much they caramelize is up to you. Some people like these cookies pale on top but golden on the edges and bottom; others bake them until the tops have also taken on a light golden color. Depending on how golden you want them and on the size and thickness of the cookies, the baking time can range from 30 minutes to an hour. Keep a close eye on the first batch, occasionally lifting up a cookie to check the color of the bottom.

brown sugar and oatmeal shortbread cookies

YIELDS ABOUT 3 DOZEN 3-INCH COOKIES

- ½ lb. (1 cup) cold unsalted butter, cut into ½-inch pieces
- ½ cup packed light or dark brown sugar
- ¼ tsp. table salt
- 10 oz. (2¼ cups) unbleached all-purpose flour; more as needed
- ½ cup quick-cooking oats

The darker the brown sugar, the deeper the cookies' flavor.

1. Using a stand mixer fitted with the paddle attachment (or in a large bowl with a hand mixer), combine the butter, sugar, and salt on low speed until the butter combines with the sugar but isn't perfectly smooth, 1 to 2 minutes. Add the flour and oats and mix on low speed, scraping the bowl frequently, until the dough has just about pulled together, about 3 minutes; don't overmix.

2. On a lightly floured surface, roll the dough to about ¼ inch thick. Aim for a uniform thickness to ensure even baking.

3. Cut the dough into bars or squares with a sharp knife or, using cookie cutters, cut out shapes as close to one another as possible. Press the scraps together, roll them out, and cut out more cookies. If the dough becomes sticky, refrigerate it briefly. Arrange the cookies on two parchment-lined baking sheets and refrigerate until chilled, at least 20 minutes.

4. Position racks in the upper and lower thirds of the oven and heat the oven to 300°F. Bake the cookies until golden on the bottom and edges and pale to golden on top, 30 minutes to 1 hour. (After 15 minutes, swap the position of the baking sheets and rotate them 180 degrees for even baking.) If the cookies are done before 30 minutes, reduce the oven temperature to 275°F for the remaining batches; if they take longer than 1 hour, increase the temperature to 325°F.   —*Carolyn Weil*

chocolate-dipped espresso shortbread cookies

YIELDS ABOUT 7 DOZEN 1½-INCH HEART-SHAPED COOKIES

FOR THE COOKIES

- ½ lb. (1 cup) cold unsalted butter, cut into ½-inch pieces
- ½ cup granulated sugar
- ½ tsp. table salt
- 10 oz. (2¼ cups) unbleached all-purpose flour; more as needed
- 2 Tbs. finely ground espresso coffee beans

FOR THE DIPPING CHOCOLATE

- 9 oz. semisweet chocolate, chopped
- 1 Tbs. vegetable shortening

These cookies are done when the tops look dry and the color has darkened slightly.

1. Using a stand mixer fitted with the paddle attachment (or in a large bowl with a hand mixer), combine the butter, sugar, and salt on low speed until the butter combines with the sugar but isn't perfectly smooth, 1 to 2 minutes. Add the flour and ground espresso and mix on low speed, scraping the bowl frequently, until the dough has just about pulled together, about 3 minutes; don't overmix.

2. On a lightly floured surface, roll the dough to about ¼ inch thick. Aim for a uniform thickness to ensure even baking.

3. Cut the dough into bars or squares with a sharp knife or, using cookie cutters, cut out shapes as close to one another as possible. Press the scraps together, roll them out, and cut out more cookies. If the dough becomes sticky, refrigerate it briefly. Arrange the cookies on two parchment-lined baking sheets and refrigerate until chilled, at least 20 minutes.

4. Position racks in the upper and lower thirds of the oven and heat the oven to 300°F. Bake the cookies until golden on the bottom and edges and pale to golden on top, 30 minutes to 1 hour. (After 15 minutes, swap the position of the baking sheets and rotate them 180 degrees for even baking.) If the cookies are done before 30 minutes, reduce the oven temperature to 275°F for the remaining batches; if they take longer than 1 hour, increase the temperature to 325°F.

5. Once the cookies have cooled, they're ready to be dipped. Set a sheet of parchment or waxed paper on a work surface. Put the chocolate and shortening in a small heatproof bowl and set the bowl over a pan of simmering water. Melt the chocolate, stirring, until it's smooth. Dip half of each cookie into the chocolate. Set the cookies on the parchment and let the chocolate set up at room temperature, about 2 hours. *—Carolyn Weil*

orange-hazelnut shortbread cookies

YIELDS ABOUT 3 DOZEN 2-INCH COOKIES

- ½ lb. (1 cup) cold unsalted butter, cut into ½-inch pieces
- ½ cup granulated sugar
- ½ tsp. table salt
- 10 oz. (2¼ cups) unbleached all-purpose flour; more as needed
- 2½ oz. (½ cup) blanched hazelnuts, toasted and ground very finely in a food processor
- 2 tsp. finely grated orange zest (from 1 orange)

These look like plain shortbread, so their orange flavor is a pleasant surprise.

1. Using a stand mixer fitted with the paddle attachment (or in a large bowl with a hand mixer), combine the butter, sugar, and salt on low speed until the butter combines with the sugar but isn't perfectly smooth, 1 to 2 minutes. Add the flour, ground hazelnuts, and zest; mix on low speed, scraping the bowl frequently, until the dough has just about pulled together, about 3 minutes; don't overmix.

2. On a lightly floured surface, roll the dough to about ¼ inch thick. Aim for a uniform thickness to ensure even baking.

3. Cut the dough into bars or squares with a sharp knife or, using cookie cutters, cut out shapes as close to one another as possible. Press the scraps together, roll them out, and cut out more cookies. If the dough becomes sticky, refrigerate it briefly. Arrange the cookies on two parchment-lined baking sheets and refrigerate until chilled, at least 20 minutes.

4. Position racks in the upper and lower thirds of the oven and heat the oven to 300°F. Bake the cookies until golden on the bottom and edges and pale to golden on top, 30 minutes to 1 hour. (After 15 minutes, swap the position of the baking sheets and rotate them 180 degrees for even baking.) If the cookies are done before 30 minutes, reduce the oven temperature to 275°F for the remaining batches; if they take longer than 1 hour, increase the temperature to 325°F. *—Carolyn Weil*

PER COOKIE: 100 CALORIES | 1g PROTEIN | 9g CARB | 6g TOTAL FAT | 3.5g SAT FAT | 2.5g MONO FAT | 0g POLY FAT | 15mg CHOL | 35mg SODIUM | 0g FIBER

If you can't find blanched hazelnuts, buy them with the skin on, and toast and skin them yourself. For information on how, see p. 152.

almond shortbread sandwich cookies

YIELDS 2½ DOZEN 2-INCH SANDWICHES

FOR THE COOKIES

- ½ lb. (1 cup) cold unsalted butter, cut into ½-inch pieces
- ½ cup granulated sugar
- ½ tsp. table salt
- 10 oz. (2¼ cups) unbleached all-purpose flour; more as needed
- 3¾ oz. (¾ cup) finely ground almonds

FOR DECORATING

- Raspberry, plum, sour cherry, or strawberry jam
- Confectioners' sugar

The jam remains soft for a day or two after assembly, so these cookies need extra care when packing.

1. Using a stand mixer fitted with the paddle attachment (or in a large bowl with a hand mixer), combine the butter, sugar, and salt on low speed until the butter combines with the sugar but isn't perfectly smooth, 1 to 2 minutes. Add the flour and almonds and mix on low speed, scraping the bowl frequently, until the dough has just about pulled together, about 3 minutes; don't overmix.

2. On a lightly floured surface, roll the dough to ⅛ to ¼ inch thick (these cookies puff a little, and a thinner cookie makes a more appealing sandwich). Aim for a uniform thickness to ensure even baking.

3. Cut the dough into bars or squares with a sharp knife or, using cookie cutters, cut out shapes as close to one another as possible. To make the sandwich tops, cut a smaller shape (try circles or hearts) in the center of half of the cookies; be sure the border is fairly wide so the cookie doesn't fall apart. Press the scraps together, roll them out, and cut out more cookies. If the dough becomes sticky, refrigerate it briefly. Arrange the cookies on two parchment-lined baking sheets and refrigerate until chilled, at least 20 minutes.

4. Position racks in the upper and lower thirds of the oven and heat the oven to 300°F. Bake the cookies until golden on the bottom and edges and pale to golden on top, 30 minutes to 1 hour. (After 15 minutes, swap the position of the baking sheets and rotate them 180 degrees for even baking.) If the cookies are done before 30 minutes, reduce the oven temperature to 275°F for the remaining batches; if they take longer than 1 hour, increase the temperature to 325°F.

5. Once the cookies have cooled, dollop a small amount of jam in the center of the cookie bottoms (on the flat side) and spread it lightly with a spoon all over but not quite to the edge. Dust the cookie tops with confectioners' sugar. Sandwich the tops and bottoms together. *—Carolyn Weil*

coconut chocolate almond biscotti

YIELDS ABOUT 25 BISCOTTI

10⅛ oz. (2¼ cups) unbleached all-purpose flour

1½ tsp. baking powder

¼ tsp. table salt

4 oz. (½ cup) unsalted butter, softened at room temperature

¾ cup firmly packed light brown sugar

2 large eggs, at room temperature

1 tsp. pure vanilla extract

½ cup firmly packed sweetened shredded coconut

1 cup chopped toasted almonds

1 cup semisweet mini chocolate chips

The classic candy combination of almond, chocolate, and coconut also makes great-tasting biscotti. They keep well, too. Layered between sheets of parchment or waxed paper in an airtight container, the cooled biscotti can be stored at room temperature for up to 3 weeks, or frozen for up to 6 weeks.

1. In a medium bowl, whisk the flour, baking powder, and salt. Using a stand mixer fitted with the paddle attachment, beat the butter and sugar on medium speed until light and fluffy, 2 to 3 minutes. Add the eggs one at a time, mixing on medium speed after each addition until incorporated. Mix in the vanilla and then the coconut until well combined.

2. With the mixer on low speed, gradually add the flour mixture and mix just until combined. The dough will be sticky. With the mixer still on low, mix in the almonds and chocolate chips. Cover the bowl with plastic wrap and refrigerate for 30 minutes.

3. Position a rack in the center of the oven and heat the oven to 350°F. Line a large cookie sheet with parchment. Divide the dough in two and place each half on the cookie sheet. Working on the sheet, shape each half into a loaf about 10 inches long, 3 inches wide, and ¾ inch high. Bake until the tops are browned, cracked, and crusty, and spring back slightly when gently pressed, 30 to 35 minutes. Let cool on the cookie sheet for about 30 minutes. Reduce the oven temperature to 325°F.

4. Transfer each loaf to a cutting board and, with a sharp serrated bread knife, cut ½-inch slices crosswise on the diagonal. When slicing, hold the sides of the loaf near each cut to keep the slices neat. Put the slices, cut side down, on the cookie sheet and bake until the biscotti are dried and the cut surfaces are lightly browned, 15 to 20 minutes. Transfer the cookie sheet to a rack and let the biscotti cool completely. The biscotti may give slightly when pressed but will harden as they cool. *—Beth Kujawski*

PER COOKIE: 170 CALORIES | 3g PROTEIN | 21g CARB | 8g TOTAL FAT | 4g SAT FAT | 3g MONO FAT | 1g POLY FAT | 25mg CHOL | 60mg SODIUM | 1g FIBER

triple chocolate biscotti

- 12 oz. (2⅔ cups) unbleached all-purpose flour; more for shaping
- 2 cups granulated sugar
- 3½ oz. (1 cup) unsweetened Dutch-processed cocoa powder
- 1½ Tbs. finely ground dark-roast coffee beans or instant espresso powder
- 1½ tsp. baking soda
- ¼ tsp. table salt
- 9 oz. (1¾ cups) hazelnuts, toasted and skinned (see p. 152 for how to toast and skin hazelnuts)
- 4 oz. (⅔ cup) chocolate chips
- 5 large eggs
- 1½ tsp. pure vanilla extract
- 12 oz. white chocolate

Covering one side of these chocolate biscotti with white chocolate gives them an elegant look and a moister texture.

1. Position racks in the center and upper third of the oven and heat the oven to 325°F. Line two baking sheets with parchment.

2. Using a stand mixer fitted with the paddle attachment (or in a large bowl with a hand mixer), beat the flour, sugar, cocoa, coffee, baking soda, and salt on medium-low speed. Mix in the hazelnuts and chocolate chips. In a separate bowl, lightly whisk together the eggs and vanilla extract. With the mixer running on low speed, slowly add the egg mixture to the bowl and mix until the dough comes together. Remove the bowl from the mixer and mix in any remaining dry ingredients from the bottom of the bowl by hand. Dump the dough onto a lightly floured work surface and knead briefly to incorporate the ingredients.

3. Portion the dough into four equal pieces and roll into logs about 2 inches in diameter. Set them 4 inches apart on prepared baking sheets and bake the logs until the sides are firm, the tops are cracked, and the dough inside the cracks no longer looks wet, 30 to 35 minutes.

4. Remove the baking sheets from the oven and reduce the oven temperature to 300°F. Let the logs cool on the baking sheets for at least 10 minutes before slicing. Cut the logs on a slight diagonal into ¾-inch-thick slices. Arrange the biscotti flat on the baking sheets and dry them in the oven for about 25 minutes, until the biscotti offer resistance when pressed. Transfer the biscotti to a rack to cool.

5. While the biscotti are cooling, chop the white chocolate and melt it in a microwave on low power or in a double boiler over simmering water. With a knife, spread white chocolate on one cut side of each cooled biscotti. Put the biscotti, white-chocolate side down, on a parchment-lined baking sheet. Allow the chocolate to harden. Peel the biscotti from the parchment and store in an airtight container. —*Emily Luchetti*

golden almond biscotti

FOR THE DOUGH

2	cups whole almonds, skin on
20	oz. (4¼ cups) unbleached all-purpose flour
1½	tsp. baking powder
½	tsp. kosher salt
1	cup turbinado sugar (also sold as Sugar in the Raw in supermarkets)
½	cup granulated sugar
¼	cup finely grated orange zest (from 3 to 4 oranges)
2	tsp. aniseed, crushed
½	lb. (1 cup) unsalted butter, cut into pieces, well chilled
4	large eggs
¼	cup strained fresh orange juice
1	tsp. pure vanilla extract
¼	tsp. pure almond extract

FOR THE GLAZE

2	egg whites, beaten until slightly foamy
6	Tbs. turbinado sugar (see note above)

Make Ahead

If stored in an airtight container, fully baked biscotti will keep for about 2 weeks.

Do the first bake and then finish the cookies as your schedule permits. Half-baked biscotti can sit as long as overnight.

MIX THE DOUGH

Position racks in the center and upper third of the oven and heat the oven to 350°F. Toast the almonds on a baking sheet until the skins just start to crack, about 15 minutes. Spread them on a cutting board to cool. Roughly chop each nut into 2 or 3 pieces (it's easier to chop them evenly if you work in small mounds). Using a stand mixer fitted with the paddle attachment (or in a large bowl with a hand mixer), combine the flour, baking powder, and salt. In a separate bowl, whisk together the sugars, orange zest, and aniseeds until well combined. Add this mixture to the flour mixture; mix to combine. With the mixer on low speed, add the chilled butter, mixing until the pieces are the size of large peas. In a small bowl, whisk together the eggs, orange juice, and vanilla and almond extracts and add to the dough, mixing until just combined; don't overmix. Add the almonds and mix for a few seconds to blend. The dough will feel sticky. Let it rest for 15 to 30 minutes before shaping.

SHAPE THE DOUGH AND DO THE INITIAL BAKING

Line two large baking sheets with parchment. Cut the dough into quarters. Using as little flour as possible on your work surface, roll each quarter into a log that's 13 inches long and 1½ inches wide, working out the air pockets as you go. (If you're working ahead, wrap the logs in plastic and refrigerate them overnight.) Set the logs on the lined baking sheets, about 3 inches apart, patting the sides to straighten and smooth. Brush the tops and sides with the beaten egg whites and sprinkle the tops with 2 Tbs. of the turbinado sugar. Bake until golden brown and firm in the center, about 35 minutes, rotating the sheets and switching their positions to ensure even baking. Set the sheets on racks until the logs are cool enough to handle and so the dough won't compress when you cut it, about 30 minutes.

BAKE A SECOND TIME, THEN GLAZE

Reduce the oven heat to 300°F and line the baking sheets with fresh parchment, if needed. With a serrated knife, saw the logs into ½-inch-thick slices, cutting crosswise. Lay the slices flat on the baking sheets. Brush the tops with more egg white and sprinkle with another 2 Tbs. of the turbinado sugar. Bake about 15 minutes, rotating the baking sheets and switching their positions as needed. Turn the biscotti over. Brush again with the egg whites and sprinkle with the remaining 2 Tbs. turbinado sugar. Bake until both sides are a rich golden brown, another 10 to 15 minutes. Set the baking sheets on racks to let the cookies cool and crisp completely on the sheets. —*Kathleen Weber*

macadamia-nut biscotti

YIELDS ABOUT 3 DOZEN
BISCOTTI

- **8 oz. (2 cups) unbleached all-purpose flour**
- **2 tsp. baking powder**
- **½ tsp. table salt**
- **6 oz. (1⅓ cups) macadamia nuts**
- **4 oz. (8 Tbs.) unsalted butter, softened at room temperature**
- **½ cup granulated sugar**
- **2 large eggs**
- **½ tsp. pure vanilla extract**

These biscotti have a light texture, similar to shortbread cookies. They don't stay fresh as long as biscotti made without butter, so plan to eat them within a couple of days.

1. Position racks in the center and upper third of the oven and heat the oven to 350°F. Sift together the flour, baking powder, and salt, and set aside.

2. Spread the macadamia nuts on a baking sheet and toast until light brown, about 10 minutes. Let cool. In a food processor, coarsely grind half of the nuts with one quarter of the flour mixture.

3. Using a stand mixer fitted with the paddle attachment (or in a large bowl with a hand mixer), beat the butter and the sugar until light and fluffy. Add the eggs one at a time, beating after each addition. Add the vanilla extract and mix until incorporated. Stir in the whole nuts, the ground nuts, and the rest of the flour mixture. Mix just until the dough comes together.

4. Dump the dough onto a lightly floured work surface, and knead in by hand any remaining dry ingredients from the bottom of the bowl. Portion the dough into three equal pieces. With floured hands, roll each piece into a log about 10 inches long and 2 inches in diameter. Place the logs 4 inches apart on greased or parchment-lined baking sheets and bake at 350°F for about 30 minutes, until lightly golden but still soft. Remove the baking sheet from the oven and reduce the oven temperature to 300°F. Let the logs cool on the baking sheet for at least 10 minutes before slicing.

5. Cut the logs on a slight diagonal into ¾-inch-thick slices. Arrange the biscotti flat on the baking sheet and bake them for an additional 15 minutes, until the biscotti offer resistance when pressed, but the cut side hasn't begun to darken. Transfer the biscotti to a rack to cool. Store in an airtight container.
—*Emily Luchetti*

Fresh macadamia nuts should be a pale yellow-white. Look for plump, unbroken nutmeats and buy from a place that has good turnover. If you can only find salted macadamia nuts, you can use them in place of fresh, but give them a quick rinse first.

chocolate-orange biscotti

YIELDS ABOUT 10 DOZEN
2½-INCH BISCOTTI

FOR THE DOUGH

2½   cups whole hazelnuts, skin on

12   oz. high-quality bittersweet or semisweet chocolate

½   lb. (1 cup) unsalted butter, softened at room temperature

4   large eggs

1   cup packed light brown sugar

1   cup granulated sugar

2   tsp. pure vanilla extract

½   tsp. pure almond extract

2   Tbs. instant espresso powder or finely ground coffee

¾   cup high-quality Dutch-processed cocoa powder, sifted

1   cup candied orange peel (to make your own, see the recipe on the facing page)

18   oz. (4 cups) unbleached all-purpose flour; more as needed

1   tsp. baking powder

1   tsp. kosher salt

FOR FINISHING

4   large egg whites

1   tsp. best-quality orange extract

¾   cup granulated sugar

These fragrant and chocolatey cookies are an inventive departure from more Christmasy-looking cookies while still being sparkly, festive, and full of delicious nuggets like hazelnuts, candied orange peel, and chocolate chunks.

MIX THE DOUGH

1. Position racks in the center and upper third of the oven and heat the oven to 350°F. Toast the hazelnuts on a baking sheet until they're well browned, about 10 minutes. Let cool. You won't need to skin them—the skins taste great—but if the nuts are bigger than ½ inch, chop them roughly. Chop the chocolate into slivers that are a scant 1 inch long and ⅛ inch wide.

2. Using a stand mixer fitted with the paddle attachment (or in a large bowl with a hand mixer), beat the butter on medium-high speed until light and creamy. Add the eggs one at a time. Add the brown and white sugars, vanilla extract, almond extract, espresso powder, and cocoa powder, scraping the bowl as needed. Add the candied orange peel, flour, baking powder, and salt. Add the hazelnuts and chocolate slivers, mixing just to combine. The dough will be stiff and a bit sticky. Let the dough rest for 15 to 30 minutes before shaping.

SHAPE THE DOUGH AND DO THE INITIAL BAKING

Line two large baking sheets with parchment. Portion the dough into six equal pieces. Using as little flour as possible on the work surface, roll each piece into logs that are 12 to 14 inches long and 1¼ inches wide, working out the air pockets as you go. (If you're working ahead, wrap the logs in plastic wrap and refrigerate them overnight). Transfer the logs to the lined baking sheets, setting the dough about 3 inches apart, patting the sides to smooth and straighten. In a small bowl, beat the egg whites with the orange extract until foamy. Brush the tops and sides of the logs with some of the whites. Sprinkle with ¼ cup of the sugar. Bake until firm in the center, about 35 minutes, rotating the sheets to ensure even baking. Set the sheets on racks until the logs are cool enough to handle and so the dough won't compress when you cut it, about 30 minutes.

BAKE THE SECOND TIME AND FINISH

Reduce the oven heat to 300°F and line the baking sheets with fresh parchment, if needed. With a serrated knife, saw the strips into ½ inch-thick slices, cutting crosswise. Lay the slices flat on the baking sheets. Brush the tops with the beaten egg white and sprinkle with another ¼ cup of the sugar. Bake for about 15 minutes, rotating the baking sheets as needed. Turn the biscotti over. Brush again with the egg white and sprinkle with the remaining ¼ cup sugar. Bake for another 10 to 15 minutes, watching carefully to make sure the chocolate doesn't burn. The centers will feel somewhat soft even when fully baked; they'll harden as the cookies cool. Set the baking sheets on racks, letting the cookies cool and crisp completely on the sheets. Store in an airtight container. *—Kathleen Weber*

candied citrus peel

YIELDS ABOUT 3 CUPS; SERVES 24

3 cups citrus peel (from about 4 large oranges, 2 large grapefruit, 8 lemons, or 5 Minneolas; see preparation instructions at right)

2½ cups granulated sugar

Make Ahead

Once fully dry, candied citrus peels can be stored in an airtight container in a cool, dry place for up to 1 month. Use leftovers to sprinkle over ice cream or as a garnish for citrus-based cocktails.

Citrus with thicker peels will produce the best candied results. Blanching peels multiple times tames their bitter flavor.

1. Using a sharp knife, cut the fruit lengthwise into eighths; then cut off the zest along with a thin layer of the white pith. Slice the peels into ¼-inch-wide strips. Save the fruit for another use.

2. Put the sliced peels in a 3-quart heavy-duty saucepan and add enough water to cover. Bring to a boil over high heat and blanch for 5 minutes.

3. Drain the peels, cover with fresh water, bring to a boil, and blanch again for 5 minutes. Repeat once more for a total of three blanchings.

4. In the same saucepan, combine 1½ cups of the sugar and 1 cup water; bring to a boil over high heat.

5. Add the peels and reduce the heat to low. Let the peels simmer very gently—the mixture should be just slightly bubbling—until they begin to look translucent, 45 to 60 minutes. Stir occasionally to ensure that the peels candy evenly and don't burn.

6. Drain the peels, reserving the syrup for another use. Set a rack over a parchment-lined rimmed baking sheet. Put the remaining 1 cup sugar in a bowl. Roll the peels in the sugar, shake them in a sieve to remove any excess, and spread them on the rack; let dry for 5 to 6 hours. Once fully dry, store the candied peels in an airtight container in a cool, dry place for up to 1 month.
—*Anita Chu*

PER SERVING: 35 CALORIES | 0g PROTEIN | 9g CARB | 0g TOTAL FAT | 0g SAT FAT | 0g MONO FAT | 0g POLY FAT | 0mg CHOL | 0mg SODIUM | 0g FIBER

classic Scottish shortbread

YIELDS ABOUT SIXTY
1X2½-INCH COOKIES

- **1** lb. (2 cups) unsalted butter, softened at room temperature
- **1** cup superfine sugar
- **18** oz. (4 cups) unbleached all-purpose flour
- **½** tsp. table salt

Make Ahead

The shortbread will keep for up to a month between layers of waxed paper in an airtight container at room temperature.

Because of its high butter content, shortbread dough can be difficult to roll out. The key is keeping it cool. If it gets too warm and starts to stick to your rolling surface, just pop it into the fridge for 20 minutes and try again.

1. Using a stand mixer fitted with the paddle attachment (or in a large bowl with a hand mixer), beat the butter until light and fluffy, about 1 minute. Slowly add the sugar and continue beating until thoroughly blended. In a large bowl, blend the flour and salt. Add the flour mixture, about 1 cup at a time, to the butter. Stop the mixer and scrape the bowl after each addition. If you're flavoring the shortbread, add the ingredients now. (See the variations on the facing page.) Continue mixing for another 2 to 3 minutes, until the dough is smooth and soft.

2. On a large sheet of parchment, draw a 10x15-inch rectangle using a pencil and ruler. Lay the paper on a jelly roll pan or baking sheet; you'll use this paper as a template to shape your shortbread. Working quickly, pat or roll the dough into an even layer. Use a ruler to score the dough into 1x2½-inch pieces. With a fork, pierce each piece in three places on a diagonal.

3. Cover the cookies tightly with plastic wrap and refrigerate for at least 2 hours or up to 4 days. The dough can also be frozen: just defrost it in the refrigerator for 24 hours before baking.

4. Position racks in the upper and lower thirds of the oven and heat the oven to 325°F. Line two baking sheets with parchment. Cut the chilled dough through the scored lines. Arrange the cookies on the baking sheets, with an inch of space between each.

5. Put the baking sheets in the oven and reduce the heat to 300°F. Bake for 20 minutes. Rotate the pans and switch their positions on the racks to ensure even baking. Bake for an additional 14 to 16 minutes. Remove the baking pans from the oven and let the pans cool on racks for 5 minutes. Then transfer the cookies to the racks to cool completely. *—Carole Bloom*

PER COOKIE: 100 CALORIES | 1g PROTEIN | 10g CARB | 6g TOTAL FAT | 4g SAT FAT | 2g MONO FAT | 0g POLY FAT | 15mg CHOL | 20mg SODIUM | 0g FIBER

Scottish Shortbread Variations

Hazelnut After all the flour has been added to the dough, mix in 4 ½ oz. (1 cup) chopped, toasted, blanched hazelnuts (other toasted and chopped nuts can be substituted). Continue with the Classic Scottish Shortbread recipe.

Spiced Blend 2 tsp. ground cinnamon, 1 tsp. ground ginger, and ½ tsp. freshly grated nutmeg. After all the flour has been added to the shortbread dough, mix in the spice blend. Continue as directed for Classic Scottish Shortbread.

Ginger After all the flour has been added to the shortbread dough, blend in 1 cup finely chopped crystallized ginger and 2 tsp. ground ginger. Continue as directed for Classic Scottish Shortbread.

Orange After all the flour has been added to the shortbread dough, mix in 1 cup finely chopped candied orange peel (to make your own, see the recipe on p. 183) and 2 tsp. orange extract. Continue as directed for Classic Scottish Shortbread.

thick Scottish shortbread

YIELDS 12 SQUARES

- 6¾ oz. (1½ cups) unbleached all-purpose flour
- 3½ oz. (¾ cup) cornstarch
- ⅛ tsp. table salt
- ½ cup plus 2 Tbs. superfine sugar
- ½ lb. (1 cup) unsalted butter, softened at room temperature for 1 hour and cut into 16 pieces
- 1 tsp. pure vanilla extract

Superfine sugar helps give these treats their delicate texture. If you can't find it, pulse granulated sugar in a food processor for about 30 seconds. If you like, serve this shortbread topped with Lemon Curd (recipe below).

1. Position a rack in the center of the oven and heat the oven to 300°F. Line an 8x8-inch pan with heavy aluminum foil, letting the foil extend over two sides of the pan. Sift the flour, cornstarch, and salt into a large bowl.

2. Add ½ cup of the superfine sugar and, with an electric mixer on low speed, mix to just blend the ingredients. Add the butter pieces and vanilla and mix until large (¼- to ½-inch) crumbs form, about 2 minutes. Very gently press the dough evenly into the prepared pan; don't pack the dough into the pan. Bake until the top of the shortbread just begins to turn golden, about 1 hour and 10 minutes. Remove from the oven and immediately sprinkle the remaining 2 Tbs. superfine sugar over the top. Cut the shortbread into 12 squares, being sure to cut through to the bottom. Let cool completely before lifting the foil and shortbread from the pan. *—Elinor Klivans*

PER SQUARE: 260 CALORIES | 2g PROTEIN | 28g CARB | 16g TOTAL FAT | 10g SAT FAT | 5g MONO FAT | 1g POLY FAT | 40mg CHOL | 25mg SODIUM | 0g FIBER

lemon curd

YIELDS ABOUT 2 CUPS

- 3 oz. (6 Tbs.) unsalted butter, softened at room temperature
- 1 cup granulated sugar
- 2 large eggs
- 2 large egg yolks
- ⅔ cup fresh lemon juice
- 1 tsp. finely grated lemon zest

Not only is lemon curd a delicious topping for Thick Scottish Shortbread, you can also make pretty sandwich cookies with it. Macaroons, butter cookies, and nut wafers all taste great with lemon curd spread between them. For lime curd, substitute fresh lime juice and zest for lemon.

1. Using a stand mixer fitted with the paddle attachment (or in a large bowl with a hand mixer), beat the butter and sugar, about 2 minutes. Slowly add the eggs and egg yolks and beat for an additional minute. Mix in the lemon juice. The mixture will look curdled, but it will smooth out as it cooks.

2. In a medium heavy-based saucepan, cook the mixture over low heat until smooth. (The curdled appearance disappears as the butter melts.) Increase the heat to medium and cook, stirring constantly, until the mixture thickens and coats the back of the spoon well enough to make a path if you run your finger through it, about 15 minutes. Don't let the mixture boil.

3. Remove the curd from the heat; stir in the lemon zest. Transfer the curd to a bowl. Press plastic wrap on the surface of the lemon curd to keep a skin from forming and chill the curd in the refrigerator. The curd will thicken further as it cools. *—Elinor Klivans*

PER TBS.: 50 CALORIES | 1g PROTEIN | 7g CARB | 3g TOTAL FAT | 1.5g SAT FAT | 1g MONO FAT | 0g POLY FAT | 30mg CHOL | 5mg SODIUM | 0g FIBER

Make Ahead

Covered tightly, lemon curd will keep in the refrigerator for a week and in the freezer for 2 months. It doesn't freeze solid, so you can spoon out as much as you need when you need it.

spirited & spiced cookies

chocolate-mint thumbprints

YIELDS ABOUT 3 DOZEN COOKIES

FOR THE COOKIES

5¼ oz. (1 cup plus 2½ Tbs.) unbleached all-purpose flour

¾ oz. (¼ cup) unsweetened Dutch-processed cocoa powder

6 oz. (¾ cup) unsalted butter, softened at room temperature

2 oz. (½ cup) confectioners' sugar, sifted

1½ tsp. pure vanilla extract

¼ tsp. table salt

FOR THE CHOCOLATE-MINT FILLING

4 oz. (¾ cup) chopped semi-sweet chocolate (or chocolate chips)

1½ oz. (3 Tbs.) unsalted butter, cut into 6 pieces

Scant ¼ tsp. pure peppermint extract

Lining the cookie sheet with parchment or liners prevents sticking, plus allows you to whisk a batch away when it comes out of the oven and begin another immediately. To get the most mint-chocolatey flavor in every bite, pipe a good amount of filling into the thumbprint depressions.

Make Ahead

The cookies will keep in an airtight container at room temperature for 4 to 5 days.

MAKE THE COOKIES

1. Sift the flour and cocoa together into a medium bowl. With a hand mixer or a stand mixer fitted with the paddle attachment, cream the butter and confectioners' sugar on medium speed until light and fluffy, about 2 minutes. Add the vanilla and salt; continue beating until blended and smooth, about another 1 minute. Add the flour mixture and mix on low speed until a soft dough forms, about 1 minute. Chill the dough in the refrigerator until firm enough to roll into balls, 40 to 60 minutes.

2. Position a rack in the center of the oven and heat the oven to 350°F. Line two baking sheets with parchment or nonstick baking liners.

3. Using your palms, roll heaping teaspoonfuls of the dough into 1-inch balls and set them 2 inches apart on the lined sheets. With a lightly floured thumb or fingertip (or the end of a thick-handled wooden spoon), press straight down into the middle of each ball almost to the cookie sheet to make a deep well.

4. Bake one sheet at a time until the tops of the cookies look dry, 8 to 9 minutes. Gently redefine the indentations with the end of a wooden spoon. Let the cookies cool on the sheet for 5 minutes and then transfer them to racks and let them cool completely.

MAKE THE FILLING

Put the chocolate and butter in a heatproof bowl set in a wide skillet of almost simmering water. Stir with a heatproof spatula until almost melted, 2 to 4 minutes. Remove the bowl from the heat and stir until melted and smooth, about another 30 seconds. Stir in the peppermint extract. Let the filling cool, stirring occasionally, until slightly thickened and a bit warmer than room temperature, 30 to 40 minutes. Spoon the filling into a small pastry bag with a small plain tip. (Or use a small plastic bag and cut a tiny bit off a bottom corner of the bag.) Pipe the filling into the center of each cookie. Let cool completely before serving or storing. *—David Crofton*

PER COOKIE: 80 CALORIES | 1g PROTEIN | 7g CARB | 6g TOTAL FAT | 3.5g SAT FAT | 1.5g MONO FAT | 0g POLY FAT | 15mg CHOL | 15mg SODIUM | 0g FIBER

lemon-rosemary christmas trees

**YIELDS ABOUT 3 DOZEN
3½-INCH COOKIES**

FOR THE COOKIES

15	oz. (3⅓ cups) unbleached all-purpose flour
1	tsp. table salt
½	lb. (1 cup) unsalted butter, at room temperature
¾	cup granulated sugar
1	Tbs. finely grated lemon zest
1	Tbs. finely chopped fresh rosemary
1	large egg
1	tsp. pure vanilla extract

FOR THE ICING

1	large egg white
6½	oz. (1½ cups plus 2 Tbs.) confectioners' sugar; more as needed
½	tsp. fresh lemon juice
	Decorating sugar or edible dragées (optional)

Rosemary gives these holiday cut-out cookies a subtle piny touch, and lemon adds brightness.

MAKE THE COOKIES

1. In a medium bowl, whisk the flour and salt. Using a hand mixer or a stand mixer fitted with the paddle attachment, cream the butter and sugar on medium speed until light and fluffy, about 2 minutes. Mix in the lemon zest and rosemary. Add the egg and vanilla; continue beating until well blended and smooth, about 30 seconds more. Reduce the speed to low and gradually add the dry ingredients. Mix until the dough is just combined; don't overmix. Divide the dough in two.

2. Roll one half of the dough between two sheets of parchment to an even 3/16-inch thickness. Slide the dough and parchment onto a cookie sheet and refrigerate until firm, about 30 minutes. Repeat with the remaining dough.

3. Position racks in the upper and lower thirds of the oven and heat the oven to 350°F. Line four cookie sheets with parchment.

4. Using a 3½-inch (or similar) Christmas tree cookie cutter, cut out the cookies and arrange them 1 inch apart on the cookie sheets. Press the scraps together, reroll, and cut (if the dough becomes too soft to handle, chill until firm). Repeat one more time and then discard the scraps. Repeat with the remaining dough.

5. Bake two sheets at a time until the cookies' edges are golden brown, 10 to 12 minutes, rotating and swapping the sheets' positions halfway through for even baking. Let the cookies cool on racks.

MAKE THE ICING

In a medium bowl, whisk the egg white, sugar, and lemon juice until smooth. If not using immediately, transfer the icing to a small bowl and press plastic wrap directly onto the surface of the icing to prevent it from drying out.

DECORATE THE COOKIES

Spoon some of the icing into a small pastry bag with a small (3/16-inch) plain tip. (Or use a small plastic bag and cut a tiny bit off a bottom corner of the bag.) Pipe the icing onto the cookies to outline the rim. (If the icing is too thick to pipe, put it back in the bowl and stir in water, a drop at a time, until it pipes easily but still retains its shape. If the icing is too thin, add confectioners' sugar, 1 tsp. at a time.) If using decorating sugar or dragées, apply them while the icing is wet. Once the icing is completely dry and hard, store the cookies in airtight containers in the refrigerator for up to 5 days. —*David Crofton*

PER COOKIE: 130 CALORIES | 2g PROTEIN | 18g CARB | 5g TOTAL FAT | 3.5g SAT FAT | 1.5g MONO FAT | 0g POLY FAT | 20mg CHOL | 70mg SODIUM | 0g FIBER

The risk of salmonella infection from consuming raw eggs is very low, but you can eliminate it entirely by using pasteurized eggs.

cardamom-honey cut-outs

YIELDS 6 DOZEN 2½-INCH
COOKIES

13½ **oz. (3 cups) unbleached all-purpose flour; more for rolling**

1 **tsp. ground cardamom**

½ **tsp. table salt**

¼ **tsp. baking soda**

½ **lb. (1 cup) unsalted butter, at room temperature**

¾ **cup granulated sugar**

¼ **cup honey**

1 **large egg**

1 **tsp. pure vanilla extract**

Royal icing (for decoration; see the recipe on p. 30)

If you cut the cookies into larger or smaller shapes, you'll need to adjust the baking time. Just be sure to bake until the edges turn light brown.

MAKE THE DOUGH

1. In a medium bowl, combine the flour, cardamom, salt, and baking soda. Whisk until well blended.

2. Using a stand mixer fitted with the paddle attachment (or in a large bowl with a hand mixer), beat the butter and sugar on medium speed until well blended and slightly fluffy, about 3 minutes. Scrape the bowl and the beater. Add the honey, egg, and vanilla. Continue mixing on medium speed until well blended, about 1 minute. Add the flour mixture and mix on low speed until the dough is well blended and comes together in moist clumps, 30 to 60 seconds.

3. Divide the dough roughly in half. On a piece of plastic wrap, shape each dough half into a smooth 5-inch disk. Wrap well in the plastic. Refrigerate until chilled and firm enough to roll out, 1 to 1½ hours.

BAKE THE COOKIES

1. Position a rack in the center of the oven and heat the oven to 350°F. Line two or more cookie sheets with parchment or nonstick baking liners. Working with one disk at a time, roll the dough on a floured work surface to about ³⁄₁₆ inch thick. Dust with additional flour as needed. Choose one or more cookie cutters of any shape that are about 2½ inches wide and cut out shapes.

Arrange the cookies about 1 inch apart on the lined cookie sheets. Gather the scraps and gently press together. Reroll and cut. Repeat with the remaining dough.

2. Bake one sheet at a time until the cookies' edges develop a ¼-inch-wide light brown rim, 11 to 13 minutes (rotate the sheet halfway through baking for even browning). Let the cookies cool on the sheet for about 10 minutes and then transfer them to a rack to cool completely. Decorate with royal icing (technique tips below). *—Abigail Johnson Dodge*

PER COOKIE: 50 CALORIES | 1g PROTEIN | 7g CARB | 2.5g TOTAL FAT | 1.5g SAT FAT | 0.5g MONO FAT | 0g POLY FAT | 10mg CHOL | 20mg SODIUM | 0g FIBER

Make Ahead

The dough may be refrigerated for up to 3 days or frozen for 1 month. Thaw overnight in the refrigerator before proceeding with the recipe.

how to decorate cookies with royal icing

Royal Icing (see the recipe p. 30) hardens to a durable, rock-hard consistency when allowed to dry. Start by making a batch of icing and then coloring it however you like. You can split the batch up and make lots of colors, or you can leave it white.

To outline a cookie, spoon some of the icing into a pastry bag fitted with a very small plain tip. If the icing is too thick to pipe evenly, put it back in the bowl and stir in water, a drop or two at a time, until it pipes easily but still retains its shape. Outline the rim of the cookies with icing or decorate it with thin lines. Set aside while the icing hardens.

To coat an entire cookie with icing, have ready a small clean artist's brush (one that you use only for food). Outline the rim of a cookie with the icing as described at left and let harden slightly. Dampen the brush in water and spread a small amount of additional icing in an even layer within the border. (You can also use the pastry bag to "flood" the area.) Set the cookie aside to dry.

To create thin and lacy freeform lines, touch the tip down as you start and lift away, draping the line as you go.

bourbon balls

YIELDS 3½ TO 4 DOZEN BALLS

- **1 cup heavy cream**
- **¼ cup bourbon**
- **½ tsp. pure vanilla extract**
- **12 oz. bittersweet chocolate, chopped**
- **8 oz. pecans, toasted and cooled (about 2 cups)**
- **8 oz. plain homemade or store-bought pound cake, cut into cubes (about 2½ cups)**
- **⅔ cup unsweetened cocoa powder, preferably Dutch-processed**
- **⅓ cup confectioners' sugar**

Save expensive single-barrel bourbons for sipping. For baking, a regular bourbon is fine.

1. In a small saucepan, bring the cream just to a boil over medium-high heat. Remove from the heat and stir in the bourbon and vanilla. Sprinkle the chocolate evenly over the cream and let sit without stirring for 5 minutes.

2. Meanwhile, pulse the pecans in a food processor until coarsely chopped. Add the pound cake and pulse until the nuts and cake are finely chopped.

3. Stir the chocolate and the cream until smooth. Pour the chocolate mixture over the pecan and pound cake mixture in the food processor and pulse until combined. Transfer to a medium bowl and refrigerate, stirring occasionally, until firm enough to scoop, about 1 hour.

4. Sift the cocoa powder and confectioners' sugar together into a medium bowl. Line a rimmed baking sheet with waxed paper or parchment. Scoop out a heaping tablespoon of the bourbon-chocolate mixture and roll it in your hands to form a ball. Transfer the bourbon ball to the cocoa-sugar mixture, roll it around to coat, and transfer to the baking sheet. Repeat with the remaining bourbon-chocolate mixture. Sift some of the remaining cocoa-sugar mixture over the bourbon balls just to dust them. Refrigerate the bourbon balls until firm, about 2 hours. For a pretty presentation, you can put them in mini muffin cups. —*Allison Ehri Kreitler*

PER BALL: 110 CALORIES | 2g PROTEIN | 9g CARB | 8g TOTAL FAT | 3g SAT FAT | 3.5g MONO FAT | 1g POLY FAT | 10mg CHOL | 30mg SODIUM | 2g FIBER

Cooking with Bourbon

When it comes to cooking and baking with liquor, bourbon is one of our favorites. Its smoky caramel and vanilla flavor adds a special nuance to savory and sweet dishes alike. It pairs particularly well with brown sugar, pecans, vanilla, chocolate, mint, apples, pears, peaches, ham, and pork. It's great in sauces, marinades, brines, glazes, cakes, pies, truffles, and cookies. Bourbon whiskey, which gets its name from Bourbon County, Kentucky, is distilled from a grain mash that's at least 51% corn (but usually 65% to 80%) and may also contain barley, rye, and sometimes wheat (as in Maker's Mark® brand). The distilled liquor is then aged in new charred oak barrels from which it gets its color and smoky, caramelly undertones.

orange butter cookies with Grand Marnier glaze

YIELDS ABOUT 3 DOZEN COOKIES

FOR THE COOKIES

10½ oz. (2⅓ cups) unbleached all-purpose flour; more as needed

¼ tsp. baking powder

½ tsp. table salt

½ lb. (1 cup) unsalted butter, softened at room temperature

1 cup granulated sugar

2 Tbs. finely grated orange zest

3 large egg yolks

1 tsp. pure vanilla extract

FOR THE GRAND MARNIER GLAZE

3½ oz. (1 cup) confectioners' sugar

2 Tbs. Grand Marnier

1½ Tbs. heavy cream; more as needed

2 tsp. finely grated orange zest

Pinch of table salt

Make Ahead

This cookie dough can be refrigerated for up to 3 days or frozen for up to 1 month. Unglazed cookies can be stored in an airtight container at room temperature for up to 5 days or frozen for up to 1 month before glazing. Store glazed cookies in an airtight container at room temperature for up to 3 days.

Citrus cookies with a Grand Marnier glaze take their cue from crêpes Suzette, the classic dessert of flambéed crêpes and boozy orange sauce.

MAKE THE COOKIES

1. In a medium bowl, whisk the flour, baking powder, and salt. Using a stand mixer fitted with the paddle attachment, beat the butter, sugar, and zest on medium speed until well blended, about 2 minutes. Add the egg yolks one at a time, mixing until blended after each addition. Add the vanilla extract along with the last yolk. Mix until well blended, about 1 minute. Add the flour mixture and mix on low speed until moist clumps form, about 1 minute.

2. Turn the dough out onto a work surface, halve it, and put each half on sheets of plastic wrap. Using the plastic as an aid, knead into a smooth dough, shape into flat 5-inch disks, and wrap in the plastic. Refrigerate until chilled, about 30 minutes.

3. Position a rack in the center of the oven and heat the oven to 350°F. Line two or more cookie sheets with parchment or nonstick baking liners.

4. Working with one disk at a time, roll the dough between lightly floured parchment or on a floured surface to about ¼ inch thick. Dust with additional flour as needed. Using a 2½-inch cookie cutter, cut out shapes. Arrange them about 1 inch apart on the cookie sheets. Gather, reroll, and cut the dough scraps up to two more times.

5. Bake one sheet at a time until the edges are golden brown, 9 to 13 minutes. Let the cookies cool on the sheet for about 5 minutes and then transfer them to a rack to cool completely.

GLAZE THE COOKIES

1. In a medium bowl, combine the confectioners' sugar, Grand Marnier, cream, zest, and salt. Mix until well blended and smooth. If necessary, add more cream a few drops at a time for a thin, spreadable consistency.

2. Top each cookie with about ½ tsp. of the glaze, using the bottom of the measuring spoon to spread the glaze to within ¼ inch of the edge.

3. Let sit at room temperature until the glaze is set, about 2 hours. Serve the cookies immediately. —*Abigail Johnson Dodge*

PER COOKIE: 120 CALORIES | 1g PROTEIN | 16g CARB | 6g TOTAL FAT | 3.5g SAT FAT | 1.5g MONO FAT | 0g POLY FAT | 30mg CHOL | 45mg SODIUM | 0g FIBER

Kahlúa truffle triangles

**YIELDS ABOUT 6 DOZEN
1½- TO 2-INCH TRIANGLES**

FOR THE CRUST

- 6¾ oz. (1½ cups) unbleached all-purpose flour; more as needed
- 3 oz. (¾ cup) confectioners' sugar
- ¼ tsp. table salt
- 6 oz. (¾ cup) cold unsalted butter, cut into 10 pieces; more for the pan
- ½ tsp. pure vanilla extract

FOR THE FILLING

- 1 lb. semisweet or bittersweet chocolate, broken into squares or very coarsely chopped
- ¾ cup whole or 2% milk
- 4 oz. (½ cup) unsalted butter, cut into 6 pieces
- 4 large eggs
- ⅔ cup granulated sugar
- 2 Tbs. Kahlúa or other coffee-flavored liqueur

Make Ahead

You can bake these up to 1 month ahead: Wrap the cooled baking pan in heavy-duty plastic wrap and freeze (no need to cut them into triangles first). The baked truffles can also be refrigerated, wrapped in plastic, for up to 2 days. Avoid piling anything on top of the pan until completely frozen.

These are wonderfully rich and chocolatey, which is why the suggested size seems small.

MAKE THE CRUST

1. Position a rack in the center of the oven and heat the oven to 350°F. Line the bottom and sides of a 9x13-inch baking pan with foil, allowing foil to overhang the long sides of the pan to act as handles for removing the cookie later. Lightly butter the foil.

2. Using a food processor, combine the flour, confectioners' sugar, and salt. Process the ingredients briefly to combine, about 15 seconds. Scatter the cold butter pieces and the vanilla over the flour mixture and process, using short pulses, until the dough begins to form small clumps, 1 to 1½ minutes. Turn the dough into the prepared pan. Using lightly floured fingertips, press the dough into the pan in a smooth, even layer. Bake until pale golden, especially around the edges, 22 to 25 minutes. Don't overbake or the crust will be hard and crisp. Transfer the pan to a rack and lower the oven temperature to 325°F.

MAKE THE FILLING

1. In a medium bowl, melt the chocolate, milk, and butter together over a pot of barely simmering water or in the microwave. Whisk until smooth and set aside to cool slightly.

2. Using a stand mixer fitted with a paddle attachment (or with a hand mixer), beat the eggs, sugar, and Kahlúa on medium-high speed until foamy and lighter in color, 2 minutes. Reduce the speed to low and gradually add the chocolate mixture. Stop the mixer and scrape the bowl and beater. Beat on medium speed until well blended, about 30 seconds.

3. Pour the chocolate batter over the baked crust and spread evenly. Bake until the sides are slightly puffed and a toothpick inserted near the center comes out wet and gooey but not liquid, 30 to 35 minutes. Transfer the pan to a rack. As it cools, the center may sink a bit, leaving the edges slightly elevated (about ½ inch). While the filling is still warm, use your fingertips to gently press the edges down to the level of the center, if necessary. When completely cool, cover with plastic and refrigerate until very cold, at least 12 hours or up to 2 days.

4. To serve, using the foil as handles, lift the rectangle from the pan and set it on a cutting board. Tipping the rectangle, carefully peel away the foil. Using a hot knife, cut the rectangle lengthwise into 1½-inch strips, wiping the blade clean before each cut. Cut each strip on alternating diagonals to make small triangles. Let sit at room temperature for about 5 minutes before serving.
—*Abigail Johnson Dodge*

PER TRIANGLE: 90 CALORIES | 1g PROTEIN | 9g CARB | 6g TOTAL FAT | 3.5g SAT FAT | 1g MONO FAT | 0g POLY FAT | 20mg CHOL | 15mg SODIUM | 1g FIBER

mocha cinnamon chocolate-chip cookies

YIELDS 48 COOKIES

- **9 oz. (2 cups) unbleached all-purpose flour**
- **½ tsp. baking powder**
- **¾ tsp. ground cinnamon**
- **¼ tsp. table salt**
- **10 oz. (1¼ cups) unsalted butter, softened at room temperature**
- **3 Tbs. instant espresso powder (or 4 Tbs. instant-coffee granules, crushed)**
- **1 cup confectioners' sugar**
- **½ cup packed light brown sugar**
- **1½ cups semisweet chocolate chips**
- **About ¼ cup granulated sugar, for dipping**

Made with cinnamon from the supermarket, these cookies are really good. Made with cinnamon from a spice retailer, they're even better. Try Chinese cassia cinnamon in this recipe.

1. Position a rack in the center of the oven and heat the oven to 350°F. Line a cooling rack with paper towels.

2. In a medium bowl, combine the flour, baking powder, cinnamon, and salt. In a larger bowl, beat the butter and coffee until well combined. Add the confectioners' sugar and brown sugar and beat until combined. Stir in the flour mixture about ½ cup at a time, mixing well after each addition. Stir in the chocolate chips.

3. Put the granulated sugar in a small, shallow bowl. Scoop out about 1 Tbs. dough and flatten it slightly into a disk. Dip one side into the granulated sugar and then set the disk, sugar side up, on an ungreased baking sheet. Repeat with the remaining dough, spacing the disks about 2 inches apart. Bake one sheet at a time until the edges of the cookies start to darken, 12 to 14 minutes. (Begin checking after 12 minutes, but don't be tempted to remove them too soon.)

4. Let the cookies cool for 1 to 2 minutes on the baking sheets. Transfer them to the paper-towel-lined rack to cool completely. Bake the rest of the dough the same way. —*Annie Giammattei*

PER COOKIE: 110 CALORIES | 1g PROTEIN | 13g CARB | 6g TOTAL FAT | 4g SAT FAT | 2g MONO FAT | 0g POLY FAT | 15mg CHOL | 15mg SODIUM | 0g FIBER

ginger crackles

YIELDS ABOUT 3 DOZEN COOKIES

- **10** oz. (2¼ cups) unbleached all-purpose flour
- **2** tsp. ground ginger
- **1** tsp. baking soda
- **¾** tsp. ground cinnamon
- **½** tsp. ground cloves
- **¼** tsp. salt
- **4** oz. (½ cup) unsalted butter, softened at room temperature
- **¼** cup shortening
- **1⅓** cups granulated sugar
- **1** large egg
- **¼** cup molasses

To freeze these ahead, put the sugared dough balls on a tray in the freezer until they're rock-hard and then stash them in zip-top bags. When it's time to bake, arrange them on cookie sheets and let them thaw while the oven heats up. The baked cookies stay fresh for up to a week if you store them in airtight containers.

1. Position a rack in the center of the oven and heat the oven to 350°F. In a large bowl, combine the flour, ginger, baking soda, cinnamon, cloves, and salt.

2. Using a stand mixer fitted with the paddle attachment (or in a large bowl with a hand mixer), beat the butter, shortening, and 1 cup of the sugar until well combined. Add the egg and molasses to the butter mixture; beat well. Add the dry ingredients and mix on low until well blended, scraping the bowl often. Shape the dough into 1-inch balls. Roll each ball in the remaining ⅓ cup sugar. Put the balls 2 inches apart (they need room to spread) on a parchment-lined baking sheet. Bake one sheet at a time until the cookies are lightly browned around the edges and puffed, about 13 minutes. Let the cookies sit on the baking sheet for 5 minutes and then transfer them to a rack to cool completely. —*Abigail Johnson Dodge*

PER COOKIE: 100 CALORIES | 1g PROTEIN | 15g CARB | 4g TOTAL FAT | 2g SAT FAT | 1.5g MONO FAT | 0.5g POLY FAT | 15mg CHOL | 55mg SODIUM | 0g FIBER

triple ginger cookies

YIELDS ABOUT 4½ DOZEN COOKIES

5½ oz. (11 Tbs.) unsalted butter, softened at room temperature

1 cup molasses

⅔ cup granulated sugar

1 large egg

1 tsp. pure vanilla extract

18 oz. (4 cups) unbleached all-purpose flour

1 tsp. baking soda

½ tsp. table salt

1 tsp. ground ginger

2 Tbs. finely chopped crystallized ginger

2 Tbs. finely chopped fresh ginger

Confectioners' sugar, for dusting (optional)

Ginger in three forms adds a warm zing to this soft yet sturdy spice cookie.

1. With an electric mixer or a wooden spoon, cream the butter and molasses until well blended. Add the sugar and mix until well blended. Add the egg and vanilla and beat until well incorporated. Sift together the flour, baking soda, and salt. Mix the ground, crystallized, and fresh ginger into the dry ingredients. Stir the flour mixture into the butter in three additions until just blended.

2. Position the racks in the upper and lower thirds of the oven and heat the oven to 350°F. Roll the dough in 1 Tbs. chunks into 1-inch balls. Arrange the balls 1 inch apart on ungreased cookie sheets. Bake until the cookies crack slightly on top but are still moist inside, about 13 minutes. Remove and let cool on racks and sprinkle with confectioners' sugar, if you like.

—Margery K. Friedman

PER COOKIE: 80 CALORIES | 1g PROTEIN | 14g CARB | 2.5g TOTAL FAT | 1.5g SAT FAT | 1g MONO FAT | 0g POLY FAT | 10mg CHOL | 45mg SODIUM | 0g FIBER

selecting and storing ginger

FRESH Look for unblemished, firm roots and avoid the older, wrinkly ones. Fresh ginger keeps in the fridge for two weeks or so. To use, gently scrape away the thin layer of skin from a portion of the root with a spoon. For finely grated fresh ginger, use a rasp-style grater.

DRIED OR GROUND Like all dried spices, ground ginger's intensity diminishes over time, so buy in small quantities and use it up within six months. If you're not sure if your ground ginger is still fresh, smell it: It should have an assertive, spicy, gingery aroma.

CRYSTALLIZED This soft, candied form of ginger is sold in many sizes, all of which are found in natural-foods stores, gourmet stores, Asian markets, and increasingly, in supermarkets' spice sections. Whether you buy ¼-inch-thick quarter-size rounds (preferred) or chopped or diced crystallized ginger, be sure it's moist, pliable, and visibly coated with sugar granules. Kept in an airtight container, it will stay moist and fragrant for months.

double ginger crackles

YIELDS ABOUT 4 DOZEN COOKIES

- **10 oz. (2¼ cups) unbleached all-purpose flour**
- **2¾ tsp. ground ginger**
- **1 tsp. baking soda**
- **¼ tsp. table salt**
- **6 oz. (¾ cup) unsalted butter, softened at room temperature**
- **1⅓ cups granulated sugar**
- **1 large egg, at room temperature**
- **¼ cup molasses**
- **3 Tbs. finely chopped crystallized ginger**

The double dose of ginger here comes from ground and crystallized ginger. Because the ginger flavor intensifies with time, these cookies keep especially well.

1. Position racks in the upper and lower thirds of the oven and heat the oven to 350°F. Line two large baking sheets with parchment or nonstick baking liners.

2. In a medium bowl, whisk the flour, ground ginger, baking soda, and salt. Using a stand mixer fitted with a paddle attachment (or in a large bowl with a hand mixer), beat the butter and 1 cup of the sugar on medium-high speed until well blended. Add the egg, molasses, and crystallized ginger; beat well. Add the dry ingredients and mix on low speed until well blended.

3. Pour the remaining ⅓ cup sugar into a shallow bowl. Using a 1-Tbs. cookie scoop (or a small one if you don't have this size) or 2 tablespoons, shape the dough into 1-inch balls. Roll each ball in the sugar to coat. Set the balls 1½ to 2 inches apart on the prepared cookie sheets.

4. Bake, rotating the sheets halfway through, until the cookies are puffed and the bottoms are lightly browned, 12 to 14 minutes. If you touch a cookie, it should feel dry on the surface but soft inside. The surface cracks will look a bit wet. Let the cookies sit on the cookie sheet for 5 minutes and then transfer them to a rack to cool completely. *—Abigail Johnson Dodge*

PER COOKIE: 80 CALORIES | 1g PROTEIN | 12g CARB | 3g TOTAL FAT | 2g SAT FAT | 1g MONO FAT | 0g POLY FAT | 10mg CHOL | 40mg SODIUM | 0g FIBER

Make Ahead

When cool, store these cookies in airtight containers for up to 5 days.

Pairing Drinks with Holiday Sweets

You can't go wrong with setting out a selection of coffees and teas for your party guests to choose from. If you'd like to serve alcohol too, the key to matching drinks with desserts is to choose liqueurs or wines that are sweeter than the dessert. Try one or more of these ideas: Coffee liqueurs like Kahlúa always taste good with chocolate or coffee-chocolate desserts. Enjoy the liqueurs in French- or Italian-roast coffee topped with fresh whipped cream, or straight up in a liqueur glass.

Fruit-based liqueurs like the legendary French raspberry liqueur Chambord work well with any dessert that has a fruit element. Serve fruit-based liqueurs chilled without ice in a liqueur glass, or add an ounce to a glass of sparkling wine or non-vintage Champagne.

A sweet fortified wine, such as a sweet sherry, is delicious with chocolate or caramel desserts; serve either at room temperature in a small wineglass.

gingersnaps

7½ oz. (1⅔ cups) unbleached all-purpose flour

1½ tsp. ground ginger

1 tsp. ground cinnamon

½ tsp. baking soda

¼ tsp. table salt

¼ tsp. ground nutmeg

¼ tsp. freshly ground black pepper

4 oz. (½ cup) unsalted butter, softened at room temperature

¾ cup packed dark brown sugar

1 large egg yolk

3 Tbs. molasses

These snaps have a crunchy texture and an almost tingly spicy warmth.

1. In a medium bowl, whisk the flour, ginger, cinnamon, baking soda, salt, nutmeg, and pepper.

2. Using a stand mixer fitted with the paddle attachment (or in a large bowl with a hand mixer), beat the butter and brown sugar on medium speed until light and fluffy, about 3 minutes. Add the egg yolk and molasses and mix until well blended, about 1 minute. Add the flour mixture and mix on medium-low speed until the dough is well blended and forms moist pebbles, 30 to 60 seconds.

3. Dump the dough onto an unfloured work surface; gently knead until it comes together. Shape into an 8-inch-long log about 1½ inches in diameter; wrap in plastic. Refrigerate until firm, about 3 hours.

4. Position a rack in the center of the oven and heat the oven to 350°F. Line two large cookie sheets with parchment or nonstick baking liners.

5. Unwrap the dough and use a thin, sharp knife to cut the log into ³⁄₁₆-inch slices. Arrange the slices about 1 inch apart on the sheets. Bake one sheet at a time until the cookies are slightly darker brown on the bottoms and around the edges, 10 to 12 minutes. Set the sheet on a rack to cool for 15 minutes. Transfer the cookies to a rack and let cool completely. When cool, store in airtight containers. —*Abigail Johnson Dodge*

PER COOKIE, BASED ON 40 SERVINGS: 60 CALORIES | 1g PROTEIN | 9g CARB | 2.5g TOTAL FAT | 1.5g SAT FAT | 0.5g MONO FAT | 0g POLY FAT | 0mg CHOL | 10mg CHOL | 35mg SODIUM | 0g FIBER

molasses crinkles

YIELDS ABOUT THIRTY-SIX 3-INCH COOKIES

- 9 oz. (2 cups) unbleached all-purpose flour
- 2 tsp. baking soda
- 1¼ tsp. ground ginger
- 1 tsp. ground cinnamon
- ½ tsp. ground cloves
- ½ tsp. table salt
- 4 oz. (½ cup) unsalted butter, softened at room temperature; more for the baking sheets
- 1 cup packed dark brown sugar
- 2 Tbs. vegetable oil
- ⅓ cup molasses
- 1 large egg
- Granulated sugar, for rolling

Molasses gives these cookies a deep, complex sweetness.

SEVERAL HOURS BEFORE BAKING

In a medium bowl, sift together the flour, baking soda, ginger, cinnamon, cloves, and salt. Using a stand mixer fitted with the paddle attachment (or in a large bowl with a hand mixer), beat the butter and brown sugar until light and fluffy. Beat in the oil until blended. Scrape the bowl, add the molasses and the egg, and beat until blended. Stir in the flour mixture until well combined. Wrap the dough in plastic and chill until firm, about 3 hours.

BAKE THE COOKIES

Position a rack in the center of the oven and heat the oven to 375°F. Lightly grease two baking sheets. Measure the dough into tablespoon-size pieces and roll each piece between your palms to form 1-inch balls. Roll the balls in granulated sugar to coat. Put the balls 2 inches apart on the prepared sheets and sprinkle the tops with more sugar. Bake one sheet a time until the center surface of the cookies is barely dry, 9 to 10 minutes; don't overbake. Let the cookies cool on the sheets for 5 minutes and then transfer them to a rack to cool completely. —*Elaine Khosrova*

Making Sense of Molasses

Molasses came about as a byproduct of sugar cane processing; it's the syrup that remains after sugar cane juice has been boiled to separate out the crystallized sugar.

Which kind of molasses works best for baking—light, robust, or blackstrap? (And do you want sulfured or unsulfured?)

Light, mild, Barbados, or robust molasses Boiled only once, this molasses has a high sugar content and a mild flavor. Some brands of single-boil molasses haven't even had any sugar removed from them—they're simply refined sugar cane juice that's been reduced to a syrup. A widely distributed brand of this type is Grandma's® Original, and it's what was used in the Molasses Crinkles above. (Grandma's Robust, which is made from the first boil, also works well with a slightly less sweet flavor.)

Dark, full, or cooking molasses This molasses is boiled twice and is slightly bitter. It will result in a cookie that's a little less sweet than one made with single-boil molasses.

Blackstrap molasses Some people prize this molasses for its nutritional value; however, it is boiled three or more times and is not really recommended for baking.

Sulfured vs. unsulfured molasses Avoid sulfured molasses. Sulfur dioxide was traditionally added to molasses as a preservative, but because it alters the flavor somewhat, use unsulfered molasses when you can.

gingersnap snowflakes

Cut this dough into festive shapes, like these snowflakes. Then fill a couple of pastry bags with the icing (for instructions, see p. 33) and let the kids go to town.

YIELDS ABOUT 24 COOKIES

FOR THE COOKIES

13½	oz. (3 cups) unbleached all-purpose flour; more for rolling
2	tsp. ground ginger
1½	tsp. baking powder
¾	tsp. baking soda
½	tsp. table salt
½	tsp. ground cinnamon
¼	tsp. freshly grated nutmeg
¼	tsp. ground cloves
¾	cup packed dark brown sugar
3	oz. (6 Tbs.) unsalted butter, softened at room temperature
½	cup unsulfured molasses
1	large egg, at room temperature
1	tsp. pure vanilla extract

FOR DECORATING

½	lb. (2 cups plus 2 Tbs.) confectioners' sugar
2½	Tbs. meringue powder
	Blue food coloring
	Edible silver dragées

MAKE THE COOKIES

1. In a large bowl, whisk the flour, ginger, baking powder, baking soda, salt, cinnamon, nutmeg, and cloves; set aside. Using a stand mixer fitted with the paddle attachment, beat the sugar and butter on medium speed until light and fluffy, about 3 minutes. Beat in the molasses, egg, and vanilla until thoroughly combined, about 1 minute. On low speed, gradually add the flour mixture until just combined.

2. Divide the dough, shape into two balls, and wrap each in plastic. Refrigerate for at least 2 and up to 8 hours.

3. Position a rack in the center of the oven and heat the oven to 375°F. Line two baking sheets with parchment. Working with one piece of dough at a time, roll it on a lightly floured piece of parchment until it's about ⅛ inch thick. Put the parchment and dough onto another baking sheet and refrigerate for 30 minutes. Cut out cookies with a 5-inch snowflake cookie cutter. Remove excess dough from around the cut-outs and transfer the cookies with a spatula to the prepared sheets, spacing them about 2 inches apart. You can gather and reroll the scraps of dough from around the cut-outs up to two times.

4. Bake one sheet at a time until the cookies begin to darken around the edges, 6 to 8 minutes. Let cool on the sheet on a rack for about 15 minutes. Transfer the cookies directly to the rack and let cool completely.

DECORATE THE COOKIES

1. Using a stand mixer fitted with the whisk attachment, mix the confectioners' sugar, meringue powder, and ¼ cup cold water on low speed until blended. Increase the speed to medium and beat until the icing holds thick, soft peaks, 3 to 4 minutes. Test the icing's consistency by piping a small amount through a piping bag fitted with a straight #2 tip. If it's too thick, add a few drops of water to the mixture in the bowl. If it's too runny, add confectioners' sugar, 1 Tbs. at a time, beating on low speed to blend. Don't overbeat, or it will stiffen and lose its gloss. Keep the icing covered with a damp cloth or plastic wrap until ready to use, and use it the same day it's made.

2. Put about three-quarters of the icing in a clean 1-quart container. Put the remaining icing in a small container and tint with the blue food coloring. (Stir in coloring a bit at a time until you reach the shade you want.)

3. Put a small amount of the white icing in a piping bag fitted with a straight #2 tip and pipe the outline of the cookie.

4. Stir water, a few drops at a time, into the remaining white icing until the icing no longer stays peaked when piped but creates a smooth surface. To test, put a small amount in another piping bag with a #2 tip (the icing will drip, so have a cloth ready). Fill in the lines on each cookie, allow the icing to spread, and don't overfill—use a small paintbrush (one that you use only for food) to help spread the icing if necessary. Let the cookies dry until the icing is set, 2 to 3 hours.

5. When the white icing is completely dry, put the blue icing in a clean piping bag fitted with a #2 tip and pipe branched lines connecting opposite tips of the snowflakes. Decorate with dragées while the blue icing is wet.
—*Daniella Caranci Verburg*

PER COOKIE: 170 CALORIES | 2g PROTEIN | 34g CARB | 3.5g TOTAL FAT | 2g SAT FAT | 1g MONO FAT | 0g POLY FAT | 15mg CHOL | 125mg SODIUM | 0g FIBER

Freshly Grated vs. Preground Nutmeg

Good cooks know there's a big difference between freshly ground spices and their preground counterparts, and this is particularly true in the case of nutmeg. See for yourself. Open the jar of ground nutmeg that's probably in your cupboard and compare it to some that's freshly grated. The freshly grated smells sweet, fragrant, almost citrusy. The preground smells sharp and musky by comparison.

This isn't to say that there's no place for preground nutmeg in the pantry alongside the whole nutmeg—it's convenient, after all—but it's best to think of them as different spices. If a recipe calls for preground nutmeg, go ahead and use it (provided it's not more than six months old). But when a recipe calls for freshly grated nutmeg, don't be tempted to substitute—the results won't be nearly as delicious.

brown sugar spice cookies

**YIELDS ABOUT 8 DOZEN
2-INCH COOKIES**

- 11¼ oz. (2½ cups) unbleached all-purpose flour; more as needed
- 2 tsp. ground cinnamon
- 1 tsp. ground ginger
- 1 tsp. ground nutmeg
- ½ tsp. table salt
- ¼ tsp. baking soda
- ¼ tsp. ground allspice
- ¼ tsp. ground black pepper
- 6 oz. (¾ cup) unsalted butter, softened at room temperature
- 1½ cups very firmly packed, very fresh dark brown sugar
- 2 Tbs. molasses
- 1 large egg yolk
- 1 large egg
- 1 tsp. pure vanilla extract
- 1 large egg white
- 8 oz. (2 cups) walnuts, toasted and coarsely chopped

These cookies, edged with toasted walnuts, are perfect with a cup of mulled cider or hot tea. When cool, store between sheets of waxed paper in a tightly covered container for up to a week, or freeze for up to 3 months.

MIX THE DOUGH

Sift together the flour, cinnamon, ginger, nutmeg, salt, baking soda, allspice, and pepper. Using a stand mixer fitted with the paddle attachment (or in a large bowl using a hand mixer), cream the butter on medium-low speed until smooth, about 2 minutes. Add the brown sugar in three additions and then add the molasses; scrape the bowl as needed. Mix for another 2 minutes. Blend in the egg yolk, egg, and vanilla, scraping the bowl again. Reduce the speed to low and add the dry ingredients in three additions, mixing just until combined. Portion the dough into thirds, wrap each third in plastic, and refrigerate until slightly firm, about 30 minutes.

SHAPE THE DOUGH

Have ready three 15-inch sheets of plastic wrap. Whisk the egg white lightly with 1 tsp. water. Put the chopped walnuts in a long, shallow pan (like a 7x11-inch Pyrex dish). Working with one piece of dough at a time on a lightly floured surface, roll into a log about 8 inches long. Set it on a sheet of waxed paper. Brush lightly all over with the egg white and then roll the log in the walnuts, pressing gently so the nuts adhere. The roll should lengthen to at least 9 inches. Position the log on a sheet of plastic wrap, centering it at the long edge closest to you. Roll tightly, twisting the ends firmly to seal. With your hands on either end of the log, push firmly toward the center to compact the dough. The finished log should measure about 9 inches long and 1¾ inches thick. Repeat with the remaining dough. Refrigerate until firm enough to slice, at least 2 hours, or freeze for up to 3 months.

BAKE THE COOKIES

Position racks in the upper and lower thirds of the oven and heat the oven to 350°F. Line two rimmed baking sheets with parchment. Working with one log at a time, use a tomato knife or other small serrated knife to slice the dough into ¼-inch rounds, using a gentle sawing motion. Set the rounds 1 inch apart on the prepared sheets and bake until the tops feel set and slightly firm, about 14 minutes, rotating the sheets as needed. Let cool on the sheets for 5 minutes. With a thin metal spatula, transfer the cookies to racks to cool completely. *—Carole Walter*

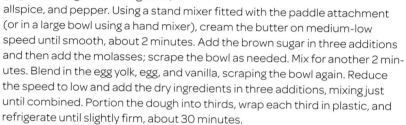

keep your logs round

To keep round logs from flattening out on the bottom while they chill, try these ideas:

- Turn frequently. Put the logs on a level shelf or flat baking sheet in the refrigerator or freezer and turn them every 15 minutes for the first hour. If necessary, remold the logs by rolling them back and forth a few times on the countertop.

- Use a cradle. A baguette pan makes a perfect cradle for chilling logs of dough. Or, take a few empty paper towel rolls, cut each in half lengthwise to make two troughs with rounded bottoms, and place a log in each half.

For both of these methods, after the logs have chilled for 15 to 20 minutes, turn them over once and chill until firm.

treasure cookies

**YIELDS ABOUT 3 DOZEN
2½-INCH COOKIES**

- 8½ oz. (1¾ cups) unbleached all-purpose flour
- ½ tsp. baking soda
- ¼ tsp. table salt
- 6 oz. (¾ cup) unsalted butter, slightly softened
- ¾ cup plus 2 Tbs. granulated sugar
- 2 large eggs
- 1 9-oz. package condensed mincemeat, crumbled

To make chewy drop cookies, underbake them slightly so that they're still quite soft and not yet browned, but no longer look wet in the center. For crispier cookies, bake them longer, letting the cookies become lightly browned all over.

1. Position a rack in the center of the oven and heat the oven to 350°F. Lightly grease two baking sheets or cover them with parchment. In a medium bowl, mix the flour, baking soda, and salt. With an electric mixer, beat the butter and sugar until light and fluffy. Beat in the eggs, one at a time, scraping down the sides of the bowl. Add the flour mixture and beat until just combined. Add the crumbled mincemeat and beat until the dough is well mixed and has darkened slightly.

2. Drop the dough by the heaping tablespoonful about 2 inches apart onto the sheets. Bake one sheet at a time until the cookies are very lightly browned, 10 to 12 minutes. Let cool on the sheets for 5 minutes; transfer to a wire rack to cool completely. *—Elaine Khosrova*

What Is Mincemeat?

Dating back to the Middle Ages as a way to preserve small amounts of meat, mincemeat still remains on supermarket shelves, although it is far less common. It is a mixture of dried fruit, nuts, citrus peel, distilled spirits, spices, brown sugar, and, yes, some sort of meat or suet. Vegetable suet is now occasionally used in some recipes. It is available in the baking section at the market.

Kahlúa fudge bites

YIELDS ABOUT 8 DOZEN
1-INCH SQUARES

FOR THE FUDGE BITES

- ¾ lb. (1½ cups) unsalted butter; more for the pan
- 9 oz. (2 cups) unbleached all-purpose flour
- ½ tsp. baking powder
- ½ tsp. table salt
- 3½ oz. (1 cup) unsweetened natural cocoa powder (not Dutch-processed)
- 3 cups very firmly packed light brown sugar
- 4 large eggs
- 2 Tbs. Kahlúa or other coffee-flavored liqueur, or 1½ tsp. pure vanilla extract

FOR THE GLAZE

- 6 oz. bittersweet chocolate, finely chopped
- 3 oz. (6 Tbs.) unsalted butter, cut into 6 pieces
- 1 Tbs. light corn syrup

These are so chocolatey and rich that it's best to cut them into small, bite-size squares.

MAKE THE FUDGE BITES

1. Position a rack in the center of the oven and heat the oven to 325°F. Lightly grease the bottom and sides of a 9x13-inch baking pan.

2. In a medium bowl, whisk the flour, baking powder, and salt to blend. Melt the butter in a large saucepan over medium heat, stirring occasionally. Remove the pan from the heat and whisk in the cocoa powder until smooth. Whisk in the brown sugar until blended. Add the eggs, one at a time, whisking until just blended. Whisk in the coffee liqueur or vanilla along with the last egg. Sprinkle the flour over the mixture and stir with a rubber spatula until just blended. Scrape the batter into the prepared pan and spread it evenly. Bake until a toothpick inserted in the center comes out with a few small, moist clumps sticking to it, about 30 minutes. (Don't overbake or the squares won't be fudgy.) Transfer the pan to a rack to let cool completely.

MAKE THE CHOCOLATE GLAZE

In a medium bowl, melt the chocolate, butter, and corn syrup in a microwave or over barely simmering water, whisking until smooth. Pour the glaze onto the center of the cooled, uncut fudge bars. Using an offset spatula, spread the glaze evenly to cover completely. Refrigerate until the glaze is set, about 30 minutes. Cut into 1-inch squares. *—Abigail Johnson Dodge*

Make Ahead

When completely cooled, the pan of uncut cookies can be covered with plastic and frozen for up to a month before thawing, glazing, and serving. Glazed bars keep for up to 4 days at room temperature in the pan if covered with plastic wrap.

ginger and lemon cookies

YIELDS ABOUT 30 COOKIES

- ½ lb. (1 cup) unsalted butter, softened at room temperature
- ¾ cup plus 2 Tbs. granulated sugar
- 3 tsp. finely grated fresh ginger
- ½ tsp. finely grated lemon zest
- ¼ tsp. table salt
- 2 large egg yolks
- ½ tsp. pure vanilla extract
- 11¼ oz. (2½ cups) unbleached all-purpose flour
- 2 Tbs. finely chopped crystallized ginger
- 1 lightly beaten egg white

These cookies can also be shaped with a cookie press or pastry bag so they look like traditional spritz cookies. Brush the tops with the egg white and sprinkle with just the sugar, eliminating the crystallized ginger.

A rasp-style grater comes in handy for grating both the ginger and the lemon zest.

1. Position a rack in the center of the oven and heat the oven to 350°F. Line three large cookie sheets with parchment or nonstick baking liners.

2. In a large bowl, combine the butter, ¾ cup of the sugar, the grated ginger, lemon zest, and salt. Using an electric mixer set on medium speed, beat the mixture until well blended and light, 2 to 3 minutes. Scrape the bowl. Add the egg yolks and vanilla; continue mixing until well blended, 30 to 60 seconds. Add the flour and mix on low speed until the dough is blended and just comes together.

3. Shape tablespoonfuls of the dough into 1-inch balls (a small ice cream scoop works well) and set the balls 1½ inches apart on the prepared cookie sheets. In a small, shallow dish, mix the crystallized ginger and the remaining 2 Tbs. granulated sugar until blended.

4. With the palm of your hand, press on one of the dough balls until it's ¼ inch thick and about 2 inches in diameter. Repeat with remaining dough balls. Brush the tops of the cookies with the egg white and sprinkle them with the ginger-sugar mixture. Press gently on the cookies with the bottom of a metal measuring cup to help the topping adhere.

5. Bake one sheet at a time until the cookies are light brown on the bottoms and around the edges, about 11 minutes on dark cookie sheets, or about 13 minutes on silver-toned sheets. Set the sheet on a rack to cool for 5 minutes and then transfer the cookies to the rack to cool completely. When cool, store in airtight containers. —*Abigail Johnson Dodge*

PER COOKIE, BASED ON 30 SERVINGS: 120 CALORIES | 1g PROTEIN | 14g CARB | 6g TOTAL FAT | 4g SAT FAT | 1.5g MONO FAT | 0g POLY FAT | 30mg CHOL | 25mg SODIUM | 0g FIBER

clove snaps

YIELDS ABOUT 3 DOZEN
COOKIES

- 6¾ oz. (1½ cups) unbleached all-purpose flour; more for rolling
- 1½ tsp. ground cloves
- ¼ tsp. ground cinnamon
- ¼ tsp. ground black pepper
- ⅛ tsp. table salt
- 4 oz. (½ cup) unsalted butter, softened at room temperature
- ¾ cup granulated sugar
- 1 large egg
- 1 tsp. packed finely grated orange zest

Like the gingersnaps on p. 202, these cookies have a delicious spicy crunch.

1. In a bowl, sift together the flour, cloves, cinnamon, pepper, and salt. Using a stand mixer fitted with the paddle attachment (or in a large bowl with a hand mixer), cream the butter at medium speed until light and fluffy, about 2 minutes. Add the sugar and blend just until combined, scraping the bowl well. Add the egg and orange zest and mix until well blended, scraping the bowl as needed. Add the sifted dry ingredients all at once and mix on low speed just until the flour is absorbed and the dough starts to come together, about 30 seconds. Turn out the dough onto a lightly floured surface and knead just until the dough forms a smooth mass. Flatten into a disk that's about ½ inch thick. Wrap tightly in plastic and refrigerate until firm, about 2 hours.

2. Position a rack in the center of the oven and heat the oven to 375°F. On a lightly floured surface, roll the dough ⅛ inch thick, making sure that it isn't sticking to the surface and that it rolls out evenly, lightly sprinkling flour under the dough if needed. With a 2-inch round (or similar-size) fluted cookie cutter, cut out shapes. Reroll the scraps and cut out more cookies. Set the cookies ½ inch apart on parchment-lined baking sheets. Bake one sheet at a time until the cookies are golden around the edges and on the bottoms, about 12 minutes, rotating the baking sheet as needed for even baking. Let the cookies cool completely on the baking sheet on racks. Store in airtight containers.

—*Robert Wemischner*

What Are Cloves?

Cloves are sharp-flavored and pack spicy depth and piquancy. Born of an evergreen tree, cloves are indigenous to Indonesia but are also cultivated in Malaysia, India, and Madagascar. The higher the quality, the more likely this nail-shaped spice will have its bud-like head intact.

How to use: Look to whole cloves for flavoring fruit-poaching syrups. Use ground cloves in concert with other spices in pumpkin pies, spice cookies, and coffee cakes, or put them front and center in the Clove Snaps above. You can also find clove oil, a fine translation of this spice's warm flavor, a few drops of which are perfect in icings, buttercreams, mousses, and other dishes where the whole or ground spice wouldn't integrate as well.

sweet & savory sandwiches

chocolate-dipped chocolate-apricot sandwich cookies

YIELDS ABOUT 3 DOZEN SANDWICH COOKIES

FOR THE COOKIES

- 9 oz. (2 cups) unbleached all-purpose flour; more as needed
- ½ tsp. baking powder
- ½ tsp. table salt
- ½ lb. (1 cup) unsalted butter, softened at room temperature
- 8 oz. (2 cups) confectioners' sugar
- 2¼ oz. (¾ cup) unsweetened, natural cocoa powder, sifted if lumpy
- 2 large egg yolks
- 1 tsp. pure vanilla extract

FOR THE FILLING AND GLAZE

- 1 cup apricot preserves
- 12 oz. bittersweet chocolate, finely chopped
- 2 tsp. canola or vegetable oil

Make Ahead

The dough can be refrigerated for up to 3 days or frozen for up to 1 month. The cookies can be stored in an airtight container at room temperature for up to 5 days or frozen for up to 1 month before filling and glazing. Filled and glazed cookies can be stored in an airtight container at room temperature for up to 2 days.

The Sacher torte—chocolate sponge cake layered with apricot jam and covered in dark chocolate icing—is reinterpreted in this recipe as cakey cookies filled with preserves and dipped in bittersweet chocolate.

MAKE THE COOKIES

1. In a medium bowl, whisk the flour, baking powder, and salt. Using a stand mixer fitted with the paddle attachment, beat the butter, sugar, and cocoa powder on low speed until blended; then raise the speed to medium and beat until light and fluffy, about 3 minutes. Scrape down the bowl and beater. Add the egg yolks and vanilla and mix on medium speed until well blended, about 1 minute. Add the flour mixture and mix on low speed until the dough comes together, about 1 minute.

2. Turn the dough out onto a work surface and portion into three equal piles on pieces of plastic wrap. Using the plastic as an aid, gently shape each one into a smooth, flat 5-inch disk and wrap in the plastic. Refrigerate until chilled, about 30 minutes.

3. Position a rack in the center of the oven and heat the oven to 375°F. Line two cookie sheets with parchment or nonstick baking liners. Working with one disk at a time, roll the dough between two sheets of lightly floured parchment or on a floured work surface until ⅛ to 3/16 inch thick. Dust with additional flour as needed. Using a 2¼-inch cookie cutter, cut out shapes. Arrange about 1 inch apart on the lined cookie sheets. Stack the scraps and gently press them together. Reroll and cut. Repeat with remaining dough disks.

4. Bake one sheet at a time until the cookies look dry and slightly cracked and feel somewhat firm when pressed, 7 to 9 minutes. Let cool on the sheet for about 5 minutes and then transfer to a rack to cool completely.

FILL AND GLAZE THE COOKIES

1. Press the preserves through a fine sieve, discarding any large pieces of apricot. Arrange half of the cookies bottom side up on a work surface. Put 1 tsp. of the preserves in the center of each cookie. Cover each with one of the remaining cookies, bottom side down. Gently squeeze each cookie together to spread the preserves until it just reaches the edges.

2. Line two or three baking sheets with parchment, aluminum foil, or waxed paper. Put the chocolate and oil in a small, deep, heatproof bowl. Heat in a microwave until almost melted, or set the bowl in a skillet of barely simmering water and stir until melted and smooth.

3. Dip each cookie halfway into the glaze until lightly covered. Lift the cookie out and gently scrape the bottom against the side of the bowl to remove excess glaze. Set on the prepared baking sheets. Let the cookies sit at room temperature or in the refrigerator until the glaze is firm.
—Abigail Johnson Dodge

PER COOKIE: 180 CALORIES | 2g PROTEIN | 24g CARB | 9g TOTAL FAT | 5g SAT FAT | 2.5g MONO FAT | 0g POLY FAT | 25mg CHOL | 50mg SODIUM | 2g FIBER

lemon-meringue sandwich cookies

YIELDS 40 SANDWICH COOKIES

FOR THE MERINGUES

¼ cup granulated sugar

2½ oz. (⅔ cup) confectioners' sugar

Pinch of table salt

2 large egg whites, at room temperature

¼ tsp. cream of tartar

¼ tsp. pure vanilla extract

¼ tsp. pure lemon extract

1 oz. (¼ cup) finely crushed gingersnap cookies

FOR THE LEMON CURD

3 oz. (6 Tbs.) unsalted butter

½ cup granulated sugar

⅓ cup fresh lemon juice (from 1½ large lemons)

2 Tbs. finely grated lemon zest (from 1 large lemon)

Pinch of table salt

6 large egg yolks

Lemon meringue pie is the inspiration for these cookies: crisp meringue buttons are sprinkled with gingersnap crumbs (the crust) and sandwiched around lemon curd. The meringues can be stored in an airtight container for up to 1 month. The lemon curd will keep in the refrigerator for up to 3 weeks.

MAKE THE MERINGUES

1. Position racks in the upper and lower thirds of the oven and heat the oven to 175°F. Line two large heavy-duty baking sheets with parchment.

2. In a food processor, process the granulated sugar until very fine, about 45 seconds. Add confectioners' sugar and salt; pulse until well blended, about 15 seconds.

3. Using a stand mixer fitted with the whisk attachment, combine the egg whites and cream of tartar. Begin mixing on medium-low speed until frothy. Increase the speed to medium high and beat until the whites form soft peaks, about 2 minutes. Continue beating while gradually sprinkling in the sugar mixture. When all the sugar is added, increase the speed to high and whip until firm, glossy peaks form, about 10 minutes. Add the vanilla and lemon extracts and beat just until blended, about 10 seconds.

4. Spoon the meringue into a large pastry bag fitted with a plain 3⁄32-inch tip (Ateco #3). Holding the pastry bag perpendicular to a lined baking sheet, pipe small flat disks about 1¼ inches in diameter and no higher than ¼ inch, spaced about ½ inch apart. As you pipe, keep the tip down into the meringue and let it spread out rather than lifting the tip up. If necessary, help the meringue spread by circling the tip in it as you pipe. Sprinkle crushed cookies evenly over the tops of the meringues. Don't worry if extra crumbs fall off. Using a fingertip, lightly press down on the crumbs to flatten any meringue peaks.

5. Bake until dried and crisp but not browned, about 2½ hours. Turn off the oven and leave the door shut; let the meringues sit in the oven until cool, about 2 hours. Remove from the oven and gently lift them off the parchment.

MAKE THE LEMON CURD

1. Melt the butter in a 4-quart saucepan over medium heat. Remove the pan from the heat and whisk in the sugar, lemon juice, zest, and salt. Whisk in the yolks until well blended. Cook over medium-low heat, whisking constantly, until the mixture is thick enough to coat a spatula and hold a line drawn through it with a finger, 4 to 6 minutes. Don't let the mixture boil.

2. Strain the curd into a clean bowl and cover with plastic wrap, pressing the plastic onto the surface to keep a skin from forming. Let cool at room temperature; then refrigerate until chilled.

ASSEMBLE THE COOKIES

Arrange half of the meringues bottom side up on a work surface. Put the chilled curd in a piping bag fitted with a plain ⅜-inch tip (Ateco #7) and pipe about 1 tsp. lemon curd onto each meringue. Gently press the remaining meringues bottom side down onto the curd. The filled cookies can be prepared and kept at room temperature up to 1 hour before serving. The longer they sit, the softer the meringues become. *—Abigail Johnson Dodge*

PER COOKIE: 50 CALORIES | 1g PROTEIN | 7g CARB | 2.5g TOTAL FAT | 1.5g SAT FAT | 1g MONO FAT | 0g POLY FAT | 35mg CHOL | 25mg SODIUM | 0g FIBER

orange cream stars

FOR THE COOKIES

3	oz. cream cheese, softened
½	lb. (1 cup) unsalted butter, softened at room temperature
1	cup granulated sugar
1	Tbs. freshly grated orange zest
1	large egg yolk
1	tsp. pure vanilla extract
12	oz. (2⅔ cups) unbleached all-purpose flour

FOR THE ORANGE CREAM FILLING

½	lb. (1 cup) unsalted butter, softened
½	cup confectioners' sugar; more for dusting
1	Tbs. freshly grated orange zest
2	tsp. fresh orange juice

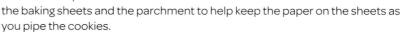

These cookies can be made ahead and frozen. The orange cream may be refrigerated for several days; soften it at room temperature before using.

MAKE THE COOKIES

1. Position racks in the upper and lower thirds of the oven and heat the oven to 350°F. Line several baking sheets with parchment. Dab a few drops of water between the baking sheets and the parchment to help keep the paper on the sheets as you pipe the cookies.

2. Using a stand mixer fitted with the paddle attachment (or in a large bowl with a hand mixer), beat the cream cheese, butter, sugar, orange zest, egg yolk, and vanilla on medium speed until fluffy, about 4 minutes. Gradually mix in the flour.

3. Fill a large pastry bag fitted with a ½-inch star tip about two thirds of the way full. Twist the opening closed and squeeze out generous 1½-inch stars, spacing them about 1½ inches apart on the prepared sheets.

4. Bake the cookies until the edges just begin to brown, about 20 minutes. Set the cookie sheet on a rack until the cookies are cool enough to remove with a spatula without distorting their shape.

ASSEMBLE THE COOKIES

Using a stand mixer fitted with the paddle attachment (or in a large bowl with a hand mixer), beat the orange cream filling ingredients until smooth, about 5 minutes. Turn half of the cookies upside down on a piece of parchment. Fit a pastry bag with a ½-inch plain tip and fill it with the orange cream. Pipe approximately ½ tsp. filling onto each cookie base. Place another cookie, right side up, sandwich style, on top. Press down lightly to adhere. Refrigerate until set. Dust the cookies lightly with confectioners' sugar before serving. —*Melissa Murphy*

PER SANDWICH: 140 CALORIES | 1g PROTEIN | 15g CARB | 9g TOTAL FAT | 5g SAT FAT | 3g MONO FAT | 0g POLY FAT | 30mg CHOL | 10mg SODIUM | 0g FIBER

how to pipe stars

Hold the bag straight up and down with the edge of the tip barely touching the baking sheet. Squeeze the bag firmly until the shape is as wide as you like.

Stop squeezing and push the tip down slightly. Give the tip a slight twist as you pull it up and away. Put your free hand on the parchment to keep it from lifting.

ginger-spice sandwich cookies with lemon cream

YIELDS ABOUT 30 SANDWICH COOKIES

FOR THE COOKIES

- **9 oz. (2 cups) unbleached all-purpose flour**
- **2 tsp. ground ginger**
- **1½ tsp. ground cinnamon**
- **½ tsp. ground cardamom**
- **½ tsp. baking soda**
- **½ tsp. kosher salt**
- **6 oz. (¾ cup) unsalted butter, softened at room temperature**
- **½ cup packed dark brown sugar**
- **½ cup granulated sugar; more for rolling**
- **¼ cup unsulfured molasses**
- **1 large egg, at room temperature**
- **½ tsp. pure vanilla extract**

FOR THE LEMON CREAM

- **4 oz. cream cheese, softened at room temperature**
- **1 Tbs. finely grated lemon zest (from 1 medium lemon)**
- **6 oz. (1½ cups) confectioners' sugar**

If you make these a day ahead of time, the cookies will soften a bit, and the flavors will mingle nicely. Fresh spices are key.

MAKE THE COOKIES

1. Position a rack in the center of the oven and heat the oven to 350°F. Line three baking sheets with parchment.

2. In a medium bowl, whisk the flour, ginger, cinnamon, cardamom, baking soda, and salt. Using a stand mixer fitted with the paddle attachment (or in a large bowl with a hand mixer), beat the butter and both sugars on medium-high speed until light and fluffy, about 3 minutes. Add the molasses, egg, and vanilla and continue to beat until incorporated, about 1 minute. Reduce the speed to low, slowly add the flour mixture, and mix until just incorporated, about 1 minute. Shape the dough into a disk, wrap in plastic, and refrigerate until firm, about 1 hour.

3. Put about ⅓ cup granulated sugar in a small bowl. Using your hands, roll teaspoonfuls of dough into 1-inch balls. Roll each ball in sugar and arrange them about 2 inches apart on the lined baking sheets. Use the bottom of a glass to flatten the cookies slightly. Bake one sheet at a time until the cookies feel dry to the touch and are beginning to firm up (they'll still feel soft inside), 10 to 14 minutes. Let cool completely on racks.

MAKE THE LEMON CREAM

With a hand mixer, mix the cream cheese and lemon zest in a medium bowl until smooth. Slowly add the confectioners' sugar and continue to mix until smooth.

ASSEMBLE THE COOKIES

Drop about 1 tsp. of the lemon cream in the center of a cookie, top with another cookie, and gently press them together. Repeat with the remaining cookies. *—Tasha DeSerio*

PER COOKIE: 150 CALORIES | 1g PROTEIN | 24g CARB | 6g TOTAL FAT | 4g SAT FAT | 1.5g MONO FAT | 0g POLY FAT | 25mg CHOL | 55mg SODIUM | 0g FIBER

Make Ahead

Store these cookies in an air-tight container for up to 2 days.

chocolate-covered sandwich cookies with dulce de leche (*alfajores*)

YIELDS ABOUT TWENTY-EIGHT
2-INCH SANDWICH COOKIES

12 oz. (2⅔ cups) unbleached all-purpose flour; more for rolling

6 oz. (1⅓ cups) whole-wheat flour

2 tsp. baking powder

1 tsp. table salt

½ lb. (1 cup) unsalted butter, softened at room temperature

¾ cup granulated sugar

1½ tsp. finely grated orange zest

2 13.4-oz. cans Nestlé® dulce de leche

1 lb. bittersweet chocolate, chopped

1 pint heavy cream

These are a take on Argentinian alfajores—delicate shortbread cookies with a gooey dulce de leche filling and a coating of dark chocolate. Store filled and coated cookies in a plastic container, separating each cookie with parchment or waxed paper, in the refrigerator for up to 2 weeks or freeze for up to 3 months.

MAKE THE COOKIES

1. In a medium bowl, whisk both flours with the baking powder and salt. Using a stand mixer fitted with the paddle attachment, cream the butter and sugar on medium speed until light and fluffy, 2 to 3 minutes. Stir in the orange zest and vanilla. Scrape down the bowl and paddle with a rubber spatula.

2. With the mixer on low, gradually add the flour mixture to the butter mixture. After adding the last of the flour but before it's fully incorporated, add ¼ to ⅓ cup cold water and mix just until a smooth dough forms, 1 to 2 minutes. Divide the dough, shape into two disks, and wrap each in plastic. Chill overnight.

3. Position a rack in the center of the oven and heat the oven to 350°F. Line two cookie sheets with parchment. Roll out the cold dough on a lightly floured surface until it's ⅛ to 3/16 inch thick. With a 2-inch plain or fluted round cookie cutter, cut the dough into rounds—you can gather and reroll the scraps once.

4. Bake one sheet at a time until the edges are very lightly browned and the cookies puff up slightly, 8 to 10 minutes. Let the cookies cool on a rack and store in an airtight container for up to 3 days or freeze for up to 1 month, until you're ready to fill and coat them.

FILL THE COOKIES

Lay out the cookies, flat side down. Put a heaping ½ Tbs. of the dulce de leche on half of the cookies. Cover each with a top cookie, flat side up.

COAT THE COOKIES

1. Put the chocolate in a small, deep, heatproof bowl. In a small saucepan over medium-high heat, bring the cream just to a boil. Pour over the chocolate and let sit for 10 minutes. Stir the mixture very gently, incorporating the cream steadily and without overworking, until glossy and completely mixed.

2. Line two cookie sheets or rimmed baking sheets with parchment. Pick up a sandwich cookie with a small offset spatula. Immerse in the chocolate mixture, flipping the cookie to coat completely. Pick up with the spatula and tap a couple of times on the side of the bowl to get rid of excess chocolate. With another spatula in the opposite hand, gently smooth out the top of the cookie and then run the spatula along the bottom. Transfer to the parchment-lined sheet. Repeat with the remaining cookies. Allow the coating to set at room temperature for a few hours and then serve. —*Andy Corson*

PER SANDWICH: 370 CALORIES | 6g PROTEIN | 45g CARB | 19g TOTAL FAT | 12g SAT FAT | 5g MONO FAT | 0.5g POLY FAT | 50mg CHOL | 160mg SODIUM | 3g FIBER

What Is Dulce de Leche?

A favorite in Latin American countries, dulce de leche (sweet milk) is made by caramelizing sweetened condensed milk. It's a delicious topping for ice cream or filling for cakes and cookies.

Before this treat became so popular, ready-made dulce de leche was hard to come by, so people made their own. If you want to make your own filling for the cookies, start with three 14-oz. cans of sweetened condensed milk. Here's how:

Fill the base pan of a double boiler (or a medium saucepan) halfway with water. Bring to a boil and then reduce the heat to medium for an active simmer. Pour the condensed milk into the double boiler's top insert (or into a stainless-steel bowl

that fits snugly on top of the saucepan) and set it uncovered over the simmering water. Every 30 minutes, check the water level in the pan, replenishing as needed, and give the milk a stir. Remove from the heat once the milk has caramelized and thickened, 2½ to 3 hours.

mocha sandwich cookies

YIELDS ABOUT 5 DOZEN SANDWICH COOKIES

FOR THE COOKIES

7½ oz. (1⅔ cups) unbleached all-purpose flour

¾ oz. (¼ cup) unsweetened Dutch-processed cocoa powder

½ tsp. baking soda

¼ tsp. table salt

4 oz. (½ cup) unsalted butter, softened at room temperature

½ cup plus 2 Tbs. granulated sugar

6 Tbs. packed light brown sugar

1 large egg

1 tsp. pure vanilla extract

FOR THE MOCHA FILLING

1 Tbs. instant espresso

2 oz. (4 Tbs.) unsalted butter, softened at room temperature

2 oz. (4 Tbs.) cream cheese

6 oz. (1½ cups) confectioners' sugar, sifted

1 tsp. pure vanilla extract

¾ oz. (¼ cup) unsweetened Dutch-processed cocoa powder, sifted

Delicate chocolate cookies stack up with a mocha-cream-cheese filling in these sweet little sandwiches. The filling can be made up to 3 days ahead and refrigerated. For the best texture, assemble the sandwiches as close to serving as possible.

MAKE THE COOKIES

1. In a medium bowl, whisk the flour, cocoa, baking soda, and salt. With a hand mixer or a stand mixer fitted with the paddle attachment, cream the butter and both sugars on medium speed until light and fluffy, about 2 minutes. Add the egg and vanilla and continue beating until blended and smooth, about 30 seconds. Reduce the speed to low and slowly add the dry ingredients, mixing until the dough is just combined.

2. Divide the dough in two and wrap one half in plastic and refrigerate. Roll the other half of the dough between two sheets of parchment to an even ⅛-inch thickness. Slide the dough onto a cookie sheet and freeze until cold and firm, about 30 minutes. Repeat with the remaining dough.

3. Position a rack in the center of the oven and heat the oven to 350°F. Line two cookie sheets with parchment. Using 1½-inch round cookie cutters, cut out the dough and arrange the rounds 1 inch apart on the prepared sheets. If the dough gets too soft, return it to the freezer for a few minutes. Carefully press the scraps together, reroll, and cut again. Repeat with the other half of the dough, and then gather all the scraps together, reroll, and cut one more time.

4. Bake in batches, two sheets at a time, until the tops look dry, about 6 minutes. Let the cookies cool on their pans for a minute and then let them cool completely on racks.

MAKE THE FILLING

1. In a small bowl, dissolve the espresso in 2 Tbs. of hot water. Let cool slightly, about 5 minutes.

2. With the mixer, cream the butter and cream cheese on medium speed until light and smooth, about 1 minute. Reduce the speed to low and slowly add half of the confectioners' sugar, mixing until just combined. Add the coffee mixture and vanilla; mix until just incorporated. Gradually mix in the remaining sugar and the cocoa. Increase the speed to medium and beat until the filling is light and fluffy, about another 1 minute.

ASSEMBLE THE COOKIES

Transfer the cooled cookies to a work surface, flipping half of them over. With an offset spatula or butter knife, spread a thin layer of the filling onto each overturned cookie. Set another cookie on top of each filled cookie, pressing gently to spread the filling. *—David Crofton*

PER SANDWICH: 60 CALORIES | 1g PROTEIN | 9g CARB | 3g TOTAL FAT | 2g SAT FAT | 1g MONO FAT | 0g POLY FAT | 10mg CHOL | 25mg SODIUM | 0g FIBER

Make Ahead

The cookies will keep at room temperature for up to 3 days or in the freezer for up to 1 month.

peanut butter and chocolate sandwich cookies

YIELDS ABOUT 30 SANDWICH COOKIES (OR 60 SINGLE COOKIES)

FOR THE PEANUT BUTTER COOKIES

2½	cups smooth peanut butter, at room temperature
1½	cups firmly packed light brown sugar
1	tsp. baking soda
2	large eggs
2	tsp. pure vanilla extract

FOR THE CHOCOLATE FILLING

10	oz. bittersweet chocolate, coarsely chopped
4	oz. (½ cup) unsalted butter, cut into 4 pieces

Make Ahead

The balls of dough may be frozen for 1 month. Thaw them overnight in the refrigerator before proceeding with the recipe.

These soft, flourless cookies house a bittersweet filling. Substitute semisweet chocolate for the bittersweet for a sweeter kick.

MAKE THE COOKIES

1. Position a rack in the center of the oven and heat the oven to 350°F. Line four cookie sheets with parchment or nonstick baking liners.

2. Using a stand mixer fitted with the paddle attachment (or in a large bowl with a hand mixer), beat the peanut butter, brown sugar, and baking soda on medium speed until well blended, about 1 minute. Add the eggs and vanilla and mix on low speed until just blended, about 25 seconds.

3. Shape level tablespoonfuls of the dough into balls about 1 inch in diameter. Arrange the balls 1½ inches apart on the prepared baking sheets. Do not press down. Bake one sheet at a time until the cookies are puffed and crackled but still moist-looking, about 11 minutes. Transfer the cookie sheet to a rack to cool for about 10 minutes. Using a spatula, move the cookies to the rack and let cool completely. Repeat with the remaining cookies.

MAKE THE FILLING

Melt the chocolate and the butter in the microwave or in a medium heatproof bowl set in a skillet with 1 inch of barely simmering water, stirring with a rubber spatula until smooth. Remove from the heat and set aside until cool and slightly thickened, 20 to 30 minutes.

ASSEMBLE THE SANDWICHES

Turn half of the cooled cookies over so they are flat side up. Spoon 2 tsp. of the chocolate filling onto the center of each cookie. Top with the remaining cookies, flat side down. Press gently on each cookie to spread the filling almost to the edge. Set on the rack until the filling is firm, 20 to 30 minutes.
—*Abigail Johnson Dodge*

PER SANDWICH: 250 CALORIES | 7g PROTEIN | 21g CARB | 17g TOTAL FAT | 6g SAT FAT | 6g MONO FAT | 3g POLY FAT | 20mg CHOL | 160mg SODIUM | 2g FIBER

peanut butter sandwich cookies

YIELDS EIGHTEEN 2½-INCH SANDWICH COOKIES

FOR THE COOKIES

- 6 oz. (1⅓ cups) unbleached all-purpose flour
- 2 oz. (½ cup) cake flour
- ½ tsp. baking soda
- ¼ tsp. table salt
- 6 oz. (¾ cup) unsalted butter, completely softened at room temperature
- ¾ cup smooth peanut butter
- ½ cup granulated sugar
- ½ cup firmly packed light brown sugar
- 1 tsp. pure vanilla extract
- 1 large egg

FOR THE FILLING

- 1½ cups confectioners' sugar
- 3 oz. (6 Tbs.) unsalted butter, softened at room temperature
- ¾ cup smooth peanut butter
- 3 Tbs. heavy cream
- ¼ cup coarsely chopped unsalted peanuts
- ¼ cup coarsely chopped semisweet chocolate, or mini semisweet chocolate chips

For the best texture, use smooth peanut butter. The chunks in chunky-style don't give as tender-crumbly a texture in the finished cookie. You'll add chunks to the filling by stirring in roasted chopped peanuts.

MAKE THE COOKIES

1. Position racks in the upper and lower thirds of the oven and heat the oven to 350°F. Line two baking sheets with parchment. In a medium bowl, sift together the two flours, baking soda, and salt. Using a stand mixer fitted with the paddle attachment (or in a large bowl with a hand mixer), cream the butter, peanut butter, and both sugars on medium speed until light and fluffy. Add the vanilla and egg; continue beating until smooth and fluffy, about 3 minutes. Stir in the flour mixture by hand just until it's incorporated; don't overmix or the cookies will be tough.

2. Drop heaping tablespoonfuls of batter, spaced about 2 inches apart, onto the lined baking sheets. With floured fingers, flatten each dab of batter into a 2-inch round.

3. Bake until the cookies are puffed and golden, 12 to 14 minutes, rotating the baking sheets if needed for even baking. Transfer the cookies to a rack to cool.

MAKE THE FILLING AND ASSEMBLE

1. While the cookies cool, cream the confectioners' sugar, butter, and peanut butter in a small bowl until smooth. Add the cream; continue beating until smooth and fluffy. Stir in the chopped peanuts and chocolate.

2. Transfer the cooled cookies to a work surface, flipping half of them over. With an offset spatula or a butter knife, spread a scant 1 tsp. of the filling onto each overturned cookie. Set another wafer on top of each filled cookie, pressing gently to spread the filling. *—Linda Weber*

PER SANDWICH: 390 CALORIES | 8g PROTEIN | 36g CARB | 25g TOTAL FAT | 11g SAT FAT | 10g MONO FAT | 4g POLY FAT | 45mg CHOL | 290mg SODIUM | 2g FIBER

Make Ahead

If you feel like assembling these cookies ahead of time, they won't get soggy—even filled—and they'll keep, sealed, in the refrigerator or at room temperature for a couple of days.

milk-chocolate pecan lace cookie sandwiches

YIELDS 15 SANDWICH COOKIES

- **2** oz. pecans (to yield ½ cup ground pecans)
- **2** oz. (4 Tbs.) unsalted butter
- **⅓** cup granulated sugar
- **2** Tbs. light corn syrup
- **1½** oz. (⅓ cup) unbleached all-purpose flour
- Pinch of table salt
- **1** tsp. pure vanilla extract
- **½** cup coarsely chopped pecans
- **4** oz. milk chocolate, chopped

Choose cookies of the same size to pair together and let the milk chocolate for the filling cool and thicken slightly before spreading it on so it doesn't drip through the lacy holes of the cookies.

1. Position racks in the center and upper third of the oven and heat the oven to 350°F. Line two baking sheets with nonstick baking liners or parchment.

2. In a food processor, grind the 2 ounces of pecans finely and measure out ½ cup. In a medium saucepan, heat the butter, sugar, and corn syrup over low heat, stirring often, until the butter melts and the sugar dissolves. Increase the heat to medium high and, stirring constantly, bring the mixture just to a boil. Remove the pot from the heat and stir in the flour and salt until incorporated. Stir in the vanilla, ground pecans, and chopped pecans. Drop the batter by 1 teaspoonful 3 inches apart on the baking sheets, about ½ dozen cookies per baking sheet.

3. Bake the cookies until evenly light brown, 11 to 12 minutes total. About 6 minutes into baking, switch the sheets from top to bottom and back to front to promote even baking. Line a wire rack with paper towels. Remove the cookies from the oven and, as soon as they're firm (which will take just a few minutes), use a wide spatula to transfer them to the rack to cool completely.

4. Melt the milk chocolate in a bowl in a microwave or over a water bath. Let it cool enough to thicken slightly. (For tips on how to melt chocolate, see p. 23.)

5. Arrange the cookies in pairs of similar size. Flip half of the cookies over. Leaving a ½-inch border around the edge, spread a thin layer of milk chocolate on the overturned cookies. Gently place the remaining cookie, bottom down, onto the milk chocolate. Let the cookies sit until the filling firms, about 30 minutes. —*Elinor Klivans*

PER SANDWICH: 160 CALORIES | 2g PROTEIN | 14g CARB | 11g TOTAL FAT | 4g SAT FAT | 5g MONO FAT | 2g POLY FAT | 10mg CHOL | 30mg SODIUM | 1g FIBER

gianduia sandwich cookies

YIELDS ABOUT 3 DOZEN
2-INCH SANDWICH COOKIES

- 9 oz. (1 cup plus 2 Tbs.) unsalted butter, softened at room temperature
- 1 cup granulated sugar
- 5 oz. (1 cup) toasted, skinned, and finely ground hazelnuts (grind the toasted nuts in a food processor)
- 4 large egg yolks, at room temperature
- 1 tsp. pure vanilla extract
- 13½ oz. (3 cups) unbleached all-purpose flour, mixed with a pinch of salt
- 1 recipe Hazelnut-Chocolate Filling (recipe on the facing page)

Make Ahead

The wafers can be baked up to 2 days before assembly and held at room temperature, tightly wrapped in aluminum foil or sealed in a plastic container. Store the assembled sandwich cookies at room temperature between layers of waxed paper, tightly covered with aluminum foil or in a plastic container, for up to 3 days.

Sandwich cookies taste best when the layers aren't too thick, so roll your wafers as thin as you can handle them—⅛ inch is good. Bring the filling to room temperature before you spread it. The cookies may crack if you try to spread the gianduia when it's stiff. The wafers for these cookies are also delicious served on their own.

MAKE THE DOUGH

1. Using a stand mixer with the paddle attachment (or in a large bowl using a hand mixer), beat the butter until fluffy, about 2 minutes. Add the sugar and beat until well blended. Add the ground hazelnuts and mix well. Stop occasionally and scrape the bowl with a rubber spatula.

2. Add the egg yolks, one at a time, mixing thoroughly after each addition. Mix in the vanilla extract, and then add the flour in two or three batches, mixing to blend well, but don't overmix. Divide the dough in two, shape each into thick disks, wrap in plastic, and chill until firm, about 3 hours. (If the dough isn't thoroughly chilled, it will be too soft to roll out and cut.)

3. Position racks in the upper and lower thirds of the oven and heat the oven to 375°F. Line four baking sheets with parchment. Work with one disk at a time; leave the other in the refrigerator. Try to work in a cool area, not too close to the warm oven. Roll the dough between sheets of lightly floured waxed paper or parchment until it's about ⅛ inch thick for sandwich cookies, ¼ inch for single cookies.

4. Cut out shapes using a cookie cutter. Use a smaller cookie cutter to make a "window" in the center of half of the shapes (these will be the top cookies of the sandwiches). Put the cookies on the lined baking sheets, leaving at least ½ inch between each wafer. Gently press the scraps together, reroll, and cut more wafers. If the dough is too warm and hard to work with, return it to the refrigerator to chill.

BAKE AND ASSEMBLE THE COOKIES

1. Bake two sheets at a time (keeping the others in the refrigerator) for 7 minutes and then switch the sheets to the opposite racks. Bake for another 6 to 7 minutes, until deep golden on the top and the bottom. Keep a close eye on the baking time, and keep in mind that the cookie tops may be finished a minute earlier than the bottoms. Let cool on racks. The wafers must be cooled completely before assembling the cookies.

2. Use a small metal spatula or a table knife to spread some of the filling onto each wafer bottom. Place one of the wafer tops on top of the filling, pressing slightly so they stick together. —*Carole Bloom*

PER SANDWICH: 180 CALORIES | 2g PROTEIN | 16g CARB | 12g TOTAL FAT | 5g SAT FAT | 5g MONO FAT | 1g POLY FAT | 40mg CHOL | 5mg SODIUM | 1g FIBER

hazelnut-chocolate filling

YIELDS ABOUT 1 CUP

- **3** oz. bittersweet or semisweet chocolate, finely chopped
- **1** oz. milk chocolate, finely chopped
- **¼** cup heavy cream
- **½** cup Hazelnut Butter (see the recipe below), at room temperature

A cut-out in the top cookies of the Gianduia Sandwich Cookies shows off this hazelnut-chocolate filling. Use the highest-quality chocolate you can find.

In a metal bowl set over a saucepan of simmering water, melt the bittersweet (or semisweet) and milk chocolate, stirring frequently with a rubber spatula to ensure even melting. In a small saucepan, heat the cream over medium heat to just below the boiling point. Remove the bowl of chocolate from the pan of water and wipe the bottom and sides dry. Pour the cream into the chocolate and stir with the spatula until very smooth. Stir in the Hazelnut Butter until well blended. Cover tightly with plastic wrap. Let cool to room temperature and refrigerate until thick but not stiff, about 2 hours, stirring occasionally with the spatula. If you make the filling in advance and it has become very firm, leave it at room temperature until it reaches a nice spreading consistency to use in cookies.   —*Carole Bloom*

hazelnut butter

YIELDS ABOUT 1 CUP

- **8** oz. (1⅔ cups) hazelnuts
- **¼** cup vegetable oil, such as canola or sunflower

This butter can be refrigerated in a sealed container for up to 3 months or frozen for up to 6 months. If frozen, thaw it slowly in the refrigerator overnight. Always bring the hazelnut butter to room temperature before use.

PREPARE THE HAZELNUTS
1. Heat the oven to 350°F. Spread the hazelnuts in a single layer on a baking sheet and toast in the heated oven until the skins are mostly split and the nuts are light golden brown and quite fragrant, 15 to 18 minutes. Don't overcook the nuts or they'll become bitter.

2. Put the warm hazelnuts in a clean dishtowel. Fold the towel around the hazelnuts and let them steam for at least 5 minutes. Then rub the nuts in the towel to remove most of the skins (try to get at least 50% of the skins off). Let the hazelnuts sit for another 10 to 15 minutes to cool completely. Toasted, peeled hazelnuts can be cooled and frozen in a sealed plastic container for up to 3 months.

MAKE THE HAZELNUT BUTTER
Put the nuts in a food processor; add the oil and pulse a few times. Then process, checking the consistency every few seconds, until the texture resembles that of natural, unhomogenized peanut butter or wet sand, 1 to 2 minutes. —*Carole Bloom*

ice-cream sandwiches

YIELDS TWELVE 2¾-INCH
ICE-CREAM SANDWICHES

FOR THE SOFT CHOCOLATE COOKIE

5¾ oz. (1¼ cups) unbleached all-purpose flour

1½ oz. (½ cup) unsweetened, natural cocoa powder

½ tsp. baking soda

¼ tsp. table salt

3 oz. (6 Tbs.) unsalted butter, softened at room temperature; more for the pan

¾ cup granulated sugar

1½ tsp. pure vanilla extract

⅔ cup cold milk

FOR SANDWICH ASSEMBLY

1 quart or 2 pints ice cream (see options, p. 229)

1½ cups press-on garnish (optional; see variations, p. 229)

You can design your own sandwich combinations by choosing the ice cream, adding flavor to the chocolate cookie (see p. 229), and picking your favorite garnish.

MAKE THE SOFT COOKIES

1. Position a rack in the center of the oven and heat the oven to 350°F. Lightly grease the bottom of an 18x13-inch rimmed baking sheet. Line the pan with parchment to cover the bottom and the edges of the pan's longer sides. Combine the flour, cocoa, baking soda, and salt in a medium bowl; whisk to blend. In a large bowl, beat the butter and sugar with an electric mixer on medium high until well blended and lightened in color, about 3 minutes. Beat in the vanilla. Add about a third of the flour mixture and beat on medium low until just blended. Pour in half the milk and beat until just blended. Add another third of the flour and blend. Pour in the remaining milk and blend, and then beat in the remaining flour.

2. Distribute the dough evenly over the prepared pan in small dollops. Using one hand to anchor the parchment, spread the dough with a spoon or spatula. Drag a rectangular offset spatula over the dough to smooth it into an even layer, rotating the pan as you work. Brush or spray a sheet of parchment the same size as the pan with oil, and lay it, oiled side down, on the dough. Roll a straight rolling pin over the paper (or swipe it with a dough scraper) to level the batter. Carefully peel away the parchment.

3. Bake until a pick inserted in the center comes out clean, 10 to 12 minutes. Set the pan on a rack and let cool to room temperature.

ASSEMBLE THE SANDWICHES

1. Lay two long pieces of plastic wrap in a cross shape on a baking sheet. Slide a knife along the inside edge of the pan containing the cookie to loosen it. Invert the cookie onto a large cutting board. Peel off the parchment. Using a ruler as a guide, cut the cookie crosswise into two equal pieces. Place one layer, top side down, in the middle of the plastic wrap (a wide, sturdy spatula will help the transfer).

2. Remove the ice cream from the freezer and take off the lid. It's important to work quickly from this point on. (If the ice cream gets too soft, pop it onto a plate and back into the freezer to harden up.) Using scissors or a sharp knife, cut the container lengthwise in two places and tear away the container. Set the ice cream on its side. Cut the ice cream into even slices, ½ to ¾ inch thick, and arrange them on top of the cookie layer in the pan, pairing the smallest piece next to the largest. Using a rubber spatula, gently yet firmly smear the ice cream to spread it evenly. (It helps to put a piece of plastic wrap on the ice cream and smear with your hands; remove the plastic before proceeding.)

3. Position the remaining cookie layer, top side up, over the ice cream. Press gently to spread the ice cream to the edges. Put a clean piece of plastic on top and wrap the long ends of the bottom sheet of plastic up and over the layers and ice cream. Put the baking sheet in the freezer and chill until the sandwich is hard, about 4 hours and up to 2 days.

4. Take the baking sheet out of the freezer. Lift the package from the pan, transfer it to a cutting board, and line the pan with a fresh piece of plastic.

Make Ahead

Individually wrapped sandwiches will keep for up to 2 weeks in the freezer.

Peel the top layer of plastic off the sandwich (you can leave on the bottom layer.) Working quickly, use a ruler and a long, sharp chef's knife to score the cookie, dividing it into twelve pieces: three rows across the short side and four rows across the long side. Cut the sandwiches, wiping the blade clean as needed. (If your kitchen is very warm, put the pieces back into the freezer to firm, or work with one strip at a time, keeping the rest in the freezer.)

5. Garnish the sandwiches, if you like: Fill a small, shallow bowl with your chosen garnish and set it next to your work surface. Press some of the garnish onto some or all of the sides of the sandwich. Set the sandwiches back on the baking sheet and return to the freezer immediately. (If your kitchen is warm, keep the sandwiches in the freezer and garnish one at a time.) Once the sandwiches are hard, wrap them individually in plastic and store in the freezer.
—*Abigail Johnson Dodge*

PER SANDWICH, WITHOUT GARNISHES: 290 CALORIES | 4g PROTEIN | 37g CARB | 15g TOTAL FAT | 9g SAT FAT | 4g MONO FAT | 1g POLY FAT | 65mg CHOL | 180mg SODIUM | 2g FIBER

continued on p. 228 ➤

continued from p. 227

how to make ice-cream sandwiches

Spread an even layer of cookie dough on a parchment-lined baking sheet. Place a greased sheet of parchment over the dough and roll until flat. Remove the parchment and bake. When cool, cut the cookie crosswise into two equal pieces.

Cut the ice cream container lengthwise on two sides and peel away the container. Set the ice cream on its side and cut into even slices.

Arrange the sliced ice cream on top of the cookie on the baking sheet, using a rubber spatula to spread it firmly and evenly across the cookie.

Place the second cookie piece on top of the ice cream and press down lightly to spread the ice cream to the edges.

Cut the large sandwich into 12 individual pieces.

Garnish the ice-cream sandwiches.

Create Your Own Ice-Cream Sandwich

You can design your own sandwich combinations by choosing the ice cream, adding flavor to the chocolate cookie, and picking your favorite garnish. The flavoring possibilities are endless.

Cookie Variations

• **Chocolate-Mint** Add ½ tsp. peppermint extract when you add the vanilla.

• **Chocolate-Orange** Add ½ tsp. natural orange flavor or orange extract when you add the vanilla.

• **Chocolate-Espresso** Mix in 1 level Tbs. instant coffee granules when you add the vanilla.

• **Chocolate-Ginger** Add ½ tsp. ground ginger to the dry ingredients.

Ice Cream Variations

• Vanilla

• Chocolate

• Coffee

• Mint chocolate chip

• Mocha swirl

• Raspberry sorbet

• Your favorite flavor

Garnishes

• Hard peppermint candies, finely crushed

• Finely chopped or grated bittersweet or semi-sweet chocolate

• Crystallized ginger, minced

• Pecans, finely chopped and toasted

• Sweetened coconut flakes, toasted

• Amaretti cookies, crushed

• Toffee chips, crushed

Winning Combinations

• Basic chocolate cookie with coconut ice cream and toasted coconut flakes

• Chocolate-mint cookie with vanilla ice cream and crushed peppermints

• Chocolate-orange cookie with raspberry sorbet

• Chocolate-ginger cookie with vanilla ice cream and minced crystallized ginger

• Chocolate-espresso cookie with coffee or mocha swirl ice cream and chopped pecans

• Chocolate-espresso cookie with dulce de leche ice cream and chopped pecans

ice-cream sandwich s'mores

YIELDS 9 SANDWICHES

FOR THE ICE CREAM

1½ cups whole milk

1½ cups heavy cream

1 Tbs. unsweetened natural cocoa powder

⅓ cup granulated sugar

7 oz. good-quality milk chocolate, finely chopped

8 egg yolks (reserve half the whites for the marshmallow topping)

FOR THE GRAHAM CRACKERS

4 oz. (½ cup) unsalted butter, softened at room temperature

2 Tbs. firmly packed brown sugar

2 Tbs. granulated sugar

2 tsp. honey

4½ oz. (1 cup) unbleached all-purpose flour; more for rolling

¼ cup whole-wheat pastry flour

Pinch of table salt

¼ tsp. baking soda

¼ tsp. ground cinnamon

FOR THE MARSHMALLOW TOPPING

4 egg whites, at room temperature

1 ¼-oz. package unflavored powdered gelatin

Pinch of table salt

¾ cup granulated sugar

¼ cup corn syrup

1 tsp. pure vanilla extract

This dessert isn't difficult to make, but it requires time to make the ice cream, graham crackers, and marshmallow topping. You can make the components and assemble most of the sandwich ahead of time. When you're ready to serve, all you have to do is broil the sandwiches.

MAKE THE ICE CREAM

1. In a heavy saucepan, combine the milk and cream. Sift the cocoa over the mixture; whisk thoroughly to combine. Sprinkle half of the sugar into the saucepan and slowly bring the mixture to a simmer; don't let it boil. Put the chopped chocolate in one bowl and fill another with ice water.

2. While waiting for the milk mixture to simmer, whisk the egg yolks with the remaining sugar. Whisk vigorously until the yolks thicken and become a paler shade of yellow, 3 to 4 minutes.

3. To combine the egg and milk mixtures, temper the egg mixture first with a portion of the hot milk. Slowly whisk half of the simmering milk into the yolks. Whisk that mixture back into the milk in the saucepan. Reduce the heat to low and stir constantly until the custard is thick enough to coat the back of a spoon (about 170°F). Pour the cooked custard over the chocolate. Stir until all the chocolate is melted. Set the custard bowl over the bowl of ice water; stir until the custard is completely cool. Pour through a fine strainer and refrigerate for several hours or overnight.

4. Pour the custard into an ice-cream machine and start to freeze following the manufacturer's directions. When it's almost completely frozen, line a 9x9-inch pan with plastic wrap, letting excess hang over the sides, and pack the ice cream into it. Level it with a spatula, cover with the plastic wrap, and freeze for several hours or overnight.

MAKE THE GRAHAM CRACKERS

1. Position a rack in the center of the oven and heat the oven to 350°F.

2. With an electric mixer, cream the butter, both sugars, and honey on medium speed until soft and fluffy. Sift together the two flours, salt, baking soda, and cinnamon and pour into the mixing bowl. Mix on slow speed until just combined. Turn out the mixture onto a clean surface. Press the crumbly-looking dough together with your hands until it just holds together. Press the dough onto a 12x16-inch piece of parchment. Roughly shape the dough into a rectangle and cover it with another 12x16-inch piece of parchment.

3. Roll out the dough paper thin by rolling from the middle of the paper outward. If the dough is difficult to roll, toss a very small amount of flour between the parchment and the dough on both sides. You'll need to patch the dough to make it fit the rectangle exactly. Slide the dough and parchment onto a cookie sheet. Gently peel away the top layer of parchment.

4. Bake the dough until the top is golden brown, slightly blistered, and dry-looking, 8 to 10 minutes. Remove the cookie sheet from the oven and, using an angel food cake cutter or a fork, mark rows of holes, ¼ inch apart, all over the dough. Trim the rough outside edges and cut the dough into 20 squares, about 3 inches each. Use a ruler and work quickly, as the crackers will be difficult to cut evenly if cool. Bake until the cut crackers are a deep golden brown, another 4 to 5 minutes. Let them cool on a rack, then store in an airtight container.

continued on p. 232 ➤

continued from p. 230

MAKE THE TOPPING AND ASSEMBLE

1. Put the egg whites in the well-cleaned bowl of an electric mixer. Sprinkle the gelatin and salt evenly over the whites and whisk by hand to combine.

2. In a small saucepan, mix the sugar, corn syrup, and ¼ cup water. Put a candy thermometer in the pan and turn the heat to medium. When the sugar mixture comes to a boil, begin whisking the whites on medium speed just until foamy. Don't overbeat. When the sugar mixture reaches 240°F, remove it from the heat. With the mixer running, pour the syrup down the side of the bowl into the frothy egg whites, being careful not to pour it directly onto the spinning whisk. When all the syrup is in the bowl, continue beating until the bowl is cool to the touch, about 15 minutes. Mix in the vanilla.

3. Transfer the marshmallow mixture to a pastry bag without a tip. Don't overfill it. Remove the ice cream pan from the freezer and uncover it. Pipe the topping back and forth over the ice cream to make a ½-inch layer. You may not need to use it all. Leave the surface bumpy. Freeze the uncovered pan until the topping is firm, about an hour. If you want to chill it overnight, cover the pan in plastic once the marshmallow is firm.

4. Assemble the s'mores following the photos on the facing page. Position a rack as close to the heating element as possible and heat the broiler on high. Slide the cookie sheet with the sandwiches under the broiler and broil (rotating the cookie sheet if necessary) until the marshmallow topping is evenly browned. Serve each sandwich with a second graham cracker.

—*Stephen Durfee*

PER SANDWICH: 620 CALORIES | 10g PROTEIN | 65g CARB | 37g TOTAL FAT | 21g SAT FAT | 11g MONO FAT | 2g POLY FAT | 280mg CHOL | 250mg SODIUM | 2g FIBER

3 Components in 3 Days

Ice cream: Two days ahead
Cook the custard for the ice cream two days before you'd like to serve the sandwiches. To develop the flavor, let the custard sit in the refrigerator for several hours or, ideally, overnight, and then freeze it in your machine the next day.

Graham crackers: One day ahead
Make the graham crackers a day ahead, while the ice cream freezes. The crackers will keep in an airtight container for several days if you want to make them before that.

Marshmallow topping: The day of serving
Make the marshmallow topping the day you're serving the sandwiches. You'll need 30 minutes to an hour to firm up the topping in the freezer before cutting portions. You can also make and pipe the marshmallow several hours in advance. The sandwiches will taste best on the day they're made, but leftovers will keep in the freezer for a few days. Keep the graham crackers separate so they don't get soggy.

how to assemble and serve the ice cream sandwich s'mores

Once the marshmallow-topped ice cream is firm, tug on the plastic wrap to lift out the ice cream block. Invert the pan and put the ice cream block on it. Peel away the plastic from the sides. Put nine graham crackers on a cookie sheet.

Arrange the graham crackers on a baking sheet. Using a long, thin-bladed knife dipped in warm water, trim the outside edges of the ice cream and cut it into nine 2½-inch squares.

With a metal spatula, carefully transfer a square of ice cream and marshmallow onto each of the nine crackers.

Broil the sandwiches and serve right away. Serve each sandwich with a second graham cracker, a sprinkling of cinnamon, and a dollop of chocolate sauce, if you like.

almond macarons

YIELDS ABOUT 30 SANDWICH
COOKIES

7⅜ oz. (1¾ cups plus 2 Tbs.)
confectioners' sugar

4⅜ oz. (1¼ cups plus 2 Tbs.)
almond flour

4 large egg whites, at room
temperature

¼ cup granulated sugar

1 recipe macaron filling of your
choice (see recipes pp. 236
and 237)

Make Ahead

The cookies are best
the day they're made,
but you can store
them in an airtight
container at room
temperature for up to
1 day or in the freezer
for up to 2 weeks.

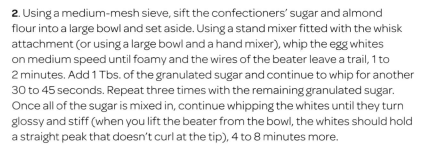

*Texture is the key to these little
cookies, which are simply two
meringues sandwiched with a
sweet filling. The subtly sweet
almond flavor of the meringues
makes them incredibly versatile:
They serve as a blank canvas
for the flavor variations on the
facing page.*

MAKE THE BATTER

1. Line three completely flat bak-
ing sheets with parchment or nonstick baking liners and set aside.

2. Using a medium-mesh sieve, sift the confectioners' sugar and almond
flour into a large bowl and set aside. Using a stand mixer fitted with the whisk
attachment (or using a large bowl and a hand mixer), whip the egg whites
on medium speed until foamy and the wires of the beater leave a trail, 1 to
2 minutes. Add 1 Tbs. of the granulated sugar and continue to whip for another
30 to 45 seconds. Repeat three times with the remaining granulated sugar.
Once all of the sugar is mixed in, continue whipping the whites until they turn
glossy and stiff (when you lift the beater from the bowl, the whites should hold
a straight peak that doesn't curl at the tip), 4 to 8 minutes more.

3. With a large rubber spatula, gently fold in half of the confectioners' sugar
mixture. Once most of it has been incorporated, fold in the remaining mixture
until just combined.

PIPE THE COOKIES

Using a piping bag fitted with a ½- to ¾-inch round tip (Ateco #806 to #809),
pipe the batter onto the prepared sheets in rounds that are about 1 inch in
diameter and ¼ to ½ inch thick, spaced about 1½ inches apart. As you pipe,
hold the bag perpendicular to the baking sheet and flick the tip of the bag as
you finish each cookie to minimize the peaks. Rap the sheet against the counter several times to flatten the mounds and pop any large air bubbles. Let rest
until the meringues no longer feel tacky, 20 to 30 minutes. Meanwhile, position
racks in the upper and lower thirds of the oven and heat the oven to 325°F.

BAKE THE COOKIES

1. Put two of the baking sheets in the oven and immediately reduce the temperature to 300°F (let the third sheet sit at room temperature). Bake, rotating
the sheets and swapping their positions after 8 minutes, until the meringues
are very pale golden, 15 to 20 minutes total. Let cool completely on the baking
sheets on racks. Meanwhile, return the oven temperature to 325°F and then
bake the third sheet as above.

2. Remove the meringues from the parchment and pair them by size.

FILL THE COOKIES

Using a piping bag with the same tip used to pipe the cookies, pipe 1 to
1½ tsp. of the filling onto half of the cookies—use just enough filling that it
spreads to the edge when topped but doesn't squish out much when bitten.
Top the filled halves with their partners. —*Joanne Chang*

continued on p. 236 ➤

how to make French macarons

Sift together the confectioners' sugar and almond flour.

Whip the egg whites on medium speed until foamy and trails form.

Add 1 Tbs. of the granulated sugar and whip, repeating until all the granulated sugar has been added. Then whip the mixture until shiny and firm.

Lift the beater from the bowl. The whites should hold a stiff, straight peak at the end of the beater.

Pipe the batter onto prepared baking sheets about 1½ inches apart, keeping peaks to a minimum. You'll need to rap the baking sheets against the counter to make the batter flat and remove the air bubbles. Then let sit until no longer sticky.

Bake the cookies only until very pale golden.

Pipe the filling onto one cookie bottom and top with another to form a sandwich.

Cookie Variations

Cinnamon Add ¼ tsp. ground cinnamon to the confectioners' sugar and almond flour while sifting; proceed as directed.

Black pepper Add ½ tsp. ground black pepper to the confectioners' sugar and almond flour while sifting; proceed as directed. Sprinkle with a little black pepper as soon as you pipe them.

Sesame Using a spice grinder, grind 2 Tbs. sesame seeds to a fine powder. Add the powder to the confectioners' sugar and almond flour while sifting; proceed as directed. Sprinkle the meringues with a few sesame seeds as soon as you pipe them.

Vanilla Add the seeds scraped from one-quarter of a vanilla bean to the egg whites after they've formed glossy, stiff peaks. Distribute the seeds evenly throughout the batter by pressing the clumps of seeds against the edge of the bowl with a spatula. Proceed as directed.

Cocoa Reduce the amount of almond flour by ⅞ ounce (¼ cup) and substitute ½ ounce (3 Tbs.) unsweetened cocoa powder; proceed as directed.

continued from p. 235

lemon curd filling

YIELDS ABOUT 1¼ CUPS

½ **cup fresh lemon juice**

1½ **oz. (3 Tbs.) unsalted butter**

3 **large eggs**

1 **large egg yolk**

½ **cup granulated sugar**

¼ **tsp. pure vanilla extract**

⅛ **tsp. kosher salt**

This smooth, creamy mixture of lemon, eggs, sugar, and butter has a refreshingly bright, tart flavor.

1. In a 3-quart nonreactive saucepan, heat the lemon juice and butter over medium-high heat until just under a boil. In a medium heatproof bowl, whisk the eggs and egg yolk and then slowly whisk in the sugar until combined. Gradually whisk the hot lemon juice mixture into the sugar and eggs.

2. Return the mixture to the saucepan and set over medium heat. Cook, stirring constantly with a wooden spoon and scraping the bottom of the pan frequently, until the curd thickens and coats the spoon, 2 to 4 minutes. Draw your finger along the back of the spoon; when the curd is done, it should hold the trail.

3. Remove the curd from the heat and strain it through a fine sieve into a bowl. Whisk in the vanilla and salt. Cover with plastic wrap, pressing the plastic onto the surface of the curd, and chill for 1 to 2 hours before using. The curd can be made up to 5 days ahead; refrigerate in an airtight container.

VARIATION: ROSEMARY-LEMON CURD
Add ¾ tsp. finely chopped fresh rosemary to the saucepan with the lemon juice and butter and bring the mixture to just under a boil. Remove from the heat and let sit for 1 hour. Bring the mixture to just under a boil again, and continue as directed.

chocolate ganache filling

YIELDS ABOUT 1¼ CUPS

¾ **cup heavy cream**

6 **oz. bittersweet or semisweet chocolate, finely chopped, or chocolate chips**

This is a classic macaron filling; it comes together in minutes—and in just one pot.

In a small saucepan, heat the cream over medium heat, swirling the pan a few times, until bubbles start to form around the edge of the pan but the cream is not yet boiling, about 4 minutes. Remove from the heat, add the chocolate, and let sit for 30 seconds. Slowly whisk the mixture until the chocolate is completely melted and smooth. Let cool to room temperature before piping onto the meringues. (The ganache may be made up to 1 week ahead. Refrigerate in an airtight container and bring to room temperature before using.)

VARIATION: CHOCOLATE-ORANGE GANACHE
Add 2 Tbs. finely grated orange zest (from 1 large orange) to the cream before heating. Heat the cream, remove it from the heat, and let sit for 1 hour. Strain through a fine sieve, pressing the zest with the back of the spoon. Reheat the cream to just under a boil and proceed as directed.

vanilla buttercream filling

YIELDS ABOUT 1 CUP

½   **cup granulated sugar**

2   **large egg whites**

4   **oz. (½ cup) unsalted butter, softened at room temperature, cut into 4 to 6 pieces**

¼   **tsp. pure vanilla extract**

    Pinch of kosher salt

1. In a small heatproof bowl, whisk the sugar and egg whites. In a 1-quart saucepan, bring 2 cups water to a simmer over medium-high heat. Set the bowl over the simmering water (don't let the bowl touch the water) and heat the mixture, whisking occasionally, until hot to the touch, 4 to 6 minutes. It will thin out a bit as the sugar melts.

2. Remove the bowl from the heat and scrape the mixture into the bowl of a stand mixer fitted with the whisk attachment. Whip on medium-high speed until the mixture is light, white, and cool to the touch, 4 to 6 minutes. Reduce the speed to low and add the chunks of butter one at a time. Increase the mixer speed to medium and beat until the buttercream is smooth, 4 to 5 minutes. Mix in the vanilla and salt.

3. Use the buttercream immediately or refrigerate it in an airtight container for up to 4 days. Before using, return to room temperature and then mix the buttercream in a stand mixer fitted with the paddle attachment on medium-low speed until smooth, 1 to 2 minutes.

VARIATION: ESPRESSO BUTTERCREAM
Substitute 2 tsp. instant espresso powder dissolved in ½ tsp. warm water, cooled, for the vanilla and mix it in along with the salt.

Secrets to Successful Macarons

• Use a scale to weigh ingredients like confectioners' sugar and almond flour—it's much more accurate than a cup measure.

• Bring the egg whites to room temperature before using; they'll whip up better. (Separate eggs when they're cold, though; it's easier to do).

• Use a flat baking sheet and a new piece of parchment (or a nonstick baking liner) to ensure that your cookies bake into a nice round shape. If the baking sheet is warped or if your parchment is creased, you may end up with amoeba-shaped cookies.

• Test the surface of the batter after it has rested for 20 to 30 minutes. It should have dried out a bit and no longer feel tacky, ensuring that each cookie forms a crisp, delicate top when baked. If the batter still feels tacky, let it rest for a few more minutes before baking.

• Rotate the cookie sheet halfway through baking so that the cookies bake to an even pale gold.

• When piping the filling onto the cookie bottoms, leave a narrow, unfilled border around the edge. When topped with another cookie, the filling will extend to the edge without overflowing.

METRIC EQUIVALENTS

LIQUID/DRY MEASURES

U.S.	METRIC
¼ teaspoon	1.25 milliliters
½ teaspoon	2.5 milliliters
1 teaspoon	5 milliliters
1 tablespoon (3 teaspoons)	15 milliliters
1 fluid ounce (2 tablespoons)	30 milliliters
¼ cup	60 milliliters
⅓ cup	80 milliliters
½ cup	120 milliliters
1 cup	240 milliliters
1 pint (2 cups)	480 milliliters
1 quart (4 cups; 32 ounces)	960 milliliters
1 gallon (4 quarts)	3.84 liters
1 ounce (by weight)	28 grams
1 pound	454 grams
2.2 pounds	1 kilogram

OVEN TEMPERATURES

°F	GAS MARK	°C
250	½	120
275	1	140
300	2	150
325	3	165
350	4	180
375	5	190
400	6	200
425	7	220
450	8	230
475	9	240
500	10	260
550	Broil	290

CONTRIBUTORS

Jennifer Armentrout is senior food editor at *Fine Cooking*.

Nancy Baggett is a food journalist and cookbook author. Her most recent book is *Kneadlessly Simple: Fabulous, Fuss-Free, No-Knead Breads*.

Rose Levy Beranbaum is a cooking instructor, cookbook author, and baker extraordinaire. She is the author of nine cookbooks, including *The Cake Bible*, and most recently, *Rose's Heavenly Cakes*.

Susan Betz is a *Fine Cooking* reader from Morgan Hill, California.

Carole Bloom studied pastry and confectionery arts in Europe. She is the author of ten cookbooks; her most recent is *Intensely Chocolate: 100 Scrumptious Recipes for True Chocolate Lovers*.

Tish Boyle is the editor of *Dessert Professional* magazine. She began her culinary education at La Varenne in Paris and has been a pastry chef, caterer, food stylist, recipe developer, and cookbook author.

Flo Braker is the author of numerous cookbooks; her most recent is *Baking for All Occasions*.

Kay Cabrera is a pastry chef and wedding cake designer living in Hawaii.

Greg Case was a pastry chef at Dean & DeLuca in New York City and Hammersley's Bistro in Boston before setting out on his own. He owns the G. Case Baking Company in Somerville, Massachusetts.

Joanne Chang is the pastry chef and owner of Flour Bakery + Café, which has two locations in Boston.

Candice Clauss is a *Fine Cooking* reader from Highlands Ranch, Colorado.

Andy Corson is a fulfillment systems coordinator at The Taunton Press and is also baker-owner of American Artisan Food & Bakery in Newtown, Connecticut.

David Crofton and his wife, Dawn Casale, are bakers and business partners at One Girl Cookies in Brooklyn, New York.

Regan Daley is a food writer from Toronto, Canada. Her cookbook, *In the Sweet Kitchen*, won several awards, including the IACP's Awards for Best Baking and Dessert Book and Best Overall Book.

Tasha DeSerio is a cooking teacher and food writer, and the co-owner of Olive Green Catering in Berkeley, California. She is also the co-author of *Cooking from the Farmer's Market*.

Paula Disbrowe was the chef at Hart & Hind Fitness Ranch in Rio Frio, Texas, from January 2002 to December 2005. Prior to that she spent ten years in Manhattan working as a food and travel writer. Her work has appeared in the *New York Times, T Living, Food & Wine, Spa, Health, Cooking Light*, and *Saveur*, among others. Her latest cookbook is *Cowgirl Cuisine: Rustic Recipes and Cowgirl Adventures from a Texas Ranch*.

Abigail Johnson Dodge, a former pastry chef, is a food writer and instructor. She studied in Paris at La Varenne and is the author of seven cookbooks, including *Desserts 4 Today*.

Stephen Durfee is the pastry chef at The French Laundry in Yountville, California.

Keri Fisher is a food writer and cookbook author who cut her teeth at restaurants in Florida and Boston.

Margery K. Friedman is a baker from Rockville, Maryland, who specializes in making custom cakes.

Annie Giammattei was associate art director at *Fine Cooking*.

Katherine Gibson is a *Fine Cooking* reader from North Scituate, Rhode Island.

Bonnie Gorder-Hinchey has over 25 years of experience as a food scientist developing products and recipes for companies including General Mills, Nestle, and Starbucks to name a few. She owns Creative Cuisine and is an adjunct professor at The Art Institute of Seattle, where she teaches culinary classes as well as classes in nutrition and general science.

Maxine Henderson is a *Fine Cooking* reader from Ypsilanti, Michigan.

Renee Henry is a *Fine Cooking* reader from Pointe-Claire, Quebec, Canada.

Patricia Ann Heyman is the author of *American Regional Cooking: A Culinary Journey* and *International Cooking: A Culinary Journey*.

Jill Hough is a cookbook author, food writer, recipe developer, and culinary instructor from Napa, California. Her first cookbook is *100 Perfect Pairings: Small Plates to Enjoy with Wines You Love*.

Wendy Kalen is a food writer who has contributed recipes to *Fine Cooking, Cooking Light, Food and Wine*, and many other magazines.

Elaine Khosrova is a food writer and recipe developer living in New York's Hudson Valley.

Elinor Klivans has written 13 cookbooks; her latest is *Fast Breads: 50 Recipes for Easy, Delicious Breads*. She also writes for the *Washington Post, Real Food, Fresh*, and *Cooking Pleasures*.

Allison Ehri Kreitler is a *Fine Cooking* contributing editor. She has also worked as a freelance food stylist, recipe tester, developer, and writer for several national food magazines and the Food Network.

Beth Kujawski is a *Fine Cooking* reader from Crown Point, Indiana.

Camilla Leonard is a *Fine Cooking* reader from Mississauga, Ontario, Canada.

Judi Terrell Linden is a *Fine Cooking* reader from Medina, Ohio.

Lori Longbotham is a recipe developer and cookbook author whose books include *Luscious Coconut Desserts* and *Luscious Creamy Desserts*.

Emily Luchetti is the executive pastry chef at Farallon and Water Bar in San Francisco.

Deborah Madison is a cookbook author, cooking teacher, and consultant. Her most recent book is *Seasonal Fruit Desserts from Orchard, Farm, and Market*.

Alice Medrich is a three-time Cookbook of the Year Award winner and teacher. Alice's most recent book, *Pure Dessert*, was named one of the top cookbooks of 2007 by *Gourmet, Bon Appetit*, and *Food & Wine* magazines.

Susie Middleton is the former editor and current editor at large for *Fine Cooking* magazine. She is also a consulting editor, writer, and photographer for *Edible Vineyard* magazine, as well as a cookbook author.

Cindy Mitchell and her husband, Glenn, own Grace Baking, an award-winning bakery in the San Fransisco Bay area.

Melissa Murphy is chef-owner of Sweet Melissa Pâtisserie in the Cobble Hill section of Brooklyn, New York.

David Norman is a former *Fine Cooking* contributor.

Denise Pierce is a *Fine Cooking* reader from Peachtree City, Georgia.

Michelle Polzine is a pastry chef at Range Restaurant in San Francisco. She was named 2010's Best Pastry Chef by *San Francisco Weekly*.

Nicole Rees, author of *Baking Unplugged* and co-author of *The Baker's Manual* and *Understanding Baking*, is a food scientist and professional baker.

Debbie Reid is a *Fine Cooking* reader from Clearwater, Florida.

Leticia Moreinos Schwartz is a cooking teacher and cookbook author based in Weston, Connecticut.

Joanne McAllister Smart has co-authored two Italian cookbooks with Scott Conant and *Bistro Cooking at Home* with Gordon Hamersley.

Molly Stevens is a contributing editor to *Fine Cooking*. She won the IACP Cooking Teacher of the Year Award in 2006; her book *All About Braising* won James Beard and IACP Awards.

Meg Suzuki is a cooking instructor and freelance writer, and former assistant test kitchen director for *Cook's Illustrated* magazine.

Daniella Caranci Verburg is a *Fine Cooking* reader from Toronto, Ontario, Canada.

Carole Walter is a master baker, cooking instructor, and cookbook author; her most recent cookbook is *Great Coffee Cakes, Sticky Buns, Muffins & More*.

Kathleen Weber is a bread baker and owns Della Fattoria bakery in Northern California.

Linda Weber is the pastry chef at Della Fattoria, the Weber family artisan bakery in Petaluma, California. She trained at Contra Costa College's culinary program and has worked at the prestigious Sonoma Mission Inn & Spa in Boyes Hot Springs, California.

Jennifer Weglowski is a *Fine Cooking* reader from Fairlawn, New Jersey.

Carolyn Weil, a former pastry chef, is a food writer and teacher.

Robert Wemischner teaches professional baking at Los Angeles Trade Technical College.

PHOTO CREDITS

Amy Albert © The Taunton Press: pp. 180, 183, 222

© Maren Caruso: p. 156

© Colin Clark: pp. 234, 235

© Carl Duncan: pp. 67, 154

© Mark Ferri: pp. 2, 10, 11, 149, 150, 155

© Ben Fink: pp. 231, 233

© Beth Galton: pp. 35, 199

Boyd Hagen © The Taunton Press: pp. vi, 160, 184

Steve Hunter © The Taunton Press: pp. 13, 25

© Rita Maas: p. 187

Scott Phillips © The Taunton Press: pp. iii, v, 4, 5, 7, 9, 12, 14, 15, 17, 18, 19, 21, 22, 23, 24, 26, 27, 28, 29, 33, 36, 38, 39, 40, 42, 44, 45, 46, 47, 48, 49, 51, 52, 53, 54, 55, 57, 58, 59, 60, 61, 63, 64, 65, 66, 69, 70, 73, 75, 77, 78, 79, 81, 82, 83, 84-85, 88, 91, 92, 93, 94, 95, 96, 97, 98, 99, 100, 101, 102, 103, 104, 105, 107, 108, 110, 111, 112, 115, 116, 117, 118, 119, 120, 121, 124, 126, 127, 128, 131, 132, 133, 134, 135, 136, 137, 138, 139, 140, 141, 142, 143, 144, 145, 147, 148, 158, 159, 162, 163, 164, 166, 167, 169, 170, 173, 174, 175, 176, 177, 179, 190, 191, 192, 193, 194, 195, 196, 197, 199, 201, 202, 203, 204, 206, 207, 209, 210, 211, 212, 214, 215, 216, 219, 220, 221, 223, 224, 227, 228, 238, 242

© Daniel Proctor: p. 123

© Alan Richardson: pp. 31, 32, 41, 188, 198

INDEX

INDEX (CONTINUED)

INDEX (CONTINUED)